Introduction

Emojis are more than just small colorful signs that decorate our messages. They take on important functions in interpersonal communication. Due to the increasing presence and use of emojis, a certain internalization of the signs is to be expected. This concerns both the use of the signs and their aesthetics. This book looks at the emergence of the new expressive possibilities as a potential for designers.

What will I get from this book?

Why does a designer need a book about emojis?

Digital communication, and with it the colorful world of signs, has changed our everyday interaction in recent years. Emojis have become an important part of our repertoire of signs and are used by billions of people every day. The pictorial signs are mostly used in informal and personal communication and can enhance writing with visual means, represent feelings, attitudes, moods, inclinations or group affiliation. The qualitatively and quantitatively increasingly complex companions of written language have long since broken out of the written media and become a pop culture phenomenon. The omnipresence and spread of emojis is often perceived ambivalently. In addition to the euphoria about the new means of expression, the decline of language, infantilization or regression in connection with emojis is also criticized, addressed and discussed. Due to their global use, emojis have become an important and powerful means of communication that reflect socially relevant issues such as equality, cultural diversity and gender stereotypes (see also pages 146–148).

A change in communication brought about by emojis and the invasion of the characters as a pop culture phenomenon can be seen as part of the so-called ›emojization‹, which addresses the rapid development, increasing use and spread of emojis. The artificial word contains the term ›emoji‹. This is made up of the Japanese ›E‹ for picture and ›moji‹

for character. Translated into English, these are ›picture characters‹. By adding the suffix ›-ization‹ to the word ›emoji‹, the increase in the development taking place is addressed. Emojization refers to the prominent role of emojis in our communication and in our everyday lives, as well as to the change in language, writing and communication resulting from the expanded expressive possibilities of digital writing.

Digital communication systems have changed the use of writing. Today, private communication and entertainment take place in the same media as task-oriented interactions. Such a mixture changes the use of writing and the attitude of users towards it. The integration of pictorial elements was previously only tolerated in informal, personal, mostly handwritten interactions. With the advent of ›computer-mediated communication‹ (CMC), the use of emojis in digital communication is now generally accepted. It must be taken into account that the communicative output of society has increased enormously since the emergence of the internet. Communicating, commenting on content and sharing everyday life digitally has become the norm. Purely textual communication would be extremely exhausting.

Due to the increasing presence and use of emojis, a certain internalization of the characters is to be expected. As Michael Giesecke noted in an email exchange, standard language has become part of our nature and its highly artificial character is usually no longer perceived. This process took time and familiarization. As emojis are a relatively new phenomenon and our understanding of forms of communication is based on existing ones, it is to be expected that the process of internalizing the signs will continue and will develop further with the emergence of other signs (see also page 15). The internalization of signs concerns both the use of signs and their aesthetics.

The central topic of this book is emojization. In order to trace its emergence, we must first ask why emojis are needed today and why it was sufficient to express ourselves for centuries using the standard linguistic sign system.

The spread and use of emojis is shaped both by technological advances and by the specific ways in which users use them, which in turn are influenced by cultural aspects. For this reason, the historical and cultural background of the characters will be discussed first. In order to find out what is new about the characters, the historical section discusses possible predecessors and the development of emojis. With the possible predecessors of emojis, the focus is on the background for the development of the signs, the use and the formal elaboration of the respective sign.

With the emergence of emojis, a kind of culture of cuteness (kawaii culture) has established itself, which is explained in the following subchapter using relevant topics. The aim of the historical and cultural chapter is to trace the rise and spread of emojis in order to illuminate and better understand their development.

This book looks at the emergence of the new means of expression as a potential for designers and shows ways of using emojis in design projects. The book offers inspiration and shows concrete areas of application to understand and utilize the creative

potential of emojis in visual communication. After the historical and cultural background of emojis, the focus is on the creative potential of the pictorial signs.

In the chapter ›Creative Variety of Emojis‹, the focus is on the creative development of the characters by designers. It offers inspiration and shows specific areas of application in order to understand and use the creative potential of emojis in visual communication.

By introducing different theoretical approaches such as semiotics or comic theory, a foundation is created to better understand the creative potential of emojis. Specific projects by designers are presented and explained in the following section. The focus is on the formal diversity and the intentions of the respective projects, which are divided into two sub-chapters: ›emoji-fonts‹ and ›(emoji)-stickers‹. This separation is based on the current options for designing emojis: either as a glyph and therefore part of a font or as an (animated) image file.

In a further chapter, the influence of the emergence, spread and formal diversity of emojis on the design of visual identities is explored. The focus of the chapter is on highlighting the creative potential of emojis in visual communication with regard to visual identities for designers and illustrating this with practical examples.

The first part focuses on projects that use emojis in different ways as an integral part of a brand.

Design projects are then presented that take different approaches to using sticker packs to support and reinforce the visual identity. These projects specifically use elements of the visual language to refer to the visual identity.

In addition to conveying historical and theoretical basics, the intention of the book is to use numerous projects to show how a development such as emojis can be used productively for one's own work as a designer.

Definition of the Terms

In the relevant literature, there are no standardized terms for designating and structuring pictorial signs from computer-mediated communication. There is no consistent terminology for the classification of various sorts of emojis. Terms like ›smiley‹, ›emoji‹, ›emoticon‹, ›kawaicon‹, and many more are used in different ways. This book attempts to use a uniform terminology based on the technique underlying the signs.

Which characters can be defined as emojis?

Can further sign types be defined within the term?

The terms described in the following graphic (Fig. 1) are used in this book. The terminological distinction is based on the underlying technique for creating and using the pictorial sign. A distinction is made between ›text-based‹, ›graphic‹ and ›AR-Emojis‹.

Text-based emojis are made up of the keyboard's character set and can be divided into ›vertical text-based‹ and ›horizontal text-based emojis‹. The latter are often referred to as ›kaomojis‹ in the relevant literature.

Graphic emojis are pictorial signs that are inserted into text or dialogs. They can be used either as part of a font or as digital stickers. The main difference is that stickers are usually sent as a separate file, while an emoji can be used as a glyph within the text. Graphic emojis have become widespread around the world, mainly due to their inclusion in Unicode in 2010 (see page 59).

From 2017, it was possible to use ›AR emojis‹, which can be used as videos in combination with a voice message or as stickers (see page 60). These 3D-animated graphic emojis react to movement by imitating the user's facial expressions in real time. The latest developments will enable the generation of emojis through the use of AI and the integration of emojis into text (see page 62). These emojis can be used as digital stickers or added to the emojis available on the emoji keyboard and thus integrated into the text. As this development has only just begun by the time the book ist completed, it can unfortunately only be discussed in the historical section and cannot be examined further due to a lack of material. Following the logic of the terminology used in the book, these emojis would be referred to as AI-Emojis.

This book is mainly about pictorial signs or constellations of signs that are perceived as images and used in the context of digital communication. If the phenomenon or the signs in general are meant, ›emojis‹ or ›pictorial signs‹ are used as an umbrella term. The term ›emojization‹ is used when discussing the rise and spread of emojis.

The characters composed of the keyboard character set are usually referred to as emoticons and the characters encoded as code points as emojis. The term emoji was coined primarily due to the spread of the NTT DoCoMo character set (see page 56). However, when looking at the historical development of emojis, there are already earlier character sets that fulfill a similar or the same range of functions. For this reason, the term ›emoji‹ is used more comprehensively in this book.

Abbreviations:

CMC = computer-mediated communication
FTF = face-to-face
AI = artificial intelligence
AR = augmented reality

Fig. 1 **structuring the terms**

EMOJIS

text-based emojis

graphic emojis

AR-Emojis

:-)

vertical

^_^

horizontal

Methodical Approach

In order to examine the emergence and formal distribution of emojis, theoretical approaches from various disciplines such as semiotics, linguistics, image and comic theory are used in addition to the presentation of different practical application examples.

On which methodological principles is this book based?

To study emojis, a multidimensional and interdisciplinary approach is beneficial, because emojis are first and foremost images that are mainly used as characters in text-based messages. Their aesthetics entail attributes that relate to comics as well as to the kawaii aesthetic. The discussions from different perspectives enable a differentiated view of the development of the signs.

Since the aim of the book is to investigate how the creative potential of emojis can be used in visual communication, a key focus is on the formal development of the characters. Signs or sign sets that can be regarded as predecessors of emojis are discussed and their form examined. Strictly talking, no direct predecessors of emojis can exist, as CMC is a new communication medium. According to Beißwenger and Pappert, there are no direct predecessors of emojis in forms of verbal or written communication outside the internet (cf. Beißwenger/ Pappert 2019: 11). Nevertheless, there are signs whose intended use corresponds to the functions of today's emojis. In order to investigate the use of emoji-like characters, the current functions of emojis must be taken as a starting point. Previous research into the functions of emojis, which mainly originates from linguistics, serves as criteria for the selection of characters for the historical reconstruction. Characters or character sets that were created before the emergence of CMC and fulfilled or were intended to fulfil the same functions as today's emojis are referred to as pre-emojis.

Due to the technology used in the past, many possible predecessors are pixel-based. In order to be able to understand the construction of the signs, selected signs are shown in their underlying grid. In order to be able to compare the shape and construction of the characters, some pixel-based characters are shown without a grid and some are shown enlarged three times so that the grid can be reproduced. Isometric representations are used to visualize the devices on which the characters were created and which had a decisive influence on their form and development. These geometric and linear visualizations allow a rational view of the different techniques used.

Emojis have developed not only through the technology used, but also through the people who use them and their cultural background. To explore this aspect further, the following subchapter will focus on kawaii culture and its connection to emojis. Japan, and Tokyo in particular, is regarded as a melting pot of kawaii culture. Therefore, own research in Tokyo serves as the basis for this subchapter. In particular, interviews were conducted with locals and people from other countries who have lived in Tokyo for a very long time and their findings were used as a basis for information. In addition to the interviews and the literature used, visual material is also used to visualize the presence and spread of kawaii culture in Tokyo.

The following chapter will examine the formal diversity of emojis. Semiotics – the theory of signs – is used to understand how a sign process works. The question arises as to how a sign process can be explained from a theoretical perspective and how emojis can be analyzed. The most important basics of Peirce's semiotics are discussed and explained using concrete messages, and various concepts from cognitive semiotics and comic theory are used to further investigate the form and how abstraction and identification are related.

The following representation of different emoji projects shows the formal diversity of emojis that has emerged in recent years. Projects were selected that were created with different intentions or through different formal elaboration. The following part examines how emojis can function as part of a visual identity. This is demonstrated by projects that use emojis or the technology of emojis as a visual identity. In doing so, care was also taken to ensure that the projects cover as wide a range of different areas of application as possible in order to illuminate the use of emojis in visual communication from different perspectives.

Fig. 2 **a pragma-linguistic approach** (according to Beißwenger/Pappert 2023: 169–170, with pictorial signs from Diglû, edited by D. E.)

interpretation cue

calculated inconsistency as a guide to search for what is meant

non-redundant marking of attitudes as a presentation of interiority

social cue

calculated redundancy as ›putting the linguistic utterance into the picture‹

acting without language

mitigation as a means of socially acceptable organisation of linguistic action

The linguistic description framework on which this work is based comes from Steffen Pappert and Michael Beißwenger (Beißwenger/Pappert 2019, 2023). The linguists analyzed the functions that emojis fulfill in specific uses. Basically, they differentiate between the ›interpretation cue‹ and the ›social cue‹ (Beißwenger/Pappert 2023: 168). The former is relevant for the interpretation of the message, i.e. without the emoji(s), the message could be interpreted incorrectly or incompletely (Beißwenger/Pappert 2019: 71 f.). The latter, on the other hand, uses visual means to make the messages socially acceptable and thus serves to build relationships (cf. ibid.: 73/104).

With the ›interpretation cue‹, the authors distinguish between two functions, which are labeled ♀ and ⊚ in this book. With the function ♀ (calculated inconsistency as a guide to search for what is meant), the authors mean that emojis are used, for example, to indicate a joke or irony. Without this indication, the message could be misinterpreted.

With the function ⊚ (non-redundant marking of attitudes as a presentation of interiority), for example, an emoji can be used to add an attitude or emotion to a statement that is not yet explicitly included in said statement.

With the ›social cue‹, the authors differentiate between three functions: ▧, ⊗ and ⅋. The function ▧ (calculated redundancy as ›putting the linguistic utterance into the picture‹) means that emojis are used like illustrations in order to present the statement again visually. With ⊗ (acting without language), the emoji completely replaces the text. In the last function ⅋ (mitigation as a means of socially acceptable organization of linguistic action), emojis are used, for example, to make a statement seem less offensive or to soften the seriousness of the message.

Detailed information on the functions can be found in Beißwenger/Pappert 2019 and 2023.

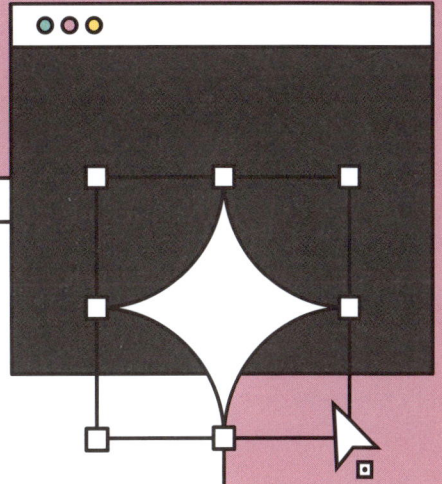

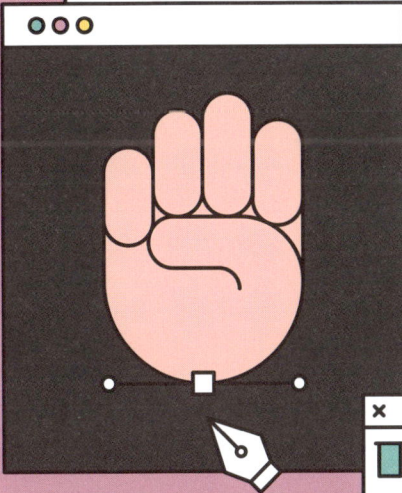

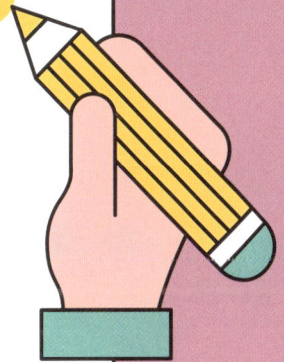

Historical and Cultural Background of Emojis

In order to investigate emojization, the first question to ask is what is new about the characters. Why was it sufficient for centuries to express oneself using the standard linguistic sign system and why are emojis used today? How do cultural characteristics influence th e development and use of emojis? To explore these and similar questions, it's useful to examine the historical and cultural background of emojis.

Where do emojis come from?

What is the historical and cultural background of emojis?

Emojization is influenced on the one hand by technical possibilities and developments and on the other by the way users use the signs, which in turn is affected by cultural aspects. For this reason, the first subchapter focuses on the historical and the second subchapter on the cultural background of the characters.

Were there already characters similar to emojis that did not spread as widely in communication as emojis? What distinguishes emojis from earlier characters that were invented with the intention of taking over functions that are attributed to today's emojis?

In order to investigate these and similar questions, it is helpful to take a look into the past.
The historical subchapter discusses potential predecessors of emojis and traces the historical development of the characters. Strictly speaking, no direct predecessors of CMC characters can exist, as CMC is a new communication medium. According to Beißwenger and Pappert, there are no direct predecessors of emojis in forms of verbal or written communication outside of the internet (cf. Beißwenger/Pappert 2019: 11). Nevertheless, there are signs whose intended use corresponds to the functions of today's emojis. The term ›pre-emojis‹ is used for these, see page 18. The question arises as to when and why the desire arose to use signs

that fulfill the current functions of emojis in writing. What strategies and systems were developed to satisfy the desire for missing para-linguistic and non-verbal means of expression?
In order to investigate the desire for the use of emoji-like characters in writing, the current functions of emojis must be taken as a starting point. The criteria for the selection of pre-emojis are based on previous research into the functions of emojis, which mainly originate from linguistics, see page 11. The focus here is on the desire to use characters in writing that also fulfill the current functions of emojis.
The intention is not to create a complete overview of pre-emojis, but to analyse and structure predecessors in order to trace and understand the development of emojization. In order to find out the background for the intention, use and formal elaboration of the respective character and to compare it with the emojis, several – also similar – examples that differ in form or content are sometimes presented and discussed.

In order to understand the rise and spread of emojization, we will trace the historical development of emojis. Text-based emojis have been established in society since the emergence of chats. Although chat cannot be seen as the digital equivalent of verbal conversation, parallels are recognizable (cf. Shirai 2009: 12 f.). The signs and abbreviations

Fig. 3 **assortment of typical kawaii accessories**

used in chats can be seen as a compensation strategy for the lack of paralinguistic and non-verbal means of expression (cf. Runkehl et al. 1998: 99). Why has this compensation strategy only been necessary since the rise of chats? Have such means of expression not always been lacking in writing? How is it possible that such a colorful world of signs has emerged from a combination of ASCII characters, which now extends to all areas of life? To what extent do cultural aspects influence the acceptance, dissemination and use of characters?

According to Janßen, it can be assumed that – just as writings were formed from verbal forms of communication – new media make use of existing ones (cf. Janßen 1995: 11). This means that new possibilities of communication build on older ones or are based on existing ones. Thus, languages are subject to a continuous process of change (cf. ibid.). According to Schmitz, new media not only change modes of communication and forms of language but also the position of human language in the totality of semiotic phenomena and human relations in general (cf. Schmitz 1995: 7).

In order to understand the development and spread of emojization, not only the historical but also the cultural background must be considered. Japan is considered to have had a formative influence on the development and spread of emojis.

Cultural behaviour not only influences the formal development of the characters (see for example page 44), but also the acceptance and use of emojis. Kawaii culture in particular has a strong influence on the formal development and use of emojis and stickers.

Since this book focuses on emojization from a design perspective, the topic of the various aspects of kawaii culture and its influence on emojis is of considerable importance. This is explored in the form of the sub-chapter ›Culture of Cuteness‹. It is not the intention of the subchapter to comprehensively address the complex historical background of kawaii culture or to cover the culture in its entirety. Rather, the spread of kawaii culture and its effects on emojis are examined. It is shown how cuteness manifests itself in everyday objects such as food, clothing, official signage and mascots. Aspects relevant to emojis are highlighted and discussed. As kawaii culture is a social phenomenon, the subchapter also focuses on personalities for whom kawaii culture has a special significance.

Historical Reconstruction

First, the question of which strategies and systems were developed to satisfy the longing for missing para-linguistic and non-verbal means of expression will be explored. In order to examine how they differ from today's emojis, they are compared with their functions. This is followed by a historical review of emojis. This focuses on the technical possibilities and how the characters were created.

What distinguishes emojis from earlier signs that were invented with the intention of taking over functions that are attributed to today's emojis?

Are emojis a new thing or are they a familiar phenomenon in a new guise?

Computer-mediated communication can be attributed to a particular upheaval in our communication behavior – similar to the modern printing press. This contributed significantly to the spread and standardization of character sets as they are used today (cf. Frutiger 2004: 164).

The emergence of the punctuation marks still used today can therefore be placed at the end of the Middle Ages (cf. ibid.: 215). The standardized written languages and character sets that emerged in Europe during the age of printing enabled the widespread dissemination of information. The standardized storage and distribution of information through the printing press laid the foundation for the emergence of mass media.

A similarly profound significance for communication is also attributed to the digital revolution. Digital communication systems combine different forms of communication to create an interactive medium in which information and entertainment technology are mixed (cf. Eichinger/Kallmeyer 2005: 138 f.). This gives rise to new forms of communication that influence our communication behavior and our use of language as profoundly as the printing press.

In both revolutionary events – the invention of printing and the digital revolution – writing played or plays a decisive role.

For this reason, the historical reconstruction begins at the point at which writing as we know it today became widespread. This is because, in addition to their functions, their connection to written dialogs is decisive for a description of text-based and graphic emojis. In order to investigate whether the desire for emoji-like characters arose before the development of CMC, the period from the beginning of the spread and standardization of writing and its characters through modern book printing to the present day is suitable.

In order to be categorized as pre-emoji, the criterion for all characters is that they were invented or used and integrated into writing before the emergence of CMC. In addition, they should take on functions that correspond to those of today's emojis. The functions already discussed in previous research serve as criteria for the selection of characters. Consequently, fonts that were designed with the intention of getting by without writing are not taken into account. Characters that have similar formal properties to emojis are addressed for the purpose of form, even if they do not meet the conditions mentioned. Similarly, characters or character sets that are considered to have historical significance for the formal development of emojis – without fulfilling the above criteria – are treated as part of an excursus.

The historical review begins with the emergence of the CMC, see page 37.

Pre-Emojis

In order to create analogies to today's emojis, the characters or character systems presented in the following are divided into groups when determining pre-emojis – analogous to the graphic of the terms (Fig. 1) used. A distinction can be made between two main groups, the ›pre-text-based emojis‹ and the ›pre-graphic emojis‹.

How can pre-emojis be structured to create analogies to today's emojis?

Pre-text-based Emojis

Signs from this group are characterized by the fact that they use the formal means of the standard language sign system. A basic distinction can be made between two different types of characters in this group. On the one hand, they are suggestions for new punctuation marks or modifications of existing characters that are intended to take on a new function, and on the other hand, they are experiments by typesetters who have created emojis by combining individual letters.

Pre-graphic Emojis

Pre-graphic emojis are independent, self-contained graphic representations or images and do not use the formal means of the standard linguistic sign system. In this group, handwritten signs, often used in letters, are thematized as functional and formal predecessors of emojis.

Fig. 4 **examples of pre-text-based emojis**

Fig. 5 **examples of pre-graphical emojis**

Pre-text-based Emojis

This group includes various designs for the creation of new punctuation marks or proposals for using existing punctuation marks to take on certain functions that coincide with the functions of emojis. This group also contains creations by typesetters who used character combinations to create pre-text-based emojis.

Which characters can be classified as pre-text-based emojis?

Around 1575, the printer Henry Denham used, for example, a mirrored question mark (Fig. 6) to indicate rhetorical questions and called it a ›percontation point‹ (cf. Houston 2013: 36). For technical reasons, some print employees used a question mark in different weights, such as italics or bold, instead of a percontation point. This led to confusion as to whether the author wanted to use a question mark or a ›percontation point‹, so that, according to Houston, the mark failed due to technical reproducibility and the fact that its form is too close to that of the question mark (cf. ibid.). It appeared in publications by Robert Herrick and Thomas Middleton, among others (cf. Parkes 1992: 218 f.).

The search for a universal language began in the 17th century (cf. Feigl/Windholz 2011: 66). In his work ›An Essay Towards a Real Character, and a Philosophical Language‹ from 1668, the philosopher John Wilkins focused on the creation of such a language. Wilkins attempted to find a universal means of communication so that language barriers would not be an obstacle to scientific progress (cf. ibid.). In doing so, Wilkins discovered that different types of pronunciation can sometimes give words a different sense or meaning (cf. Wilkins 1668: 355). He suggested compensating for this in writing with punctuation marks, for example by using the exclamation mark to express a strong passion (cf. ibid.: 356).

Fig. 6   **percontation point and and the question mark**

Fig. 7   **exclamation mark and its inverted version**

He also formulated the desideratum of an irony mark, which should be used to indicate irony or sarcasm. To compensate for this, he suggests the inverted exclamation mark (cf. ibid.: 377, 393).
According to Wilkins, the exclamation mark should take on the function ⊚, while the inverted exclamation mark assumes the function ⊚. Both signs are thus intended to take on the function of an ›interpretation cue‹.

Two centuries later, another irony mark appeared, which came from the Belgian lithographer Jean-Baptiste-Ambroise-Marcellin Jobard. Under his direction, the newspaper ›Le Courrier Belge‹ published an article on October 11, 1841, which was interrupted by an arrow-like sign (Fig. 8) (cf. Houston 2013: 215 f.). Jobard always used the sign before an ironic statement, and in the footnote, he explained that the sign is a ›point d'ironie‹ (cf. ibid.). In another work published a year later, he suggested, for example, that the arrow pointing in different directions could mark different emotional states such as irritation, indignation or hesitation (cf. ibid.: 216 f.). He believed that signs should be found to indicate different states of mind so that the readership could put themselves in the writer's shoes (cf. ibid.).
His idea of using the sign for different emotional states corresponds to the function ⊚, while the ›point d'ironie‹ took over the function ⊚. Another sign that can be classified under the function ⊚ comes from Marcel Bernhardt – known under the pseudonym Alcanter de Brahm. In 1899, he used a punctuation mark (Fig. 9) in ›L'Ostensoir des Ironies‹ to indicate irony (de Brahm 1899). He always used the sign after an ironic statement (ibid.: 2, 18, 22). According to Moeller and Wohlfart, de Brahm compared irony with regard to the use of irony in FTF communication to a kind of whip that catches you in an unexpected situation (cf. Moeller/Wohlfart 2014: 140). His sign is also called ›le petit signe flagellateur‹ (cf. Encalado 2005: 218).
Formally, the sign is similar to Henry Denham's ›percontation point‹ (Fig. 6).

By using two inverted exclamation marks (Fig. 10) to denote outrage in his novel ›Le Chiendent‹, the writer Raymond Queneau created another punctuation mark for the function ⊚.

»Je ne voudrais pas vous vexer encore un coup, mais je vais vous dire une chose; je les trouve plutôt ›à côté‹ vos réflexions sur l'onanisme. – Oh¡¡ (¡¡ c'est le point d'indignation).«

(Queneau 1933: 240)

According to Christopher Shorley, Queneau supports the arbitrariness of the content with arbitrary

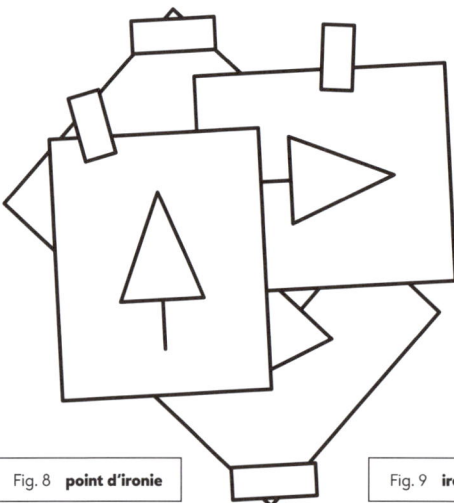

Fig. 8   **point d'ironie**

Fig. 9   **irony mark from de Brahm**

Fig. 10   **point d'indignation**

punctuation (cf. Shorley 1985: 47 f.). In addition, Queneau deliberately used white spaces in his texts in order to force the reader to follow his intended rhythm (cf. ibid.). By attempting to integrate the dramaturgy of spoken language into writing in his works, Queneau used the ›visual salience‹ of white spaces as structuring signals. A potential that is also attributed to emojis (cf. Beißwenger/Pappert 2023: 168).

The next example (Fig. 10) is a standardized character whose use differs from the intended function of the standard language character system. According to Alisa Freedman, Japanese authors in the 1920s used kanji characters to achieve an emotional effect on the reader (cf. Freedman 2020: 49). For example, in ›Shigure no eki‹ [Rainy Station], one of his ›palm-of-the-hand stories‹, Kawabata Yasunari used the iteration of the Japanese character for woman ›tsuma‹ (Fig. 11) to create the image of four single lonely women (cf. ibid.). The sign resembles a woman with a skirt and crossed legs. A kind of reverse use of the ›referencing‹ function (a sub-function of function ⊗) can be observed: Instead of an image being used for a word, here a word has been used for an image.

Another suggestion for a new punctuation mark comes from Martin K. Speckter. The owner of an advertising agency in New York was annoyed by the increasing tendency of text endings to combine the two punctuation marks question mark and exclamation mark in order to ask a surprised or rhetorical question (cf. Houston 2013: 25).

In an article in the March/April 1962 issue of ›Type Talks‹ magazine, he argued for a new punctuation mark that would convey a mixture of surprise and doubt (cf. ibid.). Speckter suggested the name ›Exclamaquest‹ and the later common name ›Interrobang‹ and presented three designs by Jack Lipton for the new character (Fig. 12). The name ›Interrobang‹ is a combination of the Latin word ›interrogatio‹ for question and the English ›bang‹, a slang word for exclamation mark (ibid.: 28). In his article, Speckter invited readers to submit name and design drafts for his new symbol, so that alternative names and drafts (Fig. 13) from designers were published in ›Type Talks‹ in the following months.

However, several publications had already reported on the interrobang, so the original name suggestion and Jack Lipton's design (Fig. 12), a combination of a question mark and an exclamation mark, had already become established. According to Houston, although the interrobang was popular with copywriters and writers, the character struggled to be accepted by the general public and struggled to be reproduced.

Fig. 11 **iterated representation of the sign ›tsuma‹**

Fig. 12 **interrobang**

In contrast to its use on a typewriter, the use of the interrobang by typesetters was difficult (cf. ibid.: 28 f.). Richard Isbell designed the typeface ›Americana‹ and incorporated the character into the glyphs, resulting in the first mass-produced lead typeface that contained an interrobang (cf. ibid.: 30).

A year later, the character even appeared on the typewriter keyboard of Remington Rand's Model 25 (ibid.: 31 f.). After that, enthusiasm for the character waned and it found no place in typesetting machines such as Lino or Monotype (cf. ibid.: 34). According to Ralf Herrmann, the interrobang was no longer current when phototypesetting emerged and was therefore not included in the standard character sets of phototypesetting machines (cf. Herrmann 2013). In some of today's digital fonts, interrobang is integrated as a glyph and it is also encoded in the ›Unicode standard‹. By indicating a surprised or rhetorical question, the interrobang fulfills the function ‽ or ⸘.

As Wilkins had already noted, Hervé Bazin was also of the opinion that written language lacked the nuances and subtlety of the spoken word (cf. Bazin 1966: 141). Bazin provided concrete suggestions to compensate for these deficits: In his book ›Plumons l'oiseau‹, he created a series of new punctuation marks, which he called ›les points d'intonation‹ (ibid.: 142) (Fig. 14–Fig. 19). He also provided pictorial explanations of the design of the signs. The sign for irony (Fig. 17) is derived from the Greek letter ›Psi‹ and, according to Bazin, represents an arrow in a bow. It is inspired by the sound of an arrow whizzing through the air – what was a whip in de Brahm's work became an arrow in Bazin's. The sign for ›love‹ is made up of two question marks that form a heart. Bazin commented on this as follows:

»Le point d'amour : Il est formé de deux points d'interrogation qui, en quelque sorte, se regardent et dessinent, au moins provisoirement, une sorte de coeur.«

(Bazin 1966: 142)

For ›le point de conviction‹ (Fig. 15), which is supposed to denote conviction, he transformed an exclamation mark into a cross.

He compared ›le point d'autorité‹ (Fig. 16) – the sign for authority – with an umbrella over the sultan (ibid.). According to Bazin, the sign for doubt

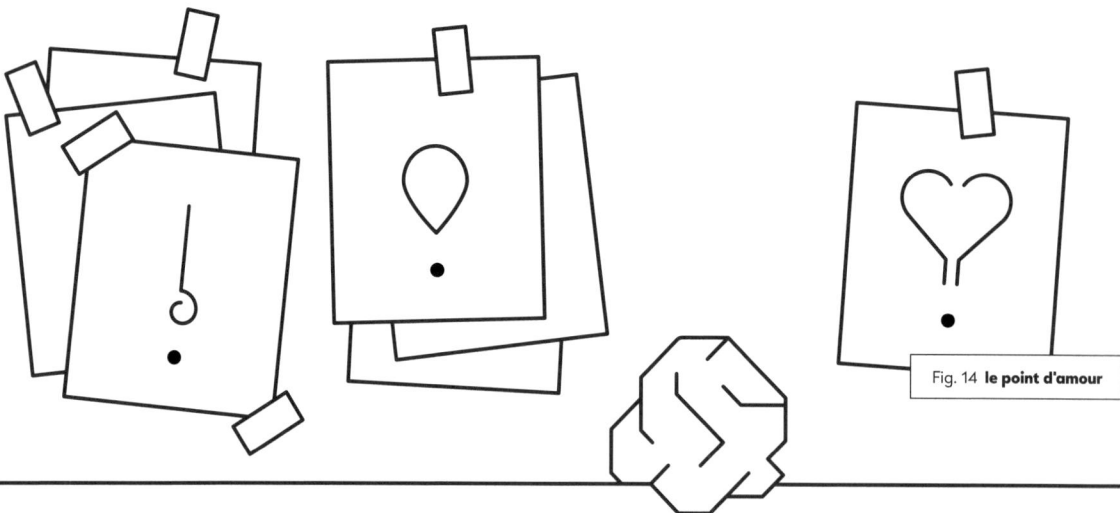

Fig. 14 **le point d'amour**

Fig. 13 **alternative design drafts for the interrobang** (according to Houston 2013: 28)

(Fig. 18) stands askew on its point, it hesitates and is about to fall. He compared ›le point d'acclamation‹ (Fig. 19) with two arms raised in victory and the ›Victory‹ sign. According to Bazin, it is a stylized representation of the two flags floating on the top of the bus during a visit by the head of state (cf. ibid.). Bazin combined elements such as the heart, cross, lightning bolt or umbrella with punctuation marks. Bazin presented examples of the use of his intonation marks and called the implementation an illustrative sketch (ibid.).

In his sketch, Bazin used his intonation marks like punctuation marks by placing them after a statement. The signs take on different functions within the linguistic description framework. In Bazin's application, the irony sign (Fig. 17) fulfills the function ♀ by marking an ironic comment. He used the sign for love (Fig. 14) twice in different places, both of which fulfill the function 🖻 by additionally depicting what is written with the heart. Bazin used ›le point de conviction‹ (Fig. 15), ›le point de doute‹ (Fig. 18) and ›le point d'acclamation‹ (Fig. 19) to indicate the inner attitude – the signs thus fulfilled the function 📍. Bazin used the punctuation mark –, which is intended to indicate authority (Fig. 16), in

three different places. The signs clarify the previous utterance and are used in a similar way to the signs from the practice 🖻.

According to Houston, Bazin's punctuation marks were not used outside of his book (cf. Houston 2013: 221). Nevertheless, it is astonishing how close his proposal for the use of signs comes to emojis.

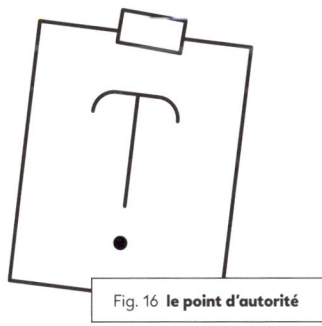

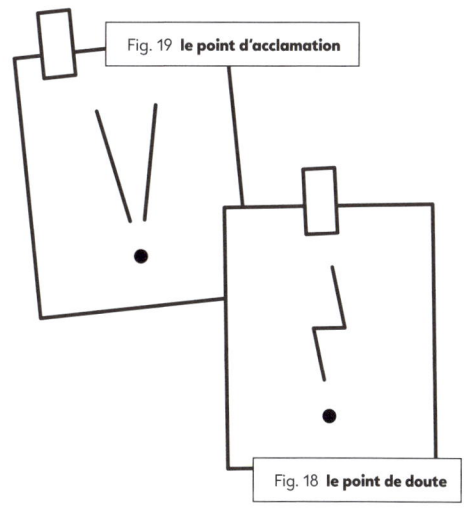

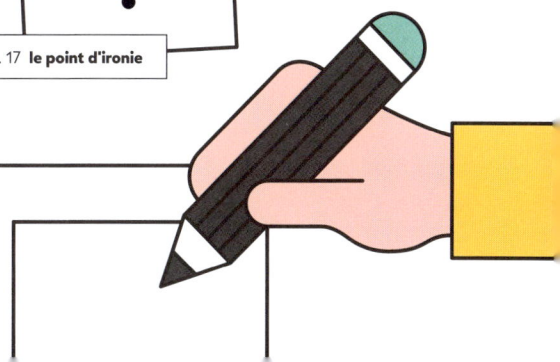

Fig. 19 **le point d'acclamation**

Fig. 18 **le point de doute**

Fig. 16 **le point d'autorité**

Fig. 17 **le point d'ironie**

Fig. 15 **le point de conviction**

Fig. 20 **joy** (Puck 1881: 65)

Fig. 21 **melancholy** (ibid.)

Fig. 22 **indifference** (ibid.)

Innovative pre-text-based emojis were created by typesetters at the American satirical magazine ›Puck‹ in 1881, who were keen to experiment. Using punctuation marks, they published different character combinations to represent four facial expressions. An ironic text accompanied the signs:

»We wish it to be distinctly understood that the letterpress department of this paper is not going to be trampled on by any tyranical crowd of artists in existence. We mean to let the public see that we can lay out, in our own typographical line, all the cartoonists that ever walked. For fear of startling the public we will give only a small specimen of the artistic achievements within our grasp, by way of a first instalment. The following are from Studies in Passions and Emotions. No copyright.«

(Puck 1881: 65)

The typesetters' representations were formally close to the text-based emojis used later. However, the characters created by the typesetters were difficult to use within a text, as they had to be typed over several lines. The pre-text-based emojis of the satirical magazine were not intended to be used within the text like the later text-based emojis. They were used for artistic expression and were used separately from the text – similar to illustrations.

Although the pre-textual emojis represent facial expressions associated with an emotion, their deployment and use is not comparable to that of today's emojis. The early attempts of typesetters with the punctuation marks that resemble today's text-based emojis are a fascinating precursor. It is interesting to note that the colon, hyphen and bracket combination was not discovered in this process for the purpose of using text-based emojis within a text. Other interesting pre-text-based emojis appeared in an editorial article entitled ›Telegraphische Zeichenkunst‹ in the ›Deutsche Postzeitung‹ (see Enzmann 2023: 44–45). The character combinations with which the pre-emojis were created were compiled using David Edward Hughes' type telegraph. They functioned according to the same principle as the later text-based emojis, but they were used separately from the text. Like the characters in the satirical magazine, they functioned more as an illustration for the text next to them than as a means of expression in writing.

Fig. 23 **astonishment** (ibid.)

There are other similar examples of such sign constellations, such as the pre-text-based emojis from 1893 in the ›Kreisblatt für den Kreis Malmedy‹ (Kreisblatt 1893). However, as these are similar in intent and form, the examples mentioned are representative of other such sign constellations.

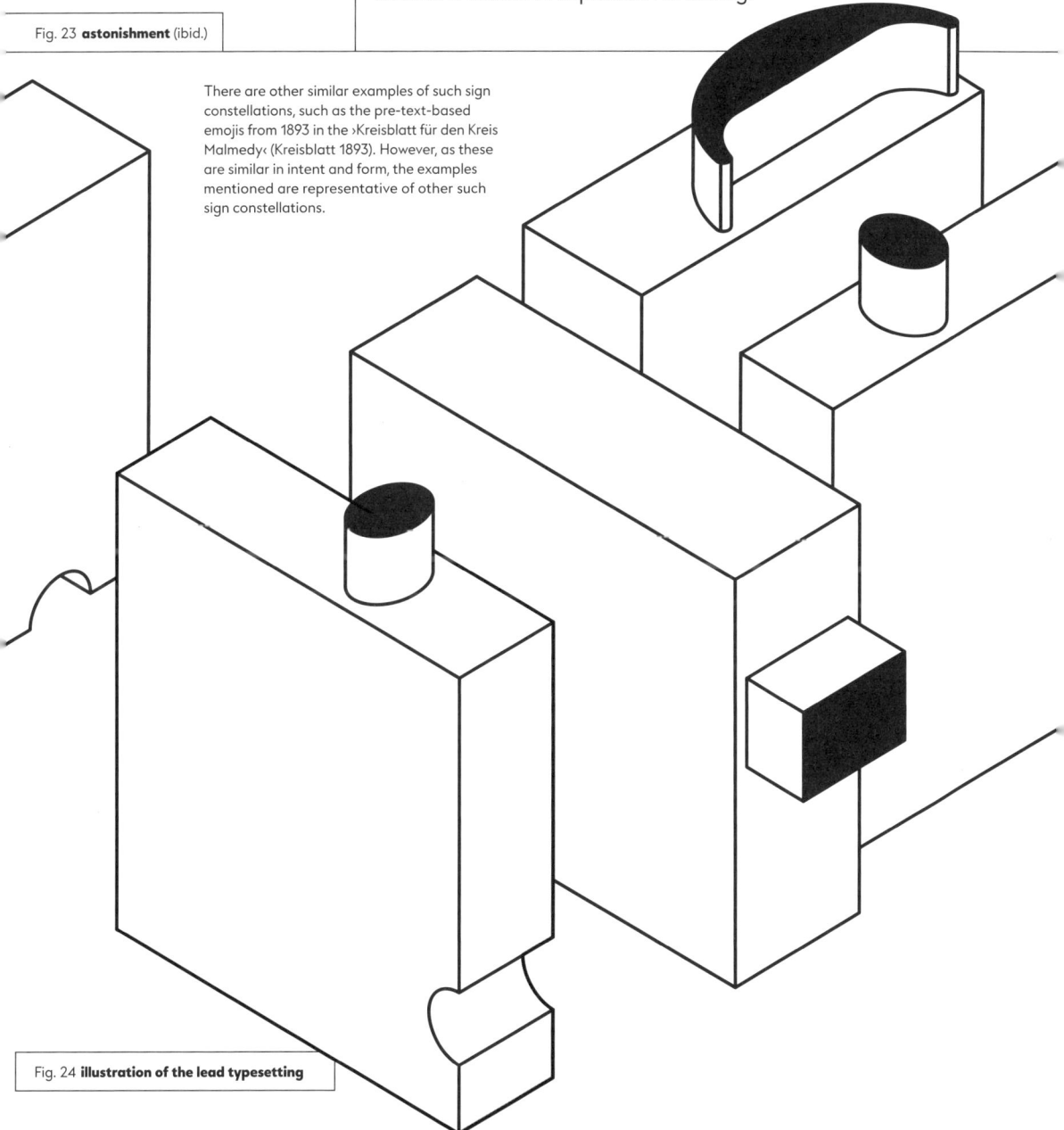

Fig. 24 **illustration of the lead typesetting**

There are numerous examples in which new sign combinations are constructed using typography to illustrate and can be regarded as pre-text-based emojis. Dadaist artists, for example, make use of such possibilities.

An interesting example comes from an ex-libris by Milan Šmíd (Fig. 25). The owl depicted on it was made by Šmíd during his apprenticeship, when students of typesetting were still learning commercial printing. This printing style was used for high-quality products such as business cards, bookplates or for special occasions such as wedding announcements or New Year's cards (Fig. 27). The ex-libris was shown as part of an exhibition presenting the work of first and second-year typesetting and printing apprentices. The exhibition took place in Prague on June 27, 1959. From a formal perspective, the owl is very close to the text-based emojis used later, but it was not integrated into the text.

A playful use of typography comes from the fairy tale ›die Scheuche‹ from 1925 (Schwitters et al. 1971), which is about a scarecrow on a farm. The figures in the fairy tale are represented by typefaces: The ›X‹ stands for the scarecrow, the B for the farmer and the ›O‹ for the rooster.

The example shown (Fig. 26) demonstrates how the typography illustrates the content of the fairy tale by anthropomorphizing constellations of punctuation marks and turning them into characters in the fairy tale. Human emotions, such as fear, were also attributed to the items of clothing.

As the punctuation marks function as characters in the fairy tale, they are comparable to text-based emojis, which are composed by combining punctuation marks to form images. the fairy tale serves as an example for the use of other such typographic character constellations.

There are several similar representations that can be regarded as forerunners of the ›ASCII art‹, including some that were created earlier (Hadley 1948: 181; Burghagen 1898: 1). From a formal perspective, such representations can be seen as predecessors of text-based emojis.

Fig. 25 **the owl on the ex-libris by Milan Šmíd** (Šmíd 2018)

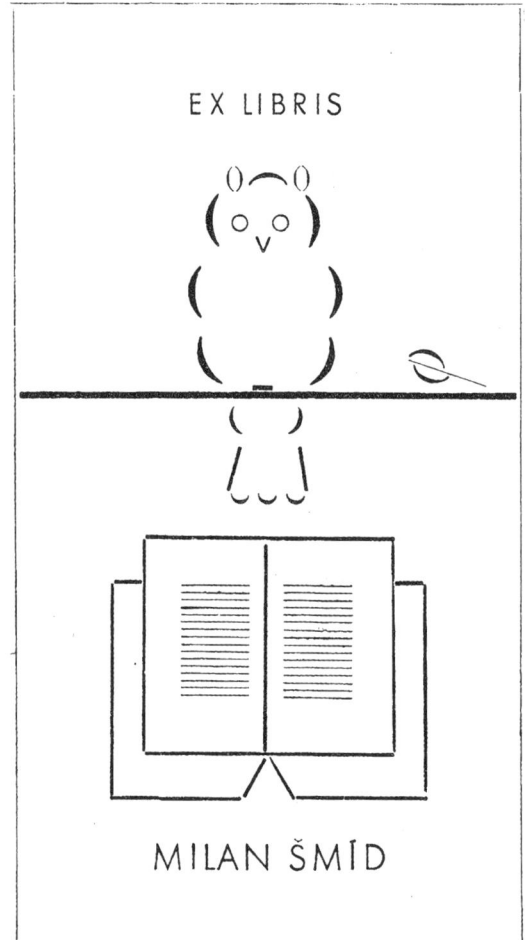

The Czech phrase ›Plnou paroudo Nového roku‹ used on Šmíd's New Year's card can be translated as ›full steam ahead into the New Year‹. It is a metaphorical expression that refers to a steam engine running at full power and speed. It expresses the wish for a dynamic and successful start to the new year.

Fig. 26 **punctuation constellations from ›die Scheuche‹** (Schwitters et al. 1971: 9)

Da forchte
sich der Hut-Schapo
da forchte sich der Frack
da forchte
sich der
B
ACH so
schöne Spitzenschal

Fig. 27 **image of a New Year's card by Milan Šmíd**

Plnou parou do Nového roku

a hodně úspěchů, zdraví a spokojenosti přeje

MILAN ŠMÍD

Pre-graphic Emojis

This category includes handwritten pictorial signs. These were found in letters and different documents.

There are several examples of the use of facial expressions in letters. One comes from Albrecht Dürer. His letter of September 8, 1506 to Nuremberg to Willibald Pirckheimer contains a depiction with disheveled hair (Fig. 29). According to Englmann, the communication partners maintained a friendship for many years, which was expressed in their letters through coded statements and so it remains a secret between the two as to what or whom the drawing is supposed to depict (cf. Englmann 2015: 19).

Fig. 28 **pre-graphical emojis by Ludwig Wittgenstein** (1968: 23)

Fig. 29 **detail of the letter by Albrecht Dürer** (Englmann 2015: 16)

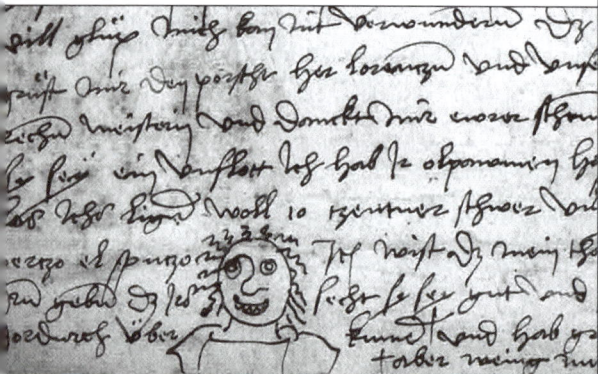

Fig. 30 **detail of the note by E.T.A. Hoffmann** (Englmann 2015: 16)

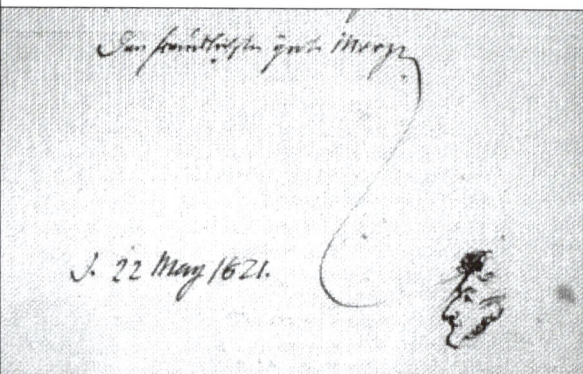

Fig. 31 **detail of the letter by Bernard Hennet** (Merta 2017)

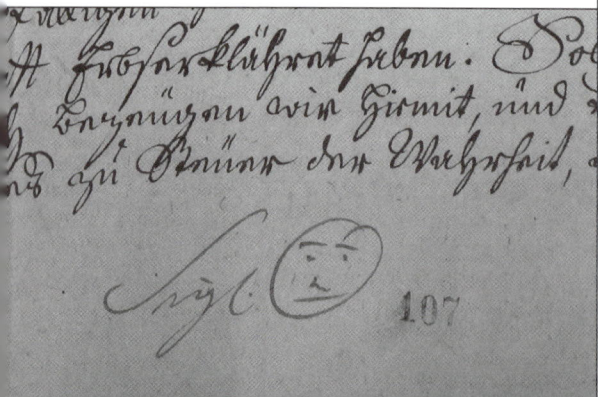

Fig. 32 **detail of the letter by Adolf Rueff** (Wiethölter 2008: 125)

A similar sign from the 18th century was discovered by the Czech organization ›Archaia Brno‹. The graphic depiction of a face (Fig. 31) was found in several letters written around 1741 by Bernard Hennet, abbot of the Cistercian monastery of Saar (›Žďár nad Sázavou‹) (cf. Merta 2017). It is not clear whether he used the sign himself or someone from the monastery, for example to confirm that the document had been read. In any case, the mark appeared next to the signature in several documents (cf. ibid.). It remains unclear what function the mark was intended to fulfill. The sign could illustrate the signature 😐 or visualize the author's mood 😊.
E.T.A. Hoffmann also used a pre-graphic emoji by signing a note to his friend Theodor Gottlieb von Hippel not with his name, but with a drawing of his profile (Fig. 30) (cf. Engelmann 2015: 82). It can therefore be assumed that the drawing was probably intended to take over the function of ⊗.

Christina Siever analyzed the illustrations in the Rebus letter of 1844 from the Swabian Adolf Rueff from Reutlingen to the sisters Alma and Bertha Froriep in Berlin as a precursor to emojis (Fig. 32) (Siever 2020: 131). The letter is interrupted by numerous illustrations that form a kind of riddle with the written text. By using pictorial signs to generate a kind of riddle, the signs took on a rebus or reference function. For example, the pictorial signs for a bear was inserted before ›liner‹ (Fig. 32) and, according to Siever, forms an ›acoustic analogy‹. The bear and the two following hares take on a reference function by replacing words or parts of words (cf. ibid.: 130).
A similar use of signs is also attributed to emoji communication, which is mainly expressed in the ⊗ function. Emojis are also used as a kind of picture puzzle. They are therefore used more for entertainment than to convey information. The most extensive example is the ›translation‹ of the literary classic ›Moby Dick‹ with emojis, in which emojis were added to the original text (see Benenson 2010). The example makes it clear that emojis cannot do without writing. According to Danesi, emojis trivialize the novel in a caricaturistic way, which leads to a reduction of critical thought (cf. Danesi 2017: 146).

However, according to him, the ›translation‹ could open up the content of the novel to a younger audience (cf. ibid.).

Signs used in rebus letters can be classified as pre-graphic emojis. Such letters were very popular throughout the 19th century (cf. Siever 2020: 130). According to Wiethölfer, epistolary iconography functions as a field of experimentation in which different forms of communication can be realized (cf. Wiethölter 2008: 122 f.). The Rebus letter mentioned here serves as a representative for other similar examples (e.g. Danesi 2017: 90).

Another suggestion for signs that belong in this group comes from Ludwig Wittgenstein. In the summer of 1938, during his lecture on aesthetics at the University of Cambridge, he compared language to a toolbox (cf. Wittgenstein 1968: 20). According to Wittgenstein, it is not only the tools themselves that matter, but also how they are used. He spoke about the use of language in aesthetic judgments and explained that if he had enough talent for drawing, he could depict a large number of facial expressions with a few strokes (cf. ibid.: 22). The text of Wittgenstein's lecture series shows three faces depicting different expressions (Fig. 28). According to Wittgenstein, words such as ›majestic‹ and ›pompous‹ could be expressed by faces. In his view, this would make our descriptions much more flexible and multifaceted than the use of adjectives.
Wittgenstein was concerned with clarifying nuances, as these are also conveyed in FTF communication with gestures or facial expressions (cf. ibid.: 20–23). He does not explain exactly how faces should be used in writing, so it remains unclear what function the faces can be assigned to. However, he was of the opinion that representations enable a more diverse and adaptable description than words and thus attributed qualities to visual communication that distinguish it from written communication (cf. ibid.: 20).

Another example that belongs in this group is ›cute handwriting‹, which mainly emerged in the 1970s. However, as this development is closely connected to kawaii culture, it is discussed in the sub-chapter ›Culture of Cuteness‹, see pages 66–67.

At this point, a brief digression on the ›Isotype‹ is necessary, as it influenced the formal development of pictograms and these in turn influenced the development of emojis. From the mid-1920s, Otto Neurath developed the ›Vienna Method of Pictorial Statistics‹ and, together with Gerd Arntz and Marie Reidemeister, developed it over the following ten years into a comprehensive pictorial language called ›Isotype‹ (International System of Typographic Picture Education) (cf. Sandner 2008: 464).

The aim of Neurath's visual language was, on the one hand, to use it as a tool for intercultural understanding. On the other hand, it was intended to disseminate knowledge in order to inform people with little education about political, social and economic issues (cf. Sandner 2008: 464).

According to Neurath, the purpose of a teaching image is to direct attention in a similar way to spoken language (cf. Neurath 1980: 41). The use of the isotype is therefore subject to strict, systematic rules (Fig. 34). According to Neurath, the arrangement of the characters or the distribution of colors must be chosen in the same way as the choice or emphasis of a word. He notes that written language lacks certain rules of rhythm:

»Special notes would be necessary to give an account of other shades of feeling, other shades of rhythm, a better idea of the distribution of weight in statements or words.«

(Neurath 1980: 41)

Neurath was of the opinion that the isotype, as an auxiliary language for teaching purposes, must pay attention to the question of rhythm. In order to effectively direct attention, factual images are characterized by the fact that they contain as few details as possible (cf. ibid.: 42). Thus, a picture produced according to the systematic rules of the Viennese method of picture statistics shows the most important things at first view; relevant details are recognizable at second and third view and if a picture provides further information at fourth and fifth view, it is considered pedagogically unsuitable from the point of view of the aforementioned Viennese school (cf. Hartmann/Bauer 2006: 49). For this reason, for example, faces were not depicted. Such a process of abstraction can lead to the stereotyping of ethnic groups, such as in the depiction of the ›five ethnic groups‹ (Fig. 33, see also pages 146–148).

During the development of visual language, a fascinating variety of signs (Fig. 35–Fig. 50) emerged. This was by no means a matter of course, because

---

Fig. 33 **signs for the five ethnic groups** (Neurath 1980: 33)

Fig. 34 **shoe + work = shoe work** (cf. ibid.: 35)

The use of the signs is subject to a clear and simply structured system. For example, the sign for ›shoe factory‹ is made up of the two signs for ›shoe‹ and ›factory‹ (cf. Neurath 1980: 35; edited by D.E.).

Fig. 35 **food**

Fig. 36 **nature**

Fig. 37 **nature**

Fig. 38 **mobility**

Fig. 39 **nature**

Fig. 40 **nature**

Fig. 41 **mobility**

Fig. 42 **at work**

Fig. 43 **at work**

Fig. 44 **people**

Fig. 45 **nature**

Fig. 46 **mobility**

Fig. 47 **people**

When selecting the Isotype signs shown on this page, care was taken to select signs whose similar motifs are also available in the emoji character set. The graphic design of the Isotype and the character sets available on mobile devices differs significantly. For example, while animals in the isotype character set are only depicted in shilouette form (Fig. 36 f., Fig. 39 f.), animals in the emoji character set are equipped with numerous details and shading. The size of the characters shown on the page depends on the amount of detail they contain to ensure good recognizability. They are designated by their corresponding category. The images (Fig. 35–Fig. 50) are from the archive of Gerd Arntz (Arntz © VG Bild-Kunst, Bonn 2024).

Fig. 48 **people**

Fig. 49 **food**

Fig. 50 **mobility**

at the time of the isotype, the graphic representation of facts was a new method that represented a complex process from a technical point of view (cf. Sandner 2008: 471 f.). The reproduction of the characters was produced in an elaborate manual process and later optimized through the use of printing techniques. Not only the production process, but also the high production costs had an influence on the appearance of the signs. Due to the limited printing conditions, it was sometimes necessary to avoid the use of several colors and instead work with different shading techniques (see Neurath 1980: 33).

The Isotype character set contains various motifs that are also available in the Emoji character set (Fig. 35–Fig. 50). However, due to the technical possibilities and the intentions of character use at the time, the two character sets differ in their graphic implementation. While the isotype was designed to visualize only what was necessary for understanding the character, emojis contain numerous details and no strict rules for use. According to Neurath, the different signs form the dictionary, the rules for the arrangement and combination of the signs form the visual grammar, and the transformation process of linguistic or numerical information into images forms the style of the visual language (cf. Sandner 2008: 474)

Neurath was of the opinion that the use of figurative language is more limited than that of spoken or written languages and reaches its limits more rapidly. He was of the opinion that figurative language was not suitable for exchanging views or expressing feelings and commands (cf. Neurath 1980: 20).

Although Neurath's vision for the use of the isotype was not fully realized, the signs created during its development serve as a source of inspiration for pictograms and international orientation systems. Neurath is also considered a pioneer of infographics and, alongside Otl Aicher, a trailblazer for the spread of pictograms. Aicher developed the signage for the 1972 Olympic Games in Munich. The pictograms he developed for the Olympic sports (Fig. 52) were based on geometric shapes and a stringent grid (Fig. 51) to enable intercultural communication. For Aicher, abstraction was associated with cultural neutrality, which leads to a global understanding (cf. Ulrich 2006: 65). This corresponds to Neurath's principle that nothing should be found in the picture that is not necessary for recognition (cf. Hartmann/Bauer 2006: 49).

Aicher was convinced that the modern world needed simple and interculturally understandable pictorial symbols to compensate for its increasing complexity (cf. Sandner 2008: 475).

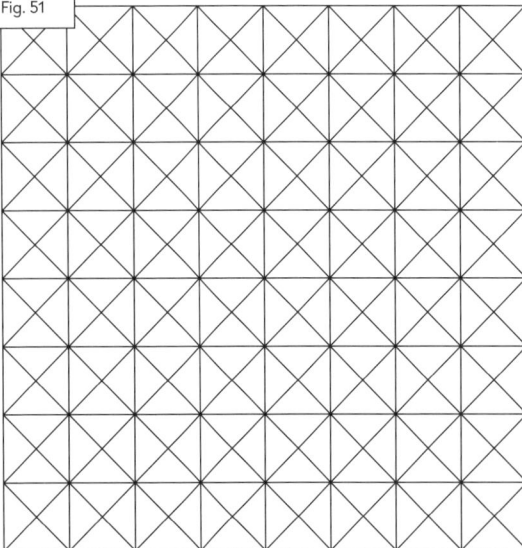

Fig. 51

Fig. 52

Aicher was commissioned in 1967 to design the 1972 Olympic Games in Munich (cf. Abdullah/Hübner 2006: 72). He was responsible for the design of the entire signage system for the Olympic Games. The design for all visual elements is based on a fascinating and well thought-out visual system (see for example Osterwalder 2020: 530–571).

Fig. 51 **the grid for pictograms and other graphic elements** (according to Osterwalder 2020: 547, edited by D.E.)

Fig. 52 **a small selection of pictograms for the Olympic sports** (Abdullah/Hübner 2006: 72 f.).

Fig. 53 **smiley by Harvey Ball** (ibid.)

Here is a digression on the famous smiley by advertising artist Harvey Ball. In 1963, the insurance company ›State Mutual Assurance Company‹ commissioned Ball to design buttons that could be pinned on to improve the working atmosphere (Kringiel 2011). Ball designed the button by creating a smiling yellow face – the smiley (Fig. 53).

The buttons were distributed to employees and customers. Ball's invention caused the yellow face to be associated with positive feelings and a good mood. According to Kringiel, the smiley was popular and quickly gained a high level of recognition, so that the motif was later reprinted countless times (cf. ibid.).

The smiley was used nine years later in the newspaper ›France Soir‹ to indicate positive news (Fig. 54). The management consultant Franklin Loufrani wanted to signal to people that good news was being spread in his newspaper. According to Loufrani, after years of negative headlines about the Vietnam War, positive news was in demand and so he suggested printing a smiley next to positive news (cf. ibid.). In January 1972, the first edition of the newspaper ›France Soir‹ appeared with a slightly modified smiley (France Soir 1972: 1). It was used as a kind of marker for good mood to indicate entire articles. It thus visualizes the positivity of what is written and is comparable to the function 🖳. By also replacing the letter ›o‹ in the France Soir lettering (Fig. 54), the smiley fulfilled the function ⊗.

In the years that followed, the smiley face became the identifying sign of both the music movement ›Acid House‹ and the band ›Nirvana‹. Nirvana used a modified, distorted version of the smiley with crossed eyes and a tongue sticking out to express their rebellious side.

Numerous companies subsequently used visual analogies with a smiling face as part of their visual language, see also page 185.

Fig. 54 **excerpt of the first ›France Soir‹ from 1972** (Stein 2022)

Fig. 55

A character set that can be regarded as a formal and functional predecessor of emojis comes from the artist and graphic designer Wolfgang Schmidt. He developed a system of characters using the human body as a starting point. He created over 200 signs from the period 1972 to 1979 and planned a system of almost 900 signs (cf. Schmidt 1992: 75).

Out of intellectual and creative interest, Schmidt defined a catalog of signs relevant to him and developed his own pictorial sign system over decades, which he called ›Lebenszeichen‹ [signs of life] (cf. Nielsen/Weirich 2021: 179).

The aim of the sign system is not to work without writing, on the contrary, his signs are intended to complement the standard linguistic sign system and, according to Schmidt, become a toy for different purposes, which he sees as belonging to the area of visual poetry (cf. Schmidt 1992: 74). The linear signs do not only refer to the human body but, according to Schmidt, are an attempt to measure the cosmos of experience (cf. Schmidt 1992: 75).

The signs were created according to a strict formal and functional system (Fig. 56, Fig. 61).

In the various applications, the signs were combined, superimposed, scaled and rearranged (cf. ibid.: 84) (Fig. 63).

Fig. 56 **constructive structure of the sign ›eye‹** (according to Schmidt 1992: 73, edited by D.E.)

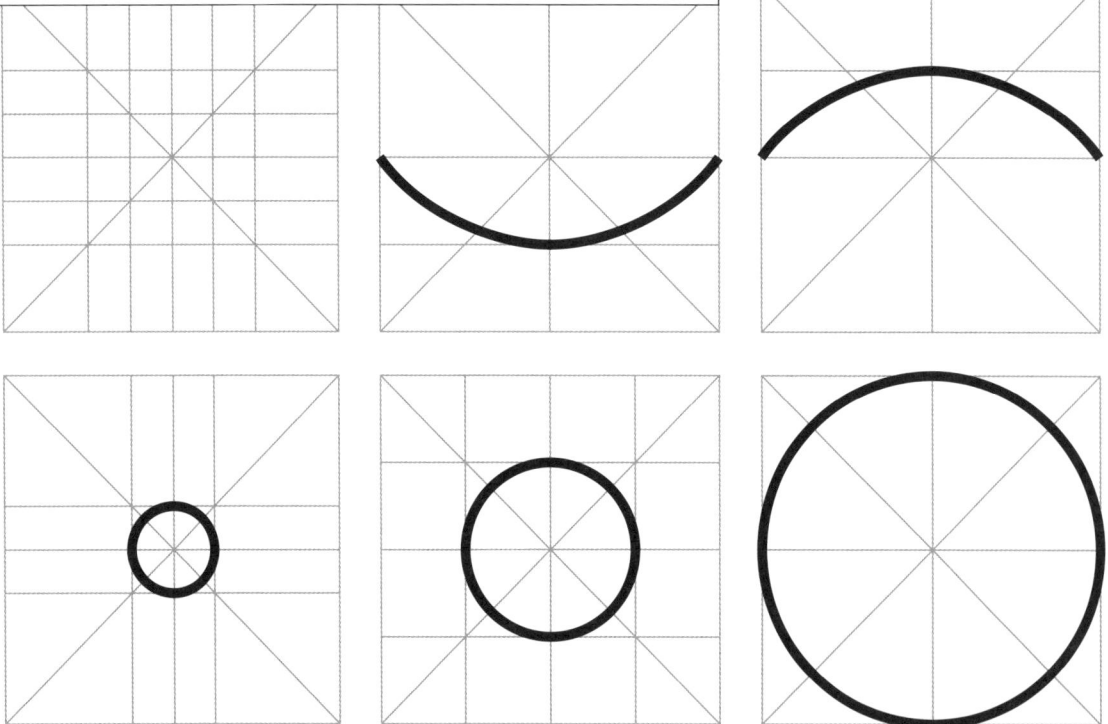

Fig. 57

Fig. 58

Fig. 59

Fig. 60

Fig. 61

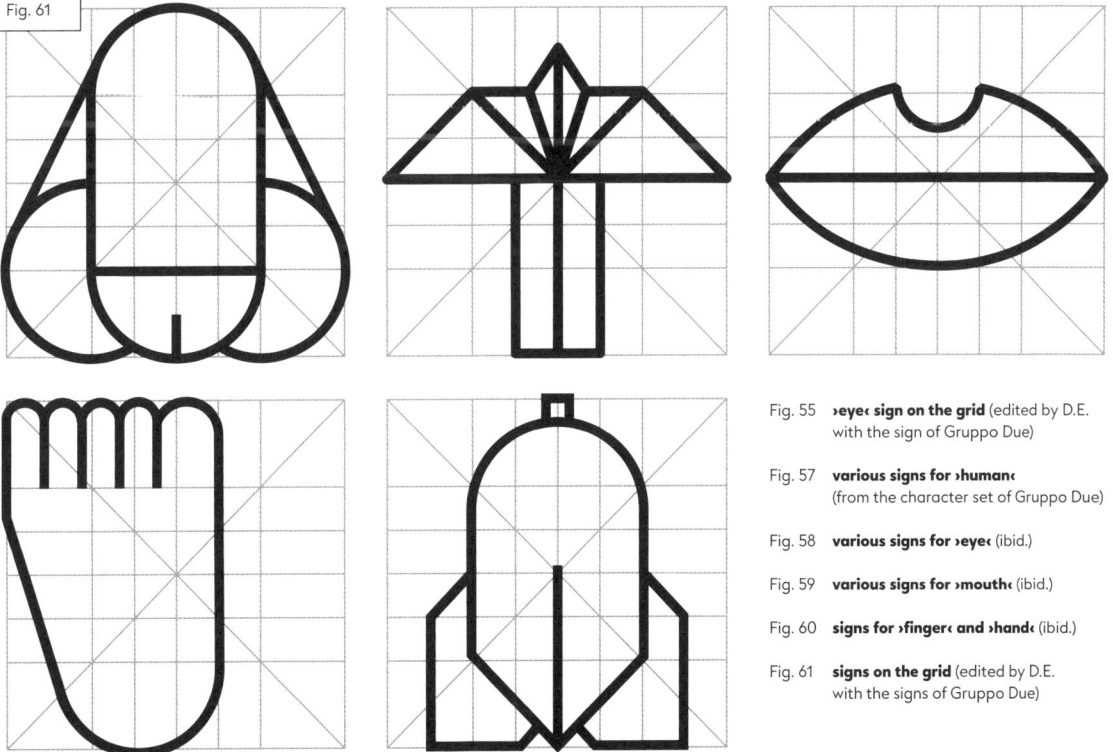

Fig. 55   ›eye‹ **sign on the grid** (edited by D.E. with the sign of Gruppo Due)

Fig. 57   **various signs for ›human‹** (from the character set of Gruppo Due)

Fig. 58   **various signs for ›eye‹** (ibid.)

Fig. 59   **various signs for ›mouth‹** (ibid.)

Fig. 60   **signs for ›finger‹ and ›hand‹** (ibid.)

Fig. 61   **signs on the grid** (edited by D.E. with the signs of Gruppo Due)

Schmidt developed the signs from his own world of life, feelings and thoughts (cf. Nielsen/Weirich 2021: 181). He worked on various possible applications and used the signs in both free and commercial projects. He even thought about translating the graphic signs into another system, such as sound signals, where the stroke widths would influence the volume of the respective sign (cf. Schmidt 1992: 85). He developed a playful approach to geometric shapes, in which the meaning was changed by adding or omitting elements (cf. Nielsen/Weirich 2021: 180). Nielsen and Weirich noted that Schmidt's visual-poetic play with signs and text is reminiscent of analog predecessors of emojis (cf. Nielsen/Weirich 2021: 179).

His formal and functional elaborations confirm this assumption. Schmidt not only designed each character with the utmost care, but also experimented with different variations (Fig. 57–Fig. 60) and possible combinations (Fig. 63). As a result, he created a fascinating system that offers a wide range of possible applications. From a formal point of view, the characters are strongly reminiscent of graphic emojis. In their functionality and combinability, the signs of life are also similar to text-based emojis, which were later developed further by the users and offer an incredible variety of possible combinations. Schmidt was a pioneer in the development of pre-emojis, not only from a graphic but also from a functional point of view.

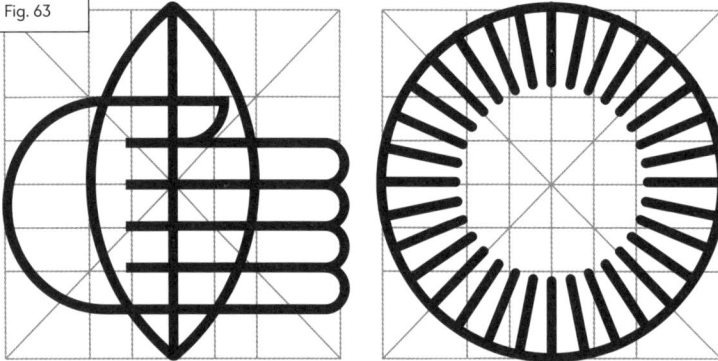

Fig. 63

Representation of the signs of life in different combinations and arrangements.
Excerpts graphically paraphrased according to Schmidt with the signs of life of Gruppo Due (Schmidt 1992: 105; Gruppo Due).

As part of Maxim Weirich's diploma project from 2019, the signs of life were digitized for the first time and were part of the exhibition ›Piktogramme, Lebenszeichen, Emojis: Die Gesellschaft der Zeichen‹ at the Leopold-Hoesch-Museum Düren from 2020/2021. In this context, a font was created that is based on the same design grid as the signs of life (Fig. 62) (Gruppo Due). Typographers Bruno Jacoby and Moritz Appich designed the ›G2 Kosmos‹ font in the ›Regular‹ and ›Extended‹ weights, with rounded and geometrically structured letters based on Schmidt's system and combining the Lebenszeichen with diacritical marks.

By comparing the signs of life with emojis and continuing Schmidt's work, the authors not only emphasize his influence on the development of visual communication, but also pay tribute to his pioneering work in this field.

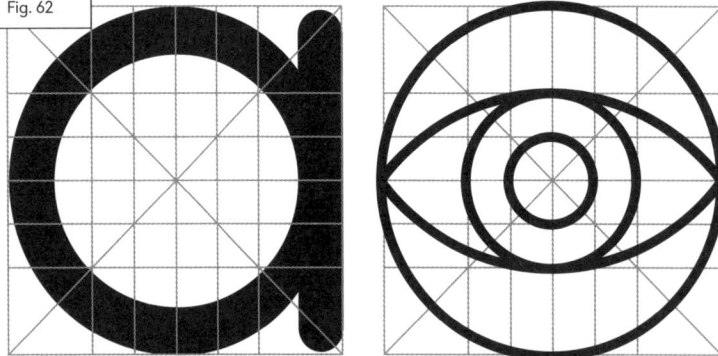

Fig. 62

Fig. 62 **letter ›a‹ from the font ›G2 Kosmos‹ in the grid of Lebenszeichen and the eye with the diacritical mark from Gruppo Due.**
The designers combined the pictorial signs with typographic properties to create a new glyph.

The History of Emojis

Since we can only speak of a historical development of emojis since the emergence of computer-mediated communication, the history of emojis begins with the emergence of CMC. In the following, character systems, characters or character constellations that have contributed to the development and spread of emojis are discussed in order to understand the emergence and expansion of emojization.

How did emojis develop and what impact did the technical conditions have on the design of the characters?

The identification of pre-emojis shows that the desire for means to supplement the standard linguistic sign system to compensate for the lack of paralinguistic and non-verbal means of expression in writing did not only arise with the advent of CMC. Approaches that were used to compensate for such deficiencies range from signs for irony, indignation or to indicate a rhetorical question, for example, to systems that enable a writer to express feelings. From a formal point of view, the main aim was to fulfill the functions of the ›interpretation cue‹ using the standard language sign system or a modified form of it, see pages 19–23.

Constellations of punctuation marks depicting a face or a figure were also developed long before CMC, see pages 24–27. The same applies to approaches that gave visual communication qualities that exceed those of written communication.

Neurath's visual language found its way into everyday life by revolutionizing the graphic representation of information and laying the foundation for the creation of pictograms, which in turn served as a formal source of inspiration for emojis. However, this did not create a system with which pictograms could be integrated into everyday language and which had the functional range of emojis.[2] In order to trace the emergence and spread of emojis, the historical development of signs is discussed in the following. According to Frutiger, forms of writing and signs do not develop from intellectual considerations alone, but from the given material – in the case of emojis through the possibilities of technology (cf. Frutiger 2004: 122). For this reason, it is necessary to address the technical conditions and possibilities in addition to the characters and character sets created. Devices with which the characters were generated are shown in the form of isometric line graphics in order to understand how the characters were created.

As the focus of this book is on the design of the signs, individual signs of the historical reconstruction are presented in a grid. To improve visual comparability, all characters based on a square grid are presented in the same unit size per grid point. Characters without a grid are displayed with a pixel size of 1 mm and characters with a grid with a pixel size of 3 mm. This makes it possible to better understand the structure and design of the signs. Characters that are not based on a pixel-based grid are displayed according to their underlying grid or construction rules.

---

1   These functions contribute to the understanding of a message by being used either as a hint, for example to mark a joke, or to visualize the writer's attitude. For an explanation of the linguistic description frame, see page 11.

2   However, this was not the aim of Neurath's visual language. It mainly served to educate and convey information. Consequently, isotypes and pictograms are predecessors of emojis from a formal, but not a functional perspective.

PLATO Programmed Logic for Automatic Teaching Operations

The ›Plato‹ project started in the 1960s at the ›University of Illinois‹ (cf. Dear 2017: 23/58). It was a research project and one of the first computer-assisted learning systems (Michel 2005: 493). Based on the definition of emojis in this book, the signs that originated in Plato can be considered some of the first emojis.

The computer system made it possible to exchange text files (›notesfile‹) in the central network. Plato was used as a kind of forum, but it only allowed limited nesting, i.e. there was no thread structure (cf. Dear 2017: 249). The number of such text files grew rapidly in the 1970s and there were notes on all kinds of topics such as film, politics or relationships (cf. ibid.). As it was difficult to handle the increasing number of text files, a forum was introduced, allowing various threads on different topics to be created.

With increased use of the computer system, users began to use overlaid letters, see pages 40–41. Other technological developments such as ›Talkomatic‹ – a kind of chat room – enabled the exchange of four-line typed messages between up to five active users. More than five users were not possible due to the limited screen size. The special thing about Talkomatic was that the chat was not transmitted line by line as in today's chat, but that each typed character was immediately visible. According to David Woolley, this enabled a livelier conversation than is practiced in today's chat with the ›send‹ button (cf. Woolley 1994).

The characters created by Plato are similar to the variety of text-based emojis created by users. Functionally and syntactically, they were able to fully fulfill the same functions as today's emojis, even if they were more cumbersome to use than today's emojis. The character combinations had to be generated anew each time they were used. The Plato pictorial signs and instructions for creating them were collected in files.

The special thing about Plato was its orange color, which, according to Dear, was described by Plato users as ›the friendly orange glow‹ (cf. Dear 2017: 111). According to Dear, even the black screen was never deep black; instead, a slight orange glow shimmered through it. Dear compared the effect to that of a campfire, which creates a pleasant atmosphere for users and therefore gave rise to the term (cf. ibid.).

A detailed historical review of the computer system can be found in Dear 2017.

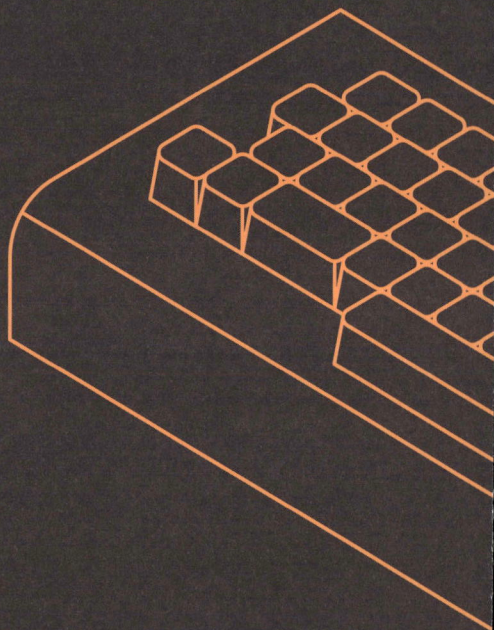

Fig. 64 **illustration of a Plato workplace**

With increased prevalence of the computer system, users began to employ superimposed letters to create a new representation so-called ›text emoticons‹ according to Dear (cf. Dear 2017: 338). Plato made it possible to move the cursor back one letter by simultaneously pressing the ›Shift‹ and ›Space‹ keys. If a key was pressed again, the typed character was placed over the last character (cf. ibid.: 339). This made it possible to create an emoji using the letter combination ›ABOTXW‹ (Fig. 65).

The computer system allowed the cursor, which was invisible at that time, to be moved up or down by one pixel by pressing additional keys (cf. Dear 2017: 340 f.). This enabled the creation of an incredible variety of text-based emojis (Fig. 67–Fig. 101).

The technical possibilities created a playful approach to pictorial signs in the Plato computer system, which were actively used in exchanges between users.

Fig. 65 **letters from Plato used to create an emoji** (Fig. 66)

Fig. 66 **visualization of the process of overlaying letters** (according to Dear 2017: 270 f.; Dear 2010, edited by D.E.)

Fig. 67 **half smile**

Fig. 68 **relieved smile** [43 px]

Fig. 69 **mask**

Fig. 70 **upside-down smile** [42 px]

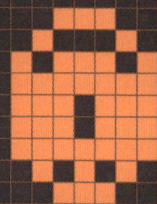

Fig. 71 **sad face**

Fig. 72 **smile**

Fig. 73 **top hat smile** [37 px]

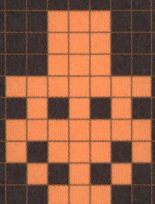

Fig. 74 **frown**

Fig. 75 **king** [85 px]

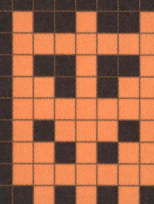

Fig. 76 **cheshire cat**

Fig. 77 **giggly face**

Fig. 78 **toothy smiley**

Fig. 79 **bomb** [48 px]

Fig. 80 **owl in a tree**

Fig. 81 **uncle sam**

Fig. 82 **lollipop** [21 px]

Fig. 83 **lyre**

Fig. 84 **waterbug**

Fig. 85 **telephone**

Fig. 86 **tv set**

Fig. 87 **bug** [25 px]

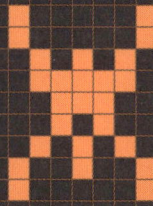

Fig. 88 **mini mask**

Fig. 89 **buddha/bell**

Fig. 90 **mask**

Fig. 91 **scorpion**

Fig. 92 **golden age flash** [43 px]

Fig. 93 **batman**

Fig. 94 **beer**

Fig. 95 **big jaw mask**

Fig. 96 **street light**

Fig. 97 **bug** [85 px]

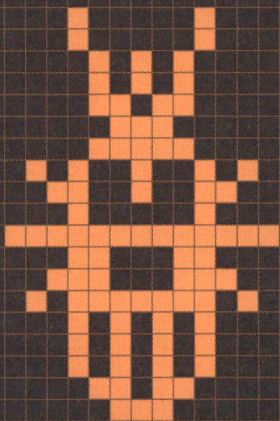

Fig. 98 **devil**

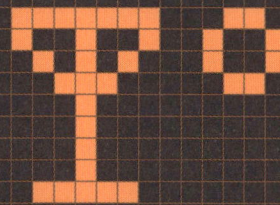

Fig. 99 **aunt bluebell**

Fig. 100 **lemon**

Fig. 101 **bloody mary**

Fig. 102 **possible use** (edited by D.E.)

All Plato emojis shown were reproduced by the author based on the following sources of Dear (2002; 2010; 2017: 270 f.).
Dear contributed to the reconstruction of the signs of the time through a personal exchange that provided a wealth of detailed and valuable information.

Scott E. Fahlman

In 1982, the most significant and groundbreaking invention in the development of text-based emojis happened. A warning message from Howard Gayle caused misunderstandings during a discussion about physics experiments in an online forum at ›Carnegie Mellon University‹, as humorous and serious comments could not be distinguished by all participants. In order to solve the problem, a day-long discussion began with the intention of finding a suitable sign with which a joke could be marked (cf. Fahlman 2002).

As the online forum at the time only allowed ASCII characters, the participants limited their search to characters and character combinations that could be created using the standard ASCII keyboard character system from the ADM-3A Terminal (Fig. 109). The debate started with characters that should be used for marking, such as the asterisk or the percent sign (cf. Fahlman 2002). After Keith Wright's suggestion to use the ampersand because it resembles a fat man twitching with laughter, the punctuation marks were compared to body-like features. Leonard Hamey, for example, suggested the hash mark to indicate jokes, as he said it represented an open mouth showing teeth in laughter. The last two suggestions probably inspired Scott E. Fahlman to create his on September 19, 1982:

»I propose that the following character sequence for joke markers:

:-)

Read it sideways. Actually, it is probably more economical to mark things that are NOT jokes, given current trends. For this, use

:-(«

(Fahlman 2002)

His suggestion was followed by Jeff Shrager's objection that it is not enough to label a joke. In his opinion, further gradations are necessary and so he proposed a coding scheme in which various aspects, such as insult, humor, information content or boredom, can be rated on a scale. After further contributions, Fahlman's proposal finally prevailed. The text-based emoji spread from the online forum at Carnegie Mellon University on November 10 of the same year. James Morris sent an email to the Xerox research center ›PARC‹ in California with the subject ›Communications Breakthrough‹ to draw attention to Fahlman's discovery. He wrote that the :-) signified a joke and the corresponding counterpart :-(indicated negative news content. He also presented further variations of the original sign and provided explanations (Fig. 103-Fig. 108). The original messages were lost for years until 2002, when the entertaining course of the discussion was restored thanks to a back-up (cf. ibid.).

Based on the combination of characters proposed by Fahlman, an incredible variety of other 90-degree text-based emojis subsequently emerged. Fahlman's intention for using his proposal was clearly aimed at labeling a joke. The subsequent proposals by Morris (Fig. 103–Fig. 108) show a further level for the communicative use of text-based emojis, as the many possible uses and combinations of the characters were recognized.

Fig. 103	Fig. 104	Fig. 105	Fig. 106	Fig. 107	Fig. 108
(:-)	@=	<:-)	oo	o>-<|=	~=

**Suggestions for further
text-based emojis**

Fig. 103 **for messages dealing
with bicycle helmets**
Fig. 104 **for messages dealing
with nuclear war**
Fig. 105 **for dumb questions**
Fig. 106 **for somebody's head-lights
are on messages**
Fig. 107 **for messages of interest
to women**
Fig. 108 **a candle, to annotate
flaming messages**

(Fahlman 2002)

For the entertaining discussion
on finding a sign to mark a joke,
see Fahlman 2002.
For a detailed explanation of the
technical situation at the time,
see Fahlman 2021. The text
below is an excerpt from it.

In 1982, the
›Computer Science
Department‹ at Carnegie
Mellon University used ADM-3A
terminals with a character selection
limited to the 7-bit ASCII character set.
This contained upper and lower case letters,
the numbers 0 to 9 and a limited selection of
punctuation marks. All computers in the department were connected via Ethernet so that
text messages could be sent from one computer
on campus to another. The use of ARPAnet, the
forerunner of today's internet, also made it possible to send email messages to an individual or
to so-called ›bulletin boards‹ or ›bboards‹.

The
last of
these created
a primitive form of
social networking with
text-only messages, without
photos or links (cf. Fahlman 2021).

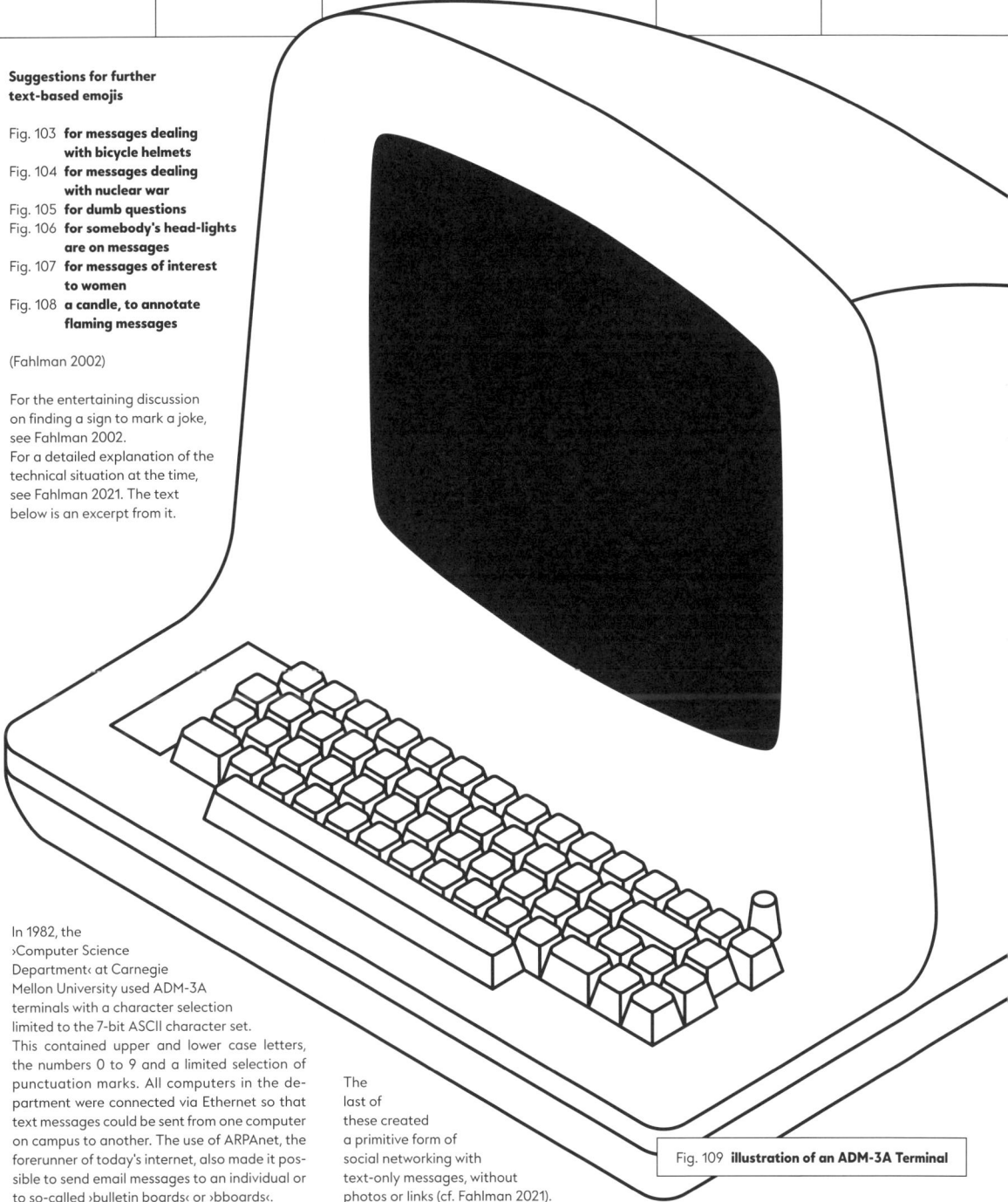

Fig. 109 **illustration of an ADM-3A Terminal**

In addition to vertical text-based Emojis, horizontal text-based Emojis, also known as ›kaomojis‹[3] have developed in Japan.

HORIZONTAL TEXT-BASED EMOJIS

Fig. 110

(^_-)

Fig. 111

(T_T)

Fig. 112

(°_°;)

Fig. 113

(^_^)

Fig. 114

(+_°)

Fig. 115

(_ _)°°

Fig. 116

(~3~)

Fig. 117

(^3^)-*

According to various sources, the first kaomoji (Fig. 113) was invented between 1985 and 1986 by Yasushi Wakabayashi (cf. Suzuki 2007: 94; Abel 2020: 31). Other sources claim that the use of vertical text-based emojis was adopted by the ›JUNET community‹ (Japan Unix Network), which connected research institutions and universities via a non-commercial computer network (cf. Oberwinkler 2020: 104 f.; Katsuno/Yano 2002: 210).

According to Katsuno and Yano, kaomojis emerged around 1986 in the second large Japanese network community ›pasokon tsūshin‹, which connected public users – and not exclusively academic users like JUNET (cf. ibid.: 207).
For Europeans, the kaomoji for ›smiling‹ (Fig. 113) does not obviously represent a smile, but rather a friendly, neutral face. Studies looking at the reasons for the different development of signs in Eastern and Western cultures have found that the reasons are based on a cultural background: as facial expressions are traditionally used with restraint in Japan, the participants in the conversation focus more on the eyes of the other person in order to infer the other person's feelings. In contrast, Western conversation participants concentrate more on the mouth (cf. Yuki et al. 2007: 303-310). According to the study by Yuki et al., the culturally influenced use of para-linguistic elements of FTF communication influences the visualization of facial expressions through kaomojis in the respective cultural area.
The facial expressions in kaomojis are much more

Fig. 118 **sparkling smile** (Enzmann 2023a: 76)

キタ――――。°゚+.ヽ(´∀`*)ノ゚+.° ――――!!

3   Literally translated, ›kaomoji‹ means ›face characters‹ (cf. Shirai 2009: 69), also known as ›kawaicons‹ (ibid.: 137).

Horizontal / vertical text-based Emojis
Fig. 110 / Fig. 119 **winking**
Fig. 111 / Fig. 120 **crying**
Fig. 112 / Fig. 121 **scare**
Fig. 113 / Fig. 122 **smiling**

Fig. 114 / Fig. 125 **being drunk**
Fig. 115 / Fig. 126 **sleeping**
Fig. 116 / Fig. 127 **kissing in love**
Fig. 117 / Fig. 128 **kiss mouth**
(Schlobinski/Watanabe 2006: 29f.)

VERTICAL TEXT-BASED EMOJIS

Fig. 119

;-)

Fig. 120

:'-(

Fig. 121

:-O

Fig. 122

:-)

Fig. 125

#*)

Fig. 126

zzz

Fig. 127

:-*

Fig. 128

:-{}

differentiated than in vertical text-based emojis, as they contain several nuances. In addition, Japanese chatters are creative in their use of text-based emojis. They invent some and add explanations (cf. Shirai 2009: 74), resulting in an enormous variety of different character combinations. On the one hand, this can be attributed to the different cultural understanding of facial expressions, but also to the writing systems used and the technical possibilities of Japanese mobile phones (cf. Schlobinski/Watanabe 2003: 409). To understand this, a brief consideration of the writing systems used and the digital text processing technologies that make kaomojis possible is helpful. Kavanagh explained this as follows: In the Japanese writing system, the Latin alphabet is used alongside the Chinese char-

acters kanji and kana. Kana consists of hiragana and katakana (cf. Kavanagh 2020: 150). According to Kavanagh, the reason why the horizontal text-based emojis are more varied than the vertical text-based emojis is that users have access to different character sets and the Japanese language offers great flexibility and variety in terms of orthography. Software also enables the direct transfer of individual characters into different character sets, making it easier to use the different writing systems. Japanese users can access character sets that contain an extremely wide variety of different characters and therefore have a greater number of options for creating text-based emojis (cf. ibid.). In addition to the options for using different character sets, Shirai emphasizes that users often make

Fig. 123 **hugging** (ibid.)

(つ^▽^)つc(•﹏•c)

Fig. 124 **angry** (ibid.)

ヽ(`д´;)/

an effort to express themselves ›kawaii‹, see also pages 68–69 (cf. Shirai 2005: 53). It is a gesture of politeness to make an effort when creating text-based emojis. Thus, the diversity of horizontal text-based emojis is due to cultural, technical and linguistic factors (ibid.).

In addition to the meaning of the elements used, the use of culturally specific gestures – such as bowing to say thank you (›dogeza‹) – also plays an important role in the interpretation of text-based emojis. In Japanese culture, it is customary to apologize instead of saying thank you, as inconvenience can be caused by receiving a favour. Thus, the dogeza-performing kaomoji (Fig. 134) is used to ask for something, to apologize or to show thankfulness (cf. Karpinska et al. 2020: 72; Shirai 2005: 56). Using horizontal text-based emojis, a way was found to represent adjectives such as ›delicious‹ (Fig. 133) or a state such as freezing (Fig. 129) (cf. Oberwinkler 2020: 113). They are also able to represent complete scenes, such as the depiction of a horizontal turning movement (Fig. 130), two kissing individuals (Fig. 131) or the sequence of a bow (Fig. 132). Matsuda compares such signs to scenes in the theater, as they represent an entire communication situation in which it is suggested that the interacting parties are present in the same place. The author notes that such signs function as the scenic backdrop of a particular utterance and as such resemble the functions of onomatopoeic expressions, which also deictically refer to scenes (cf. Matsuda 2020: 206).

Fig. 129 **trembling and ice-cold cheeks** (Oberwinkler 2020: 113)
Fig. 130 **horizontal rotary movement** (Matsuda 2020: 204)
Fig. 131 **kissing** (ibid.: 201)
Fig. 132 **procedure of a bow** (Kavanagh 2020: 158)
Fig. 133 **delicious** (Oberwinkler 2020: 113)
Fig. 134 **dogeza-performing kaomoji** (Karpinska et al. 2020: 72)

Fig. 129

{{{(+_+)}}}

Fig. 130

(^_^)(^_)(^)( )(^)(_^)(^_^)

Fig. 131

(*^3(*^O^*)

Fig. 132

(*-)(* _ _)

Fig. 133

(^Q^)

Fig. 134

m(__)m

Icons

In order to do the tracing of emojis and possible predecessors justice, a brief excursus on the development of icons is necessary at this point.

Fig. 136 **detail of the ›design icon‹ in the grid**

The word ›icon‹ comes from the Greek ›eikon‹, which means similarity or image (Abdullah/Hübner 2006: 207). Since conventional written instructions in the computer field were too cumbersome to make technical expressions understandable across languages and without subject-specific terms, the term ›icon‹ was introduced (cf. ibid.). Icons thus became an important component of graphical user interfaces. In contrast to pictograms, according to Abdullah and Hübner, icons have a high entertainment factor, but at the same time fulfill important routine functions on mobile phones, computers and other electronic interfaces; especially when there is not enough space for text. Icons can also be animated and are therefore capable of conveying more information than a single image (cf. ibid.: 206 f.).

The ›Xerox Alto‹ contained the first ›Graphical User Interface‹ (GUI), which already included icons for ›folders‹ or ›documents‹ (Fig. 135). The use of graphic elements such as icons or windows and the use of a mouse enabled intuitive interaction with the computer and thus laid the foundation for the design of modern user interfaces.

Fig. 135 **icons for the first GUI** (Bergerhausen/Helmig: 44)

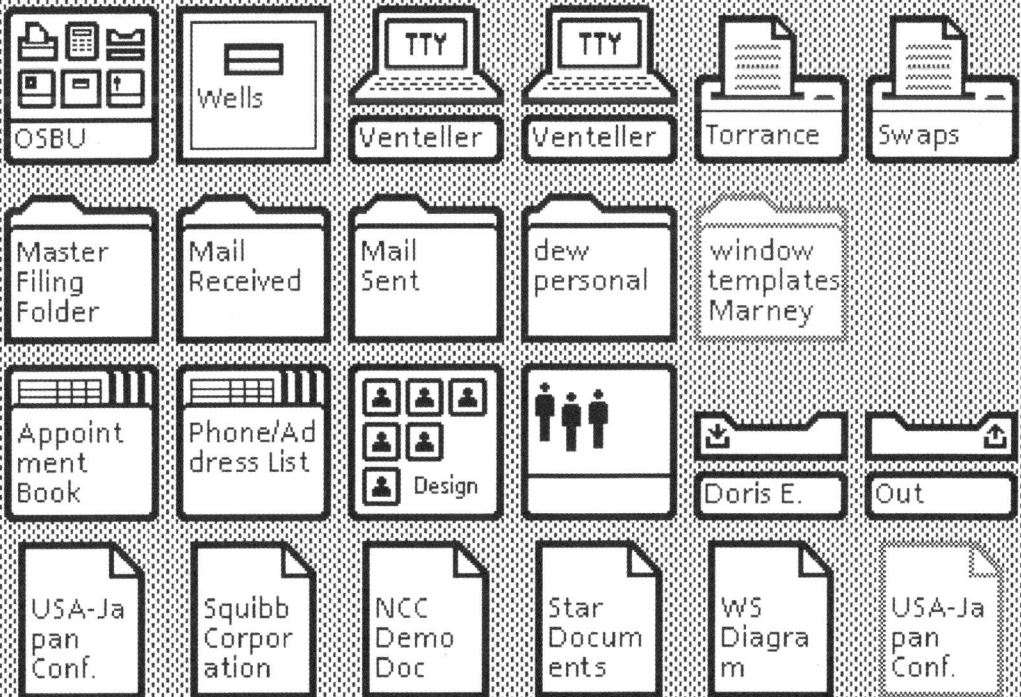

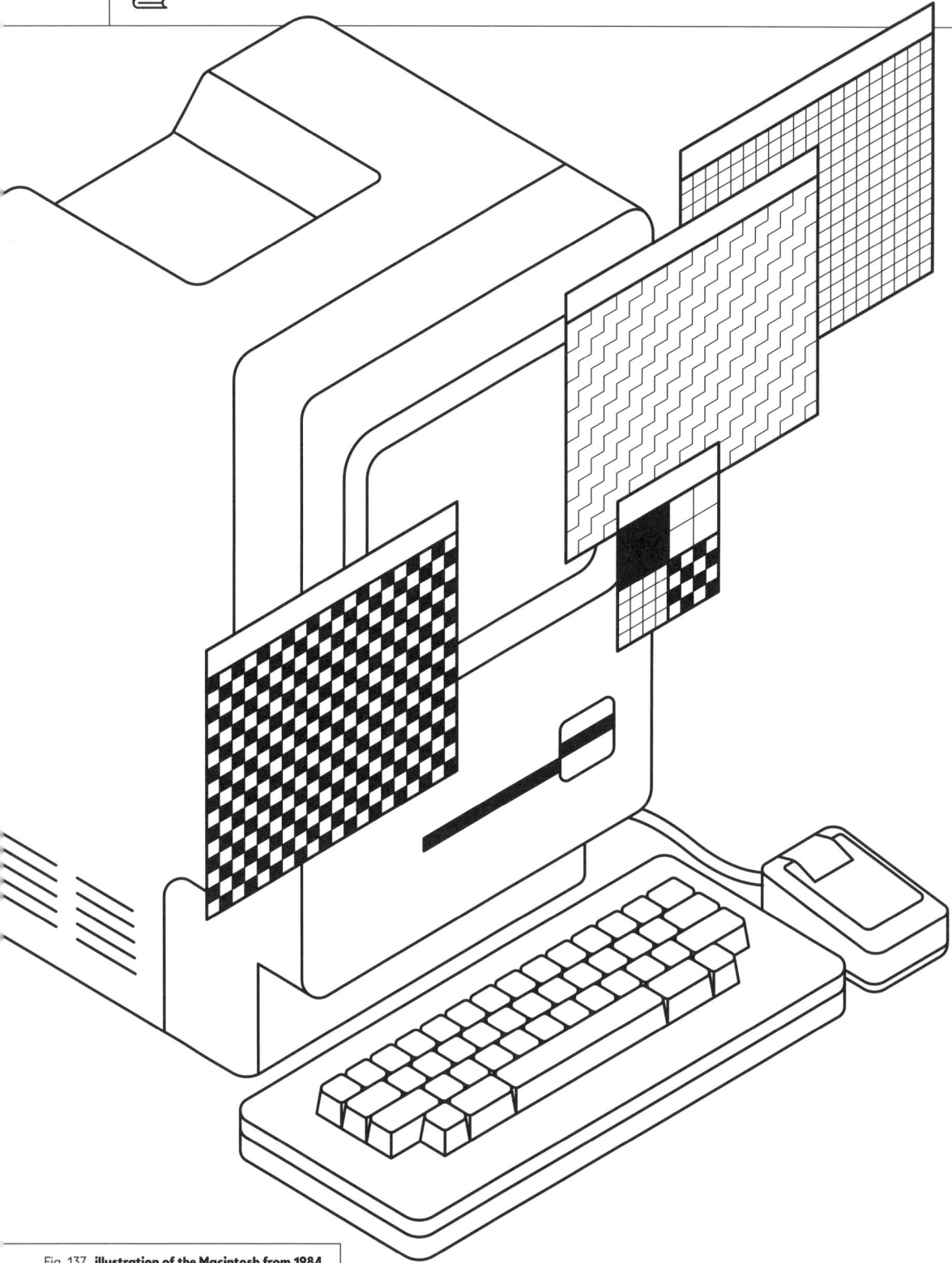

Fig. 137 **illustration of the Macintosh from 1984**

Susan Kare

Fig. 138

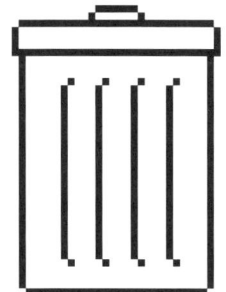

Susan Kare is considered the pioneer of icons. She worked at Apple from 1983 to 1986 and designed icons and fonts for the Macintosh, which was launched in 1984 under the direction of Steve Jobs. Her groundbreaking work is still recognizable today.

Based on a grid and the arrangement of several pixels, Kare created a series of icons that simplified the use of computers.

»Icon design is like solving a puzzle, trying to marry an image and idea that, ideally, will be easy for people to understand and remember.«

(Kare in: Le Moign 2022)

Her aim was to transform the cold, impersonal image of a machine (Fig. 137) (cf. Abdullah/Hübner 2006: 208–209). By anthropomorphizing the Macintosh icon (Fig. 203), for example, she created a kind of imaginary counterpart, see also page 114.

Kare realized that the signs had to work without typography and be designed as pictograms so that they would function even in the smallest of spaces (cf. ibid.). Due to the technical conditions, she had a pixel grid at her disposal as a design basis on which she developed her characters (see page 50 f.). Some of her icons are still used today in a slightly modified form – for example the wastepaper basket (Fig. 141), the hand gestures (Fig. 143) or the icon for the command key (Fig. 145).

Fig. 138 **happy mac**   Fig. 143 **dragging hand**
Fig. 139 **bomb**   Fig. 144 **font suitcase**
Fig. 140 **print**   Fig. 145 **command**
Fig. 141 **trash**   Fig. 146 **index finger**
Fig. 142 **arrow**   (cf. Abdullah/Hübner 2006: 208-209)

Fig. 139

Fig. 140

Fig. 141

Fig. 142

Fig. 143

Fig. 144

Fig. 145

Fig. 146

In addition to the icons, Kare designed various bitmap fonts. These include the dingbat font ›Cairo‹, which contains numerous signs (Fig. 147–Fig. 178) that can be inserted into texts. This made it possible to use pictorial signs in writing.[4] However, the functionality was tied to the font used in each case. To insert a character into the text, the user had to select the Cairo font and press the corresponding key for the respective character. Different characters are assigned to lowercase letters, uppercase letters, numbers and some special glyphs. The graphic emojis shown on the page are designated with their respective keyboard assignments. It is remarkable how many motifs are included that are also available as emojis today, such as the bow (Fig. 162), the shamrock (Fig. 153) or the numerous animal motifs. Some of the pictorial signs even feature subtle shading, indicated with just a few pixels, such as the fried egg (Fig. 177) or the pot of the cactus (Fig. 152). Some characters, such as

Fig. 147 **b**

Fig. 148 **]**

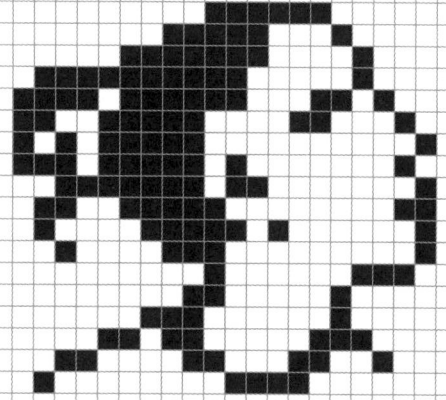

Fig. 149 **o** [134 px]

Fig. 150 **p**

Fig. 151 **S**

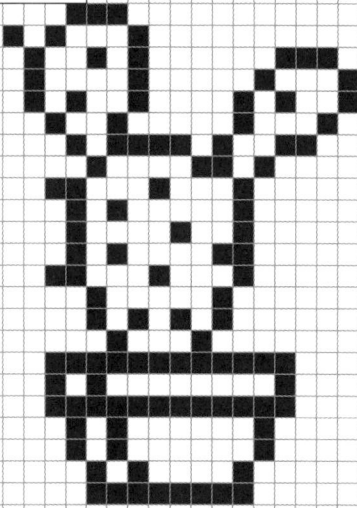

Fig. 152 ***** [109 px]

Fig. 153 **w**

Fig. 154 **d**

Fig. 155 **g**

Fig. 156 **{**

Fig. 157 **j** [61 px]

Fig. 158 **t**

Fig. 159 **m**

Fig. 160 **<**

Fig. 161 **a**

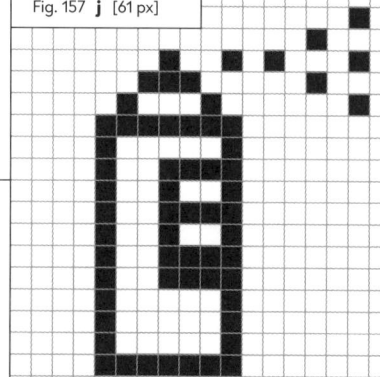

the paintbrush (Fig. 163) or the spray can (Fig. 157), were also used as tools in the Macinthosh programs and are still included as motifs today. With just a few pixels, Kare created an astonishing variety of different characters at a high level of creativity. Her creations achieved worldwide fame, with the dogcow (Fig. 172) even reaching cult status among Apple fans. Through her work, Kare became part of Apple's design history. Her work had a significant impact on the design of user interfaces and con-tributed to icons playing an important role in user interaction with computers. The characters she de-signed are considered classics and are exhibited in the Museum of Modern Art (MoMA).

4　The Cairo font was not the first font to include pictorial signs. The American company IBM launched the ›IBM Personal Computer‹ (IBM PC) on the market in 1981. The computer's original character set already contained pictorial signs, like facial expressions, playing card suits, gender symbols, musical notes and various arrows (cf. Enzmann 2023: 71). In the 1990s in particular, a series of Wingdings, Webdings and Zapf Dingbats fonts were created that integrated pictorial characters.

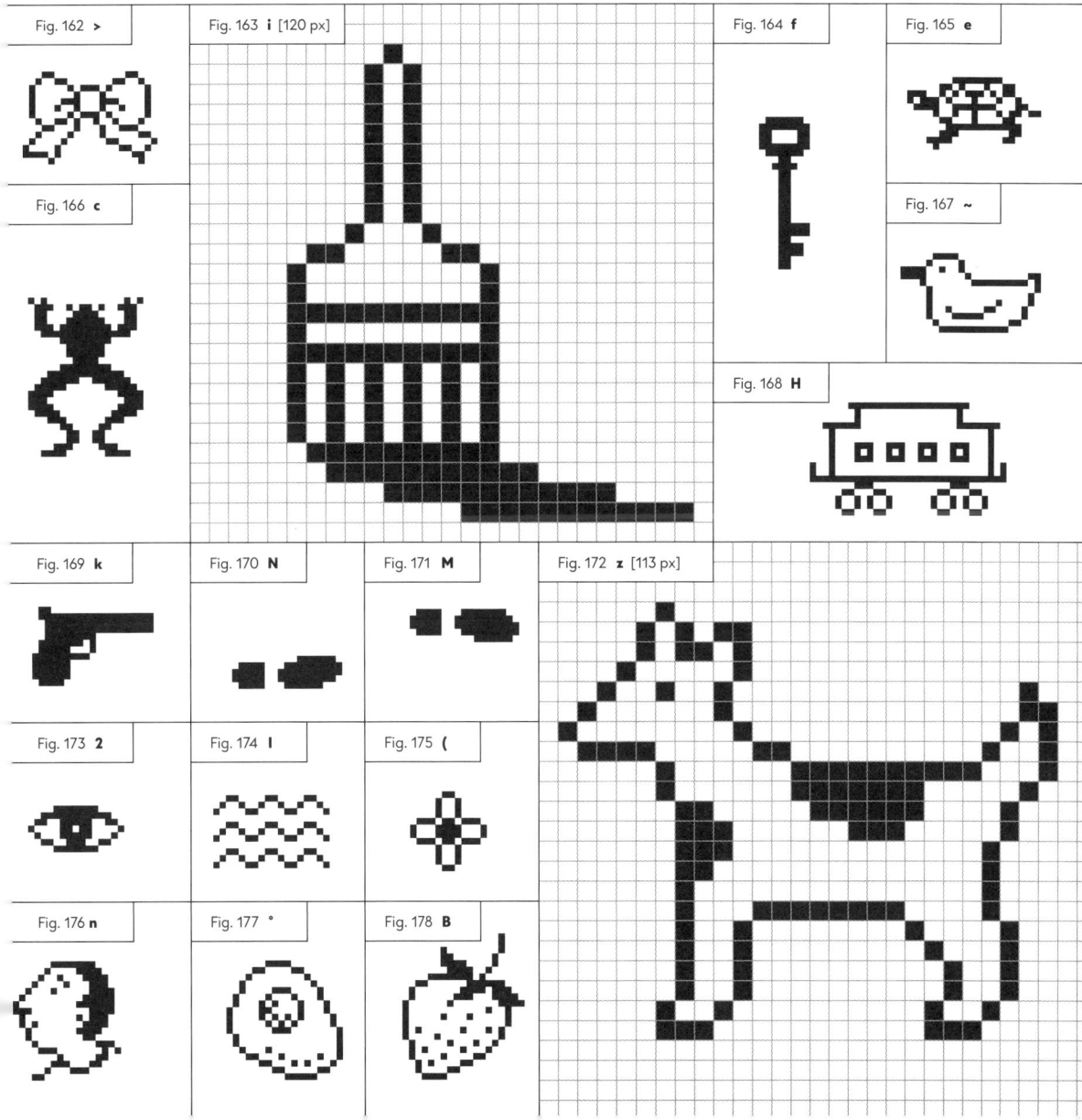

Fig. 162 >

Fig. 163 i [120 px]

Fig. 164 f

Fig. 165 e

Fig. 166 c

Fig. 167 ~

Fig. 168 H

Fig. 169 k

Fig. 170 N

Fig. 171 M

Fig. 172 z [113 px]

Fig. 173 2

Fig. 174 I

Fig. 175 (

Fig. 176 n

Fig. 177 °

Fig. 178 B

COCONET

One of the least known innovations when it comes to the history of emojis are the picture characters developed by Brian Dear, which were introduced in the COCONET system in 1988. The characters were popular with users and, considering the time, their function was surprisingly similar to today's emojis.

Fig. 179	Fig. 180	Fig. 181

Fig. 182	Fig. 183	Fig. 184

Fig. 185	Fig. 186	Fig. 187

In 1987, Dear and his wife Patricia Dear founded Coconut Computing, Inc. According to an email from Dear (5/17/2023), their intention in founding the company was to bring the ideas of social computing, collaboration and communication that had been developed on the PLATO system at the University of Illinois to the modern PC in the form of graphical software that would allow anyone to launch an online service, conferencing system or message board. In addition to instant messaging, the system offered options for message forums and e-mail platforms. For the message board and email platforms, Dear developed a series of pictorial signs[5] with different facial expressions (ibid.).

»The emoticons I came up with for COCONET were inspired by the far more primitive ones on the PLATO system that required a lot of knowledge and then experimentation to create on-the-fly.«

(Brian Dear, personal communication, July 1, 2024)

Compared to previous ways of using emojis – which either required different combinations of letters or were based on a specific font such as the Cairo font – COCONET enabled the selection and insertion of faces in messages through an ›emoticon picker‹ that acted as a pop-up window.

»When a user wanted to place an emoticon in their message, just pop up a window and quickly select the emoticon they wanted, and then move it around anywhere in the message. Done. It was vastly simpler than PLATO. And users loved it and embraced it instantly.«

(Brian Dear, ibid.)

Similar to what is possible today when writing an email on a computer, Dear's picker contained different facial expressions, including, for example, sobbing (Fig. 182), laughing (Fig. 179), blinking (Fig. 183), sticking out the tongue (Fig. 202) and rolling the eyes (Fig. 192). The pictorial signs were not part of the text, but small picture characters that could be placed anywhere in a message independently of each other (ibid.). The signs were introduced in 1988 on the COCONET system, a public online service for San Diego, California. The COCONET characters were, according to Dear, an instant success and very popular with users because they were easy and intuitive to use.

---

5   Dear named the pictorial signs ›COCONET's Emoticons‹ after interviewing Dr. Janet Asteroff, who wrote her dissertation on paralinguistic communications and symbols on computer systems in the 1980s.

The pictorial signs (Fig. 179–Fig. 203) were graphically reconstructed by D. E. using the available image material provided by Dear. Due to slight blurring of the material, individual pixels may not be in their original positions.

Fig. 188 [180 px]

Fig. 189 [156 px]
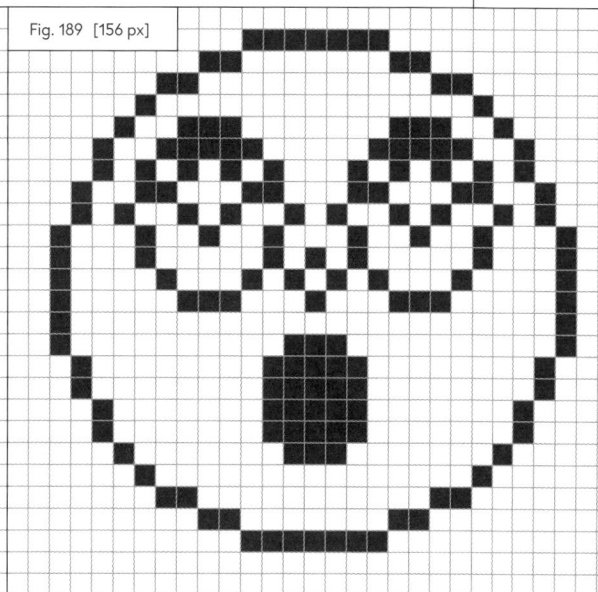

Fig. 190

Fig. 191

Fig. 192

Fig. 193

Fig. 194

Fig. 195

Fig. 196

Fig. 197

Fig. 198

Fig. 199

Fig. 200

Fig. 201

Fig. 202 [134 px]

Fig. 203 [131 px]
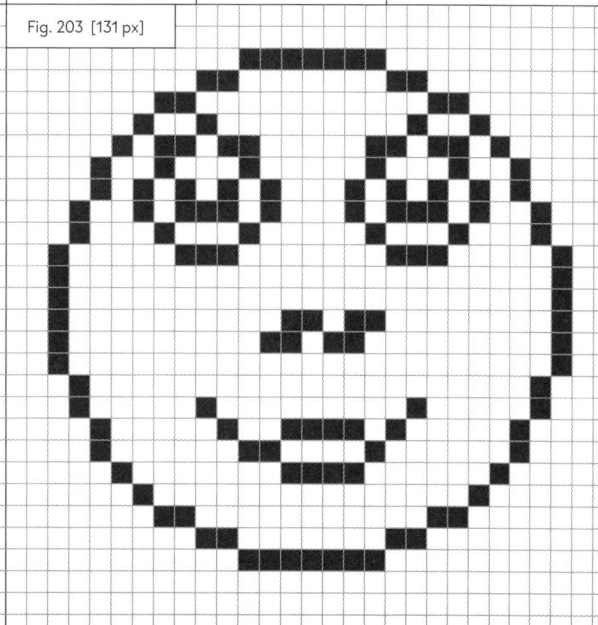

SoftBank & NTT Docomo Emojis

There is no consensus among researchers as to which sign is considered the first emoji. On the one hand, this has to do with the use of the term emoji. Depending on how the term is defined, it is possible to speak of emojis before or from the emergence of CMC. Another important aspect is that it is difficult to identify the genuine creator when different companies were working on the same or similar technological developments. It therefore remains unclear which mobile device was the first to include a graphic emoji character set.

For a long time, the graphic emojis from the character set of the Japanese telecommunications company ›NTT Docomo‹, which were introduced as part of the ›i-mode‹ project in 1999, were considered to be the first emoji character set on a mobile device, see page 56. However, ›SoftBank‹ – then known as ›J-Phone‹ – released the ›SkyWalker DP-211SW‹ with graphic emojis as early as November 1, 1997, making it possibly the first mobile phone to enable the transmission of emojis. The set from SoftBank contains four emojis for facial expression in addition to many other emojis. The character set already contains graphic emojis that are still widely used today, such as ›pile of poo‹, ›thumbs up‹ or ›spouting whale‹. Various animals and electronic devices are also already represented.

Fig. 204 **pile of poo**
Fig. 205 **disappointed face**
Fig. 206 **smiling face with smiling eyes**
Fig. 207 **red heart**
Fig. 208 **grinning face with big eyes**
Fig. 209 **angry face**
Fig. 211 **spouting whale**
Fig. 212 **cat face**

Fig. 213 **mouse face**
Fig. 214 **thumbs up**
Fig. 215 **mobile phone**
Fig. 216 **dog face**
Fig. 217 **penguin**
Fig. 218 **laptop**
Fig. 219 **camera**
(Emojipedia a)

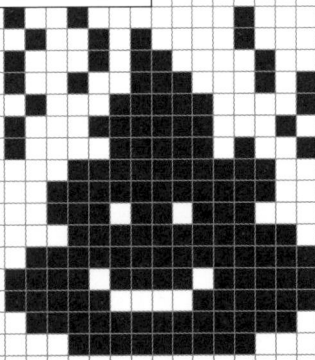

Fig. 204 [142 px]

Fig. 205

Fig. 206

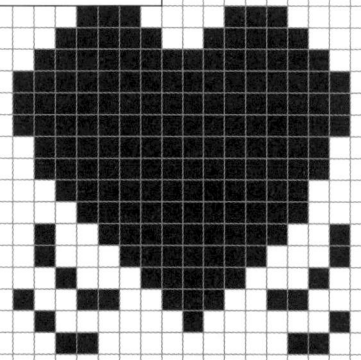

Fig. 207 [151 px]

Fig. 208

Fig. 209

Fig. 210 **illustration of the one of the early J-Phone models with the emoji picker**

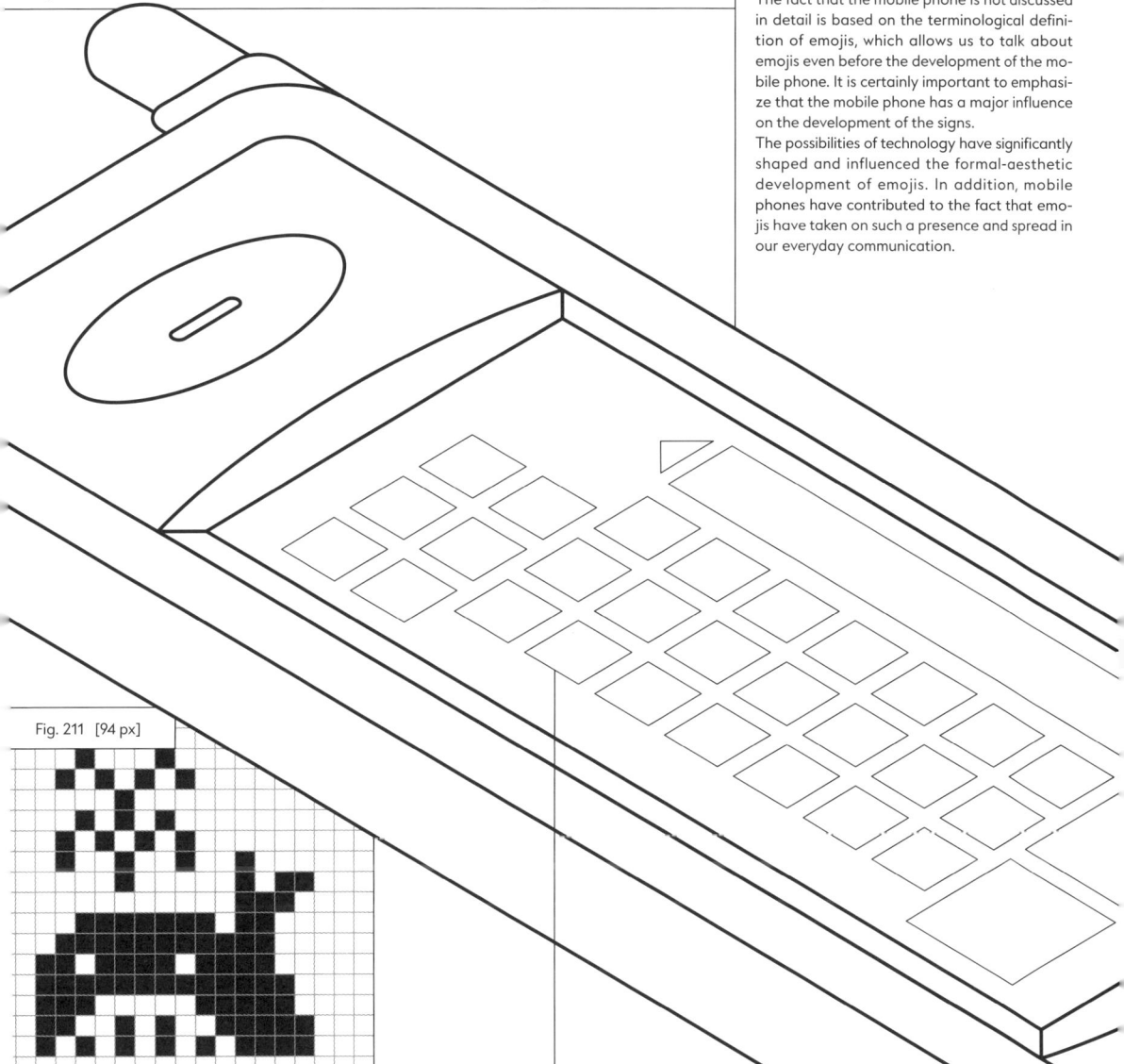

The fact that the mobile phone is not discussed in detail is based on the terminological definition of emojis, which allows us to talk about emojis even before the development of the mobile phone. It is certainly important to emphasize that the mobile phone has a major influence on the development of the signs.

The possibilities of technology have significantly shaped and influenced the formal-aesthetic development of emojis. In addition, mobile phones have contributed to the fact that emojis have taken on such a presence and spread in our everyday communication.

Fig. 211 [94 px]

Fig. 212

Fig. 213

Fig. 214 [78 px]

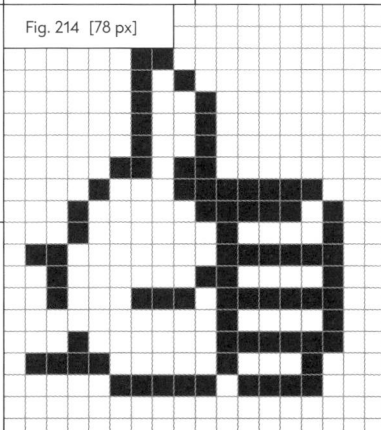

Fig. 215

Fig. 216

Fig. 217

Fig. 218

Fig. 219

Fig. 220

Fig. 221

Fig. 222 [20 px]

Fig. 223

Fig. 224

Fig. 225

Fig. 226

Fig. 227 [24 px]

Fig. 228 [48 px]

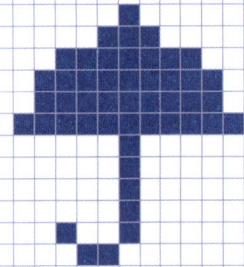

Fig. 229

Fig. 230

Fig. 231

Fig. 232 [48 px]

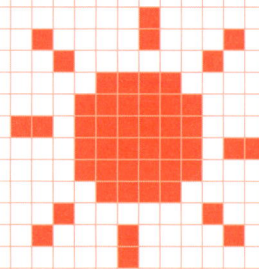

Fig. 233

Fig. 234

Fig. 235

Fig. 236

Fig. 237

In the 1990s, pagers were very popular for Japanese young people. NTT Docomo's decision to include a heart in its standard character set may have enabled the use of a graphic emoji on a mobile device for the first time (cf. Blagdon 2013). According to Blagdon, the intensive use of the heart emoji gave NTT Docomo the idea of developing a pictogram-like character set for the market. Although it was possible to use text-based emojis on the pager without any problems, they required a large number of signs, which were limited on the pager (cf. Freedman 2020: 49 f.). The solution was to replace several letters or words with a single sign. The resulting graphic emoji character set made it possible to use other pictogram-like characters in text messages in addition to the standard language

character system. This allowed users to convey additional levels of meaning despite the limited number of characters (cf. Arens 2002: 9 f.). NTT Docomo's character set was introduced as part of the ›i-mode‹ project. The NTT Docomo character set was designed by Shigetaka Kurita. He asked designers to further work out his character designs, but no one was interested, so Kurita designed the emojis himself (cf. Blagdon 2013). The character set contains five emojis for facial expressions that can be used to express anger (Fig. 226), sadness (Fig. 220), dizziness (Fig. 221), happiness (Fig. 222) and disappointment (Fig. 225) (Arens 2002: 99). What is striking about the emoji depicting a happy face (Fig. 222) is that the mouth is not smiling. Only the eyes express a smile, as in the horizontal text-

Fig. 220 **sad face**
Fig. 221 **dizzy**
Fig. 222 **happy face** (emoji in the grid)
Fig. 223 **good idea**
Fig. 224 **mood**
Fig. 225 **disappointed face**
Fig. 226 **angry face**
Fig. 227 **dash (running dash)** (emoji in the grid)
Fig. 228 **rain** (emoji in the grid)
Fig. 229 **typhoon**
Fig. 230 **cloudy**
Fig. 231 **fog**
Fig. 232 **fine**
Fig. 233 **sweat**
Fig. 234 **thunder**
Fig. 235 **snow**
Fig. 236 **drizzle**
Fig. 237 **good (upward arrow)**
Fig. 238 **cold sweat** (emoji in the grid)
Fig. 239 **shining new** (emoji in the grid)
Fig. 240 **bump (collision)**
Fig. 241 **kiss**
Fig. 242 **angry** (emoji in the grid)
Fig. 243 **cute** (emoji in the grid)
Fig. 244 **punch**
Fig. 245 **bomb**
(Arens 2002: 79–113).

A list of all ›i-mode‹ emojis can be found at Arens (cf. ibid.).

i-mode adapts websites to the capabilities of the mobile phone and thus guarantees their display and range of functions on the cell phone. Within three years, ›i-mode‹ had found over 30 million customers, which is a quarter of the Japanese population (Arens 2002: 9 f.). According to Arens, the rapid spread was facilitated by the low number of PCs, the high fixed network costs and the Japanese population's enthusiasm for technology, as well as the long commuting times that many people in Japan have to bridge (cf. ibid.).

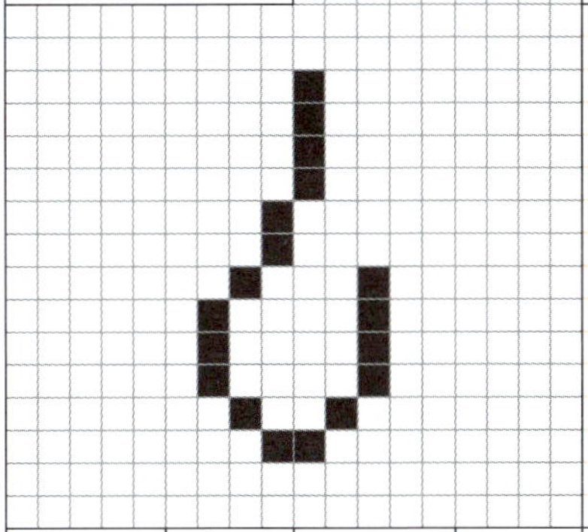

Fig. 238 [18 px]

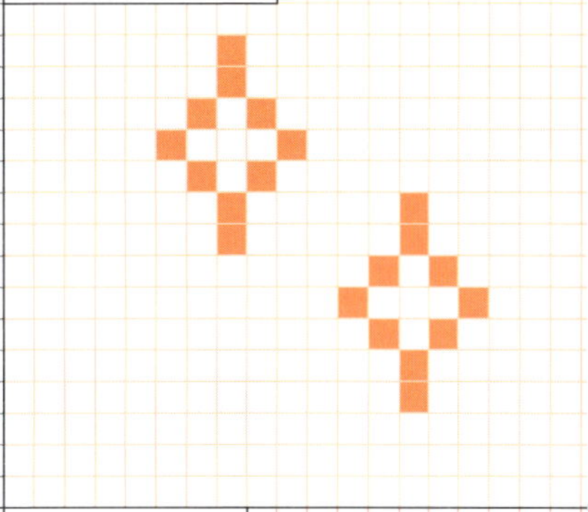

Fig. 239 [20 px]

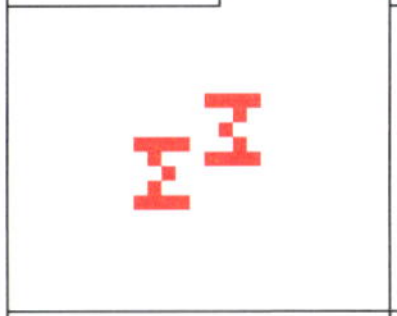

Fig. 240

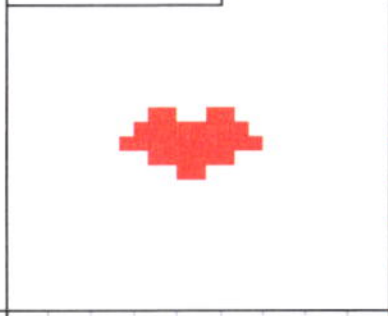

Fig. 241

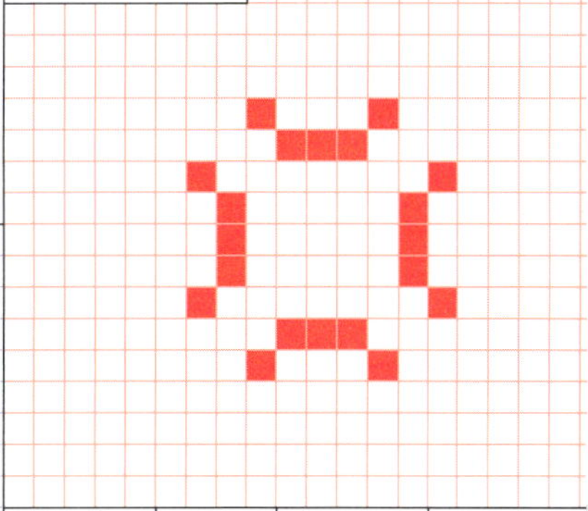

Fig. 242 [20 px]

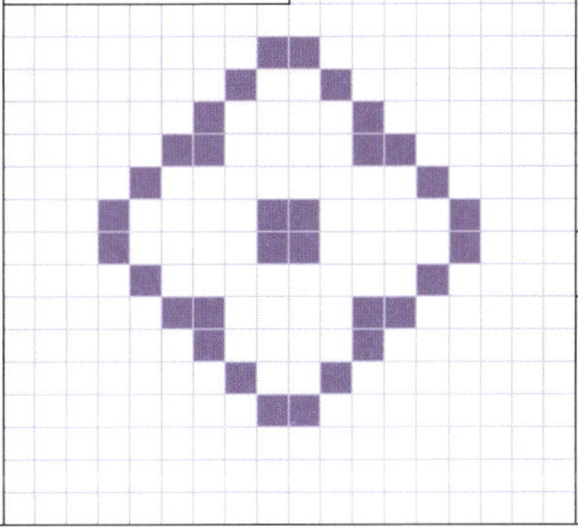

Fig. 243 [32 px]

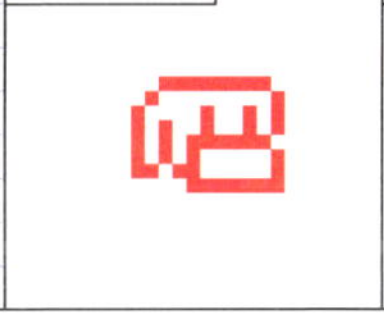

Fig. 244

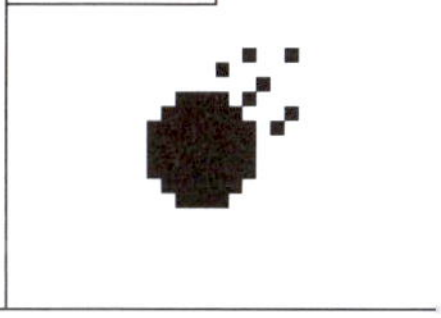

Fig. 245

based emoji (Fig. 113). As Kurita explains, the weather service gave him the idea of designing emojis, as the weather service was difficult to understand due to the pure representation of the word (cf. Blagdon 2013; Arens 2002: 79-80). Kurita used pictograms, manga and kanji characters as inspiration for the design of the graphic emojis (see Blagdon 2013). The example of the emoji ›angry‹ (Fig. 242) shows the relationship to manga. Representations of anger are marked with a vein cross in manga and anime. The ›dash‹ emoji (Fig. 227) and the ›cold sweat‹ emoji (Fig. 238) are also reminiscent of typical manga or comic representations, see also page 109.

The character set designed by Kurita contains graphic emojis that can be divided into various areas such as sports, means of transport, buildings, food, music, technology, weather, zodiac signs, playing card suits, body parts, clothes, animals or emotions.

Kurita saw emojis as pictograms that complement or replace text. He did not envisage detailed pictorial representations that went beyond pictographic representations (cf. ibid.). Due to a lack of originality, Kurita's emojis could not be protected by copyright. This allowed other providers to use the signs or design their own.

The emojis of ›KDDI‹ and those of SoftBank, together with the character set of NTT Docomo, have reached a considerable number of users. Both the SoftBank and NTT Docomo emoji sets look different and may have been in development at similar times (cf. Burge 2019, cf. Alt 2016: item 15 of 1122).

Graphic further development of Emojis

Internet cafés emerged in the 1990s, and the Internet gradually became a part of private life (cf. Hammond/Richey 2014: 140 f.). The development of technology and the spread of the internet improved chat as a communication medium, encouraging the emergence and spread of a wide variety of digital pictorial signs.

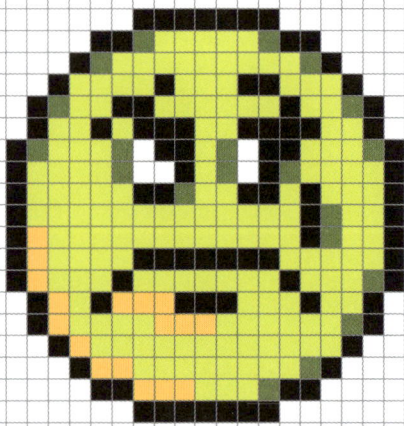

Fig. 249 **reconstruction of AIM 3.5 crying face grid**

Fig. 246 **MSN Messenger 6.1**
Fig. 247 **Yahoo! Messenger 5.6**
Fig. 248 **AIM 3.5**
(cf. Enzmann 2023a: 86)

[92 px]
[20 px]
[17 px]
[138 px]

In addition to the graphic emojis of mobile devices, there were two other ways of integrating pictorial signs into chat dialogs at the time, namely either using a font or using images provided by the respective instant messenger (cf. Petronzio 2012). Font signs were linked to their respective fonts, and instant messenger signs to their services. The former were restricted by medium, the latter by platform. The graphic emojis of mobile devices, on the other hand, use code points; they are therefore not tied to a font or platform and can also be sent in unformatted texts (see Alt 2016: item 703 of 1122). Emojis have often only been referred to as emojis since the use of code points, but in this book the term is used as explained on page 9. From the late 1990s to the early 2000s, the smiley-like and mostly animated graphic emojis of instant messaging platforms were popular and partially replaced the text-based emojis. In the course of emojization, a large variety of different signs emerged (see also pages 94–95).

Fig. 246

Fig. 247

Fig. 248

Unicode

In 2010, one of the most significant and controversial developments in the history of emojis took place. According to Bergerhausen and Poarangan, there has rarely been so much controversy and bitter debate among experts as when graphic emojis were included in Unicode 6.0 (cf. Bergerhausen/Poarangan 2011: 47).

Opponents argued that emojis go beyond Unicode's concept of writing and criticized the incorporation of characters into a global standard without any discernible logic. Those in favor pointed to the fact that the characters would be used by millions on their mobile phones every day and would have to be included so that graphic emojis sent from mobile devices in messages and emails would be compatible with graphic emojis on computers. Another reason was the search machines, which could not handle the characters without encoding. In October 2010, the graphic emojis were included in the Unicode block ›Miscellaneous Symbols and Pictographs‹ in the standard (cf. ibid.). One year after the Unicode coding, an emoji keyboard was available on the iPhone and in 2013 also on Android smartphones (cf. Siever 2016: 35). Now nothing stood in the way of emoji use and they spread internationally. According to Giannoulis and Wilde, emojis – in contrast to many other attempts to create a ›visual Esperanto‹ – gained their popularity through their compatibility, i.e. through processes of technological standardization (cf. Giannoulis/Wilde 2020: 4). The official term for graphic emojis is defined in Unicode. However, Unicode does not determine what the characters should look like in detail. Therefore, the same graphic emojis can be designed differently on different devices and depending on the communication platform (Fig. 250–Fig. 257). Anyone can apply to add a new sign to Unicode, but the process is lengthy and time-consuming.

Emojis reached another peak in 2015:

»The Oxford Word of the Year 2015 is... 😂 That's right – for the first time ever, the Oxford Dictionaries Word of the Year is a pictograph 😂, officially called the ›Face with Tears of Joy‹ emoji, though you may know it by other names.«

(Oxford Languages 2024)

Visualization of the ›face with tears of joy‹ emoji across different platforms:
(Emojipedia b)

Fig. 250 **Apple iOS 17.4**
Fig. 251 **Facebook 15.0**
Fig. 252 **Huawei HarmonyOS 4.0**
Fig. 253 **Microsoft Windows 11 23H2**
Fig. 254 **Samsung One UI 6.1**
Fig. 255 **SoftBank 2014**
Fig. 256 **X Twemoji 15.0.1**
Fig. 257 **WhatsApp 2.24.8.85**

Fig. 250	Fig. 251	Fig. 252	Fig. 253
😂	😂	😂	😂
Fig. 254	Fig. 255	Fig. 256	Fig. 257
😂	😂	😂	😂

AR-Emojis

With the release of the iPhone X at the end of 2017, AR-Emojis came onto the market. These 3D-animated emojis react to movement by mimicking the user's facial expressions in real time. Subsequent updates continue to offer options for creating customized AR-Emojis.

With AR-Emojis – called ›Animojis‹ by Apple – such as the fox (Fig. 258), videos can be created and sent with a sound recording of your own voice.

With iOS 12, customizable faces – called ›Memojis‹ by Apple – were added: users can create their own animated 3D emoji with a 3D avatar (Fig. 259). The other updates offer additional options for hairstyles, headgear, glasses, etc. AR-Emojis can be sent as stickers or videos. The stickers adopt facial expressions and gestures from the graphic emojis, such as ›face blowing a kiss‹ (Fig. 262) or ›face with tears of joy‹ (Fig. 265).

Samsung also launched AR-Emojis (Fig. 260) with the Galaxy S9. Apple's AR-Emojis are created by the user using existing elements, while Samsung's AR-Emojis can be generated based on a selfie (see Sevilla 2018). While Apple's AR-Emojis mainly focus on the face, Samsung's involve the whole body.

Fig. 258 **Apple iOS 11** (Emojipedia k)

Fig. 260 **Samsung Experience 9.0** (Sevilla 2018)

Fig. 261 **illustration of the iPhone X**

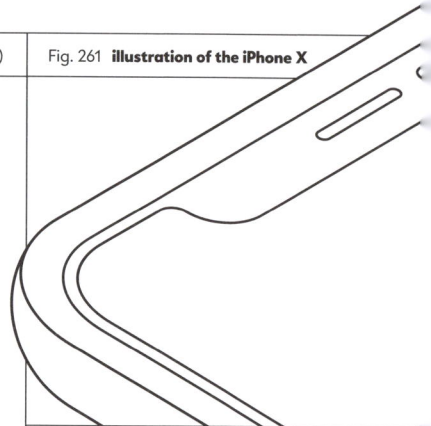

Fig. 259 **Apple iOS 12** (Otterstein 2018)

AR-EMOJIS AS STICKERS

Fig. 262

Fig. 263 **illustration of a memoji creation**

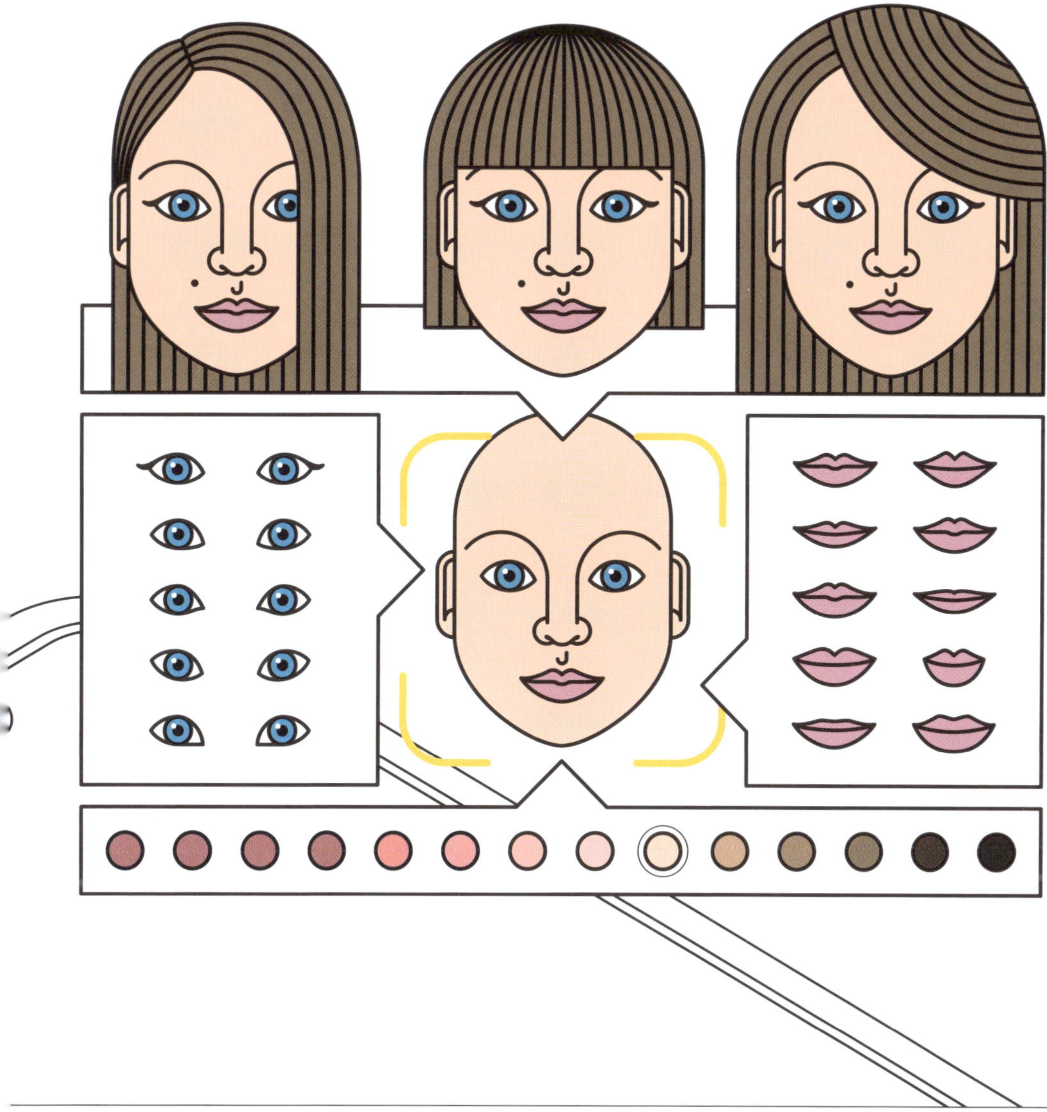

(created with Apple iOS 17.5.1, see also pages 70–71)

Fig. 264

Fig. 265

Fig. 266

Genmoji

With the preview of the new iOS18 operating system in 2024, Apple introduced a completely new tool – Genmojis (Apple 2024a). With a description or based on photos, emojis can be generated using Apple Intelligence. These can be used in the standard emoji keyboard or as stickers.

The development of emojis has continuously increased in both quality and quantity. The emoji library has become increasingly complex, but there have been ongoing discussions about expanding the character set.

With the preview of the new iOS18 operating system, Apple presents a promising solution to this problem: the so-called Genmojis (generated emojis). Based on a description, for example ›T-rex wearing a tutu on a surfboard‹, a Genmoji is created (see Fig. 267), with various options to choose from (cf. Apple 2024a). If the generated emoji is liked, it can either be used as a sticker or inserted directly into the emoji keyboard so that the genmoji can be used within the text.

Apple demonstrates various examples in its preview of the new operating system. For example, Fig. 268 is generated based on the description ›Squirrel DJ‹, Fig. 269 appears based on ›Lox bagel‹ and Fig. 271 is created by entering ›Smiley relaxing wearing cucumbers‹ (cf. ibid.).

Genmojis can be created not only on the basis of descriptions, but also on the basis of photos (see Fig. 272). This makes the expansion of the emoji character set almost unlimited, and there are no longer any limits to emojization – at least as far as the motifs are concerned.

According to Apple (2024a), the new ›Image Playground‹ system function will also make it possible to generate images that can be sent as stickers, among other things (see Fig. 273), as this function will be integrated directly into the Messages app. Users can choose between different concepts and styles, such as birthday, accessories or places.

Based on the request, Apple Intelligence creates an image based on the different components. Different styles can be selected.

Fig. 267 (Apple 2024a)

Fig. 268 (ibid.)

Fig. 269 (ibid.)

Fig. 270 **illustration of a image playground creation**

Fig. 271 (Apple 2024b)

Fig. 272 (ibid.)

Fig. 273 (ibid.)

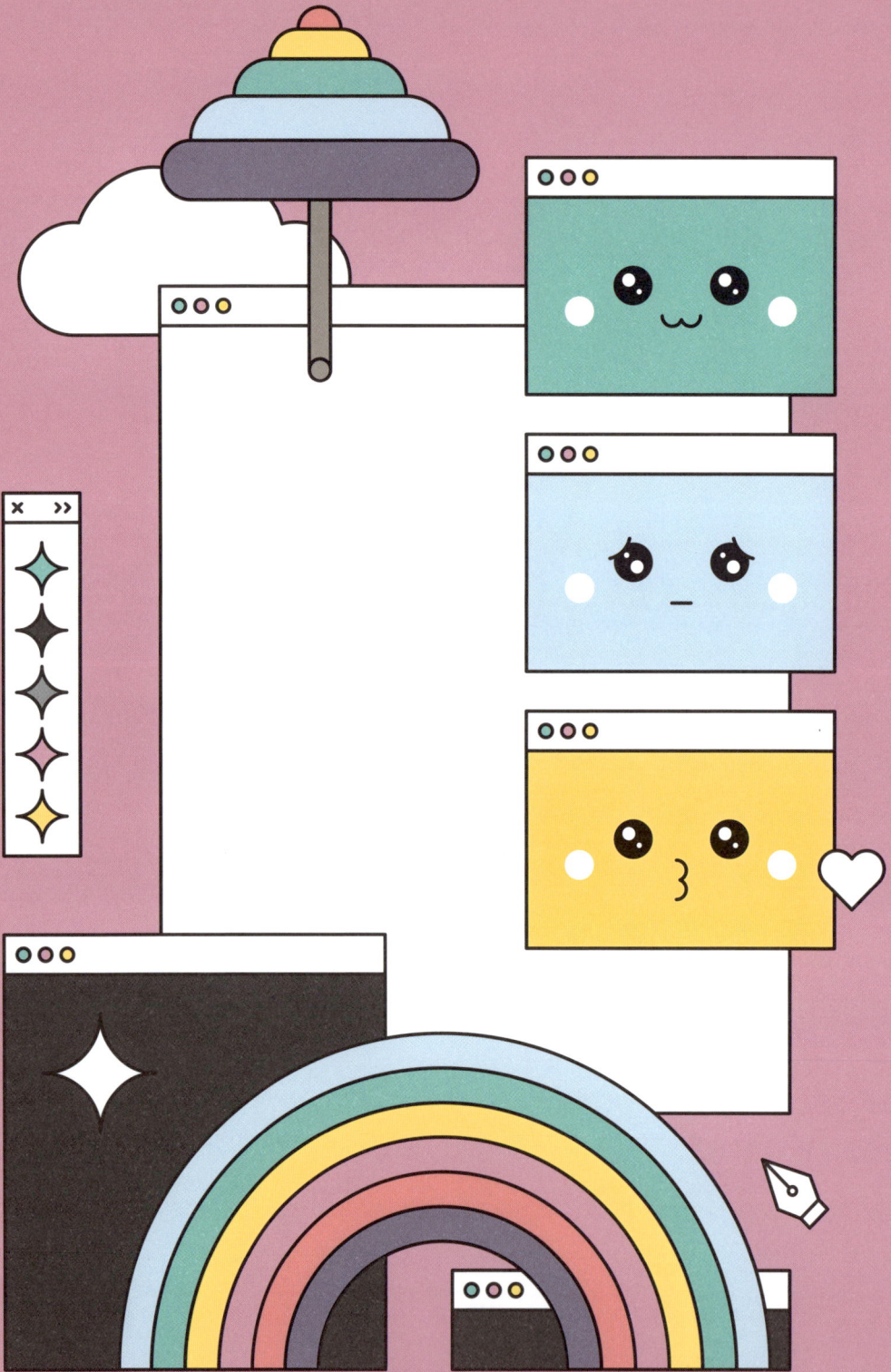

Culture of Cuteness

With the rise of emojis, a kind of culture of cuteness has become increasingly established. Tokyo is viewed as the centre of the rise and spread of ›kawaii‹ aesthetic, which is characterized by its adorableness and cuteness. It has deeply influenced various aspects of Japanese society and the international perception of Japan. Kawaii culture shapes fashion, design, art, media, consumer goods and even some behaviors. The aim of this subchapter is to explore the spread of cuteness. What influence do cultural aspects have on the use of digital signs?

What influence do cultural aspects have on the use of digital signs?

How do cultural characteristics influence the development and use of emojis?

Kawaii is commonly translated as ›cute‹ or ›sweet‹. However, the word cannot simply be translated into another language, as it has multiple layers of meaning and these have changed over time (cf. Nittono 2016: 80).

In research, kawaii was almost exclusively associated with infantility (cf. ibid.). Hiroshi Nitton, however, describes kawaii as a psychological concept that goes beyond cuteness (cf. Nittono 2016: 80). He translated the following definitions for the adjective kawaii from the Japanese dictionary, Nihon Kokugo Daijiten:

»(1) looks miserable and raises sympathy. pitiable. pathetic. piteous. (2) attractive. cannot be neglected. cherished. beloved. (3) has a sweet nature. lovely. (a) (of faces and figures of young women and children) adorable. attractive. (b) (like children) innocent. obedient. touching. (4) (of things and shapes) attractively small. small and beautiful. (5) trivial. pitiful. (used with slight disdain).«

(Nittono 2016: 81)

The diverse, sometimes contradictory meanings of Kawaii have developed through the different words of origin, like ›kawayui‹, ›kawaisou‹ or ›kawairashii‹ (cf. ibid.). This is how a multi-layered understanding of kawaii developed.

The rise of kawaii can be contextualized from different points in time. In this chapter, I take a contemporary, visual look at kawaii in order to create a relation to emojis.

Fig. 274	Fig. 275	Fig. 276	Fig. 277	Fig. 278	Fig. 279

There is an emoji for ›Kawaii‹, which was already represented in the NTT-Docomo character set (cf. Arens 2002: 100).
According to the i-mode definition, the character stands for ›cute‹ and according to Emojipedia it represents a flower-shaped diamond (ibid., Emojipedia e). In some representations, the flower (Fig. 275, Fig. 276) and in others (Fig. 278, Fig. 279) the diamond is more pronounced.

Fig. 274 **NTT Docomo 1999** (Emojipedia e)
Fig. 275 **NTT Docomo 2013** (ibid.)
Fig. 276 **Google Android 4.4** (ibid.)
Fig. 277 **Google Android 11.0** (ibid.)
Fig. 278 **Apple iOS 5.1** (ibid.)
Fig. 279 **Apple iOS 13.3** (ibid.)

The spread of Kawaii Culture

In the 1970s, young people began to write in a new way – called ›cute handwriting‹ or ›Maru-Moji‹. According to Kinsella, handwriting marked the beginning of the spread of ›kawaii‹ youth culture (cf. Kinsella 1995: 222). This culture now extends to different areas of life, see also page 28.

How has kawaii culture spread and what impact has it had on different areas of everyday life in Japan?

The result of the handwriting can be assigned to the pre-graphic emojis, see page 28 cute handwriting mainly spread among young people in the 1970s. They rounded off the Japanese characters (see Fig. 281–Fig. 284) and wrote from left to right in a line instead of from top to bottom. While the Japanese characters varied in thickness, the young people wrote the characters in a constant thickness (cf. Kinsella 1995: 222). According to Kinsella, characteristic features of the handwriting are the overlapping and crossing of lines that otherwise do not touch, modifications at the ends of strokes, the strong emphasis on the circle and the altered placement of nigorative characters (cf. ibid.: 223). This can be seen, for example, in the kanji character for love (Fig. 283) or for tomorrow (Fig. 284), as Shirai explained in a lecture (Shirai 2019). Modifications are also evident in hiragana and katakana

Fig. 280 ›this is so cute‹ in Maru-Moji (accoding to Wikimedia Commons 2019, edited by D.E.)

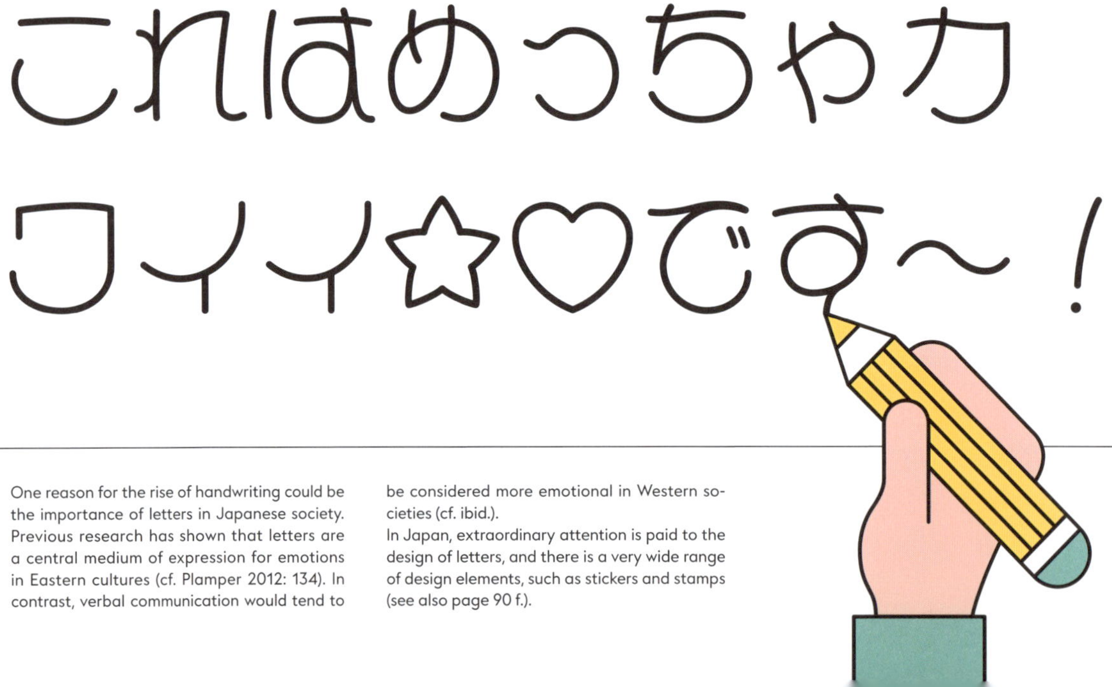

これはめっちゃカ
ワイイ☆♡です〜！

One reason for the rise of handwriting could be the importance of letters in Japanese society. Previous research has shown that letters are a central medium of expression for emotions in Eastern cultures (cf. Plamper 2012: 134). In contrast, verbal communication would tend to be considered more emotional in Western societies (cf. ibid.).

In Japan, extraordinary attention is paid to the design of letters, and there is a very wide range of design elements, such as stickers and stamps (see also page 90 f.).

Fig. 281 **kanji character ›love‹** (cf. Shirai 2019)

Fig. 282 **kanji character ›morning‹** (cf. ibid.)

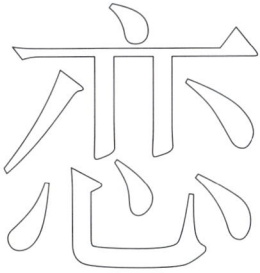

Fig. 283 **Fig. 281 in cute handwriting** (cf. ibid.)

Fig. 284 **Fig. 282 in cute handwriting** (cf. ibid.)

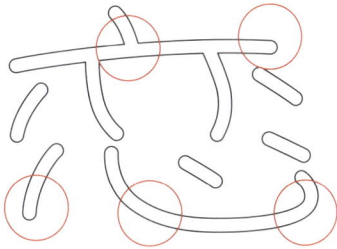

(cf. ibid.). The characters stylized by the rounding were supplemented with small pictorial elements (Fig. 285–Fig. 290) such as hearts, stars and inserted faces, while individual English words such as ›Love‹ were also inserted (cf. Kinsella 1995: 220). The elements inserted into the handwriting are not only similar to emojis, but also to cartoon or manga representations, see also page 109.

The handwriting style was very popular in Japan and spread, especially among young people, but it was forbidden in most schools. There is no standardized term for handwriting. For example, it is called ›marui ji‹/›marumoji‹ [round script/round writing], ›koneko ji‹ [kitten writing], ›manga ji‹ [comic writing] or ›burikko ji‹ [fake childlike writing] (ibid.: 222, Kavanagh 2020: 152 f.).

Although cute handwriting is more difficult to read than conventional letters, this did not deter the young people from using it. This makes it clear that the use of the writing is not purely about conveying information, but that its use includes other important aspects. This shows the relationship between the writing and emojis or the rebus letters already discussed, see page 28.

According to Shirai, young people use cute handwriting to make the letters and sentences appear softer (cf. Shirai 2019). In this way, they use aesthetic qualities to achieve their intended effect. According to Kinsella, the young people had found their own way of rebelling against traditional Japanese culture and expressing their feelings (cf. Kinsella 1995: 224).

Fig. 285

Fig. 286

Fig. 287

Fig. 288

Fig. 289

Fig. 290

When the new style appeared in magazines, comics and advertising in the 1980s and even word processing programs adopted the style, this handwritten writing variant became popular in the media (cf. Kavanagh 2020: 153). According to Kinsella, handwriting marked the beginning of the spread of kawaii youth culture (cf. Kinsella 1995: 222). The style developed from the infantile pink romanticism of the early 1980s to a humorous, kitschy, androgynous style in the early 1990s (cf. ibid.: 220). Characteristics of this style are reflected in clothing, food, toys, personal appearance and behavior. According to McVeigh, the Japanese consumption of Kawaii has become a »›standard‹ aesthetic of everyday life« (McVeigh 2000: 135). According to Barry Kavanagh, the Japanese consumption of kawaii has often been wrongly condemned as a subculture that is mainly attributed to women and children. According to him, the Japanese consumption of kawaii has often been wrongly condemned as a subculture that is mainly attributed to women and children. This is despite the fact that the extent

and reach of kawaii culture extends to the whole of Japanese society and even includes government documents and signs (cf. Kavanagh 2020: 153), see also pages 74–75. Cute handwriting can be seen as the handwritten precursor of emojis. From a formal perspective, handwriting is capable of taking over the functions of graphic emojis in full. This is because, as with emojis, handwriting combines pictorial elements with the standard character system. In contrast to graphic emojis, characters can be added, adapted or invented.

The kawaii aesthetic has a very prominent position in Japan and is of considerable importance in the formal development of emojis. According to Shirai, harmony and conflict avoidance are of great importance in Japanese culture (Shirai 2024). The ›kawaiization‹ of the characters is intended to achieve a trivialization and a kind of innocence. The Japanese therefore strive to make their horizontal text-based emojis as kawaii as possible. According to Shirai, horizontal text-based emojis are still widely used despite the possibilities of today's technology

Fig. 291

(^_^)

Fig. 292

(T_T)

Fig. 293

(^_-)

Fig. 294

:-)

Fig. 295

:'-(

Fig. 296

;-)

Fig. 297

Fig. 298

Fig. 299

Fig. 300

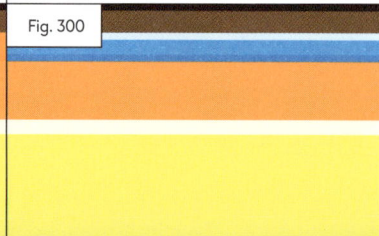

Fig. 291 / Fig. 294 **smiling**
Fig. 292 / Fig. 295 **crying**
Fig. 293 / Fig. 296 **winking**
(Schlobinski/Watanabe 2006: 29f.)

Fig. 297 **smiling face with smiling eyes**
Fig. 298 **crying face** (Apple iOS 17.4)
Fig. 299 **estimated ratio of the colors used in smiling face with smiling eyes** (Fig. 297)
Fig. 300 **estimated ratio of the colors used in crying face** (Fig. 298)

Fig. 301 **constructive structure of the smiling face with smiling eyes** (Fig. 297)
Fig. 302 **constructive structure of the crying face** (Fig. 298)

(cf. Shirai 2019). The comparison of the characters from the historical reconstruction, see page 44 f., makes it clear that the horizontal text-based emojis (Fig. 291–Fig. 293) appear more kawaii than their vertical counterparts (Fig. 294–Fig. 296) due to the diversity of the eyes and the emphasis on the broad heads that the brackets give them. The circle or rounding is another characteristic of the Kawaii aesthetic that can also be found in graphic emojis. If graphic emojis are reduced to their basic shapes and these are determined geometrically (Fig. 301, Fig. 302), it becomes clear that the signs are built on the circle with the principle of the center.

»The feelings are addressed more strongly by the circle than by any other sign.«

(Frutiger 1989: 46)

According to Frutiger, the principle of the center conveys completeness; thus abstract signs are usually based on symmetry (cf. ibid.: 266).
Another characteristic of the graphic emojis is their colorfulness. The quantity ratio and the color composition of the graphic emojis (Fig. 297, Fig. 298) could look as shown in Fig. 299 and Fig. 300. The signs consist of rich, bright colors, some of which blend into one another using a gradient. In the 1970s, the ethnologists Roy D'Andrade and Michael Egan came to the conclusion in a comparative cultural study that people in different parts of the world tend to associate bright and rich colors with positive emotions, while dark and pale colors tend to be associated with negative emotions (cf. Plamper 2012: 105). Looking only at the colors used in the graphic emojis, there is no discernible difference between those with negative and positive associations. From a color perspective, both graphic emojis therefore convey surface appearances of

»a positive mood«

(Danesi 2017: 58).

Beißwenger and Pappert (2023: 168) describe this potential as framing, which is inherent in emojis.

Fig. 301

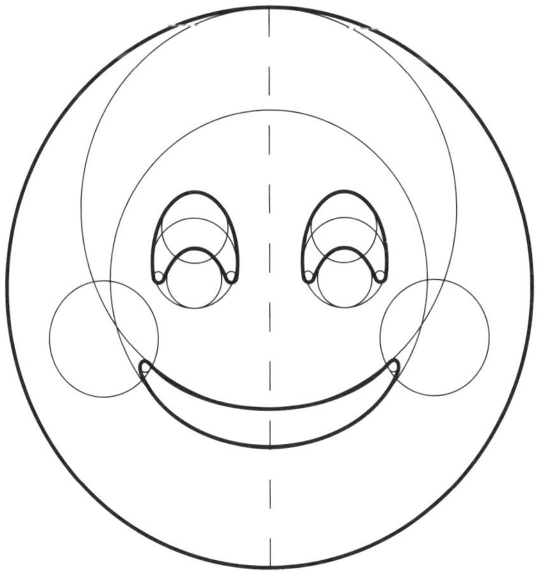

Fig. 302

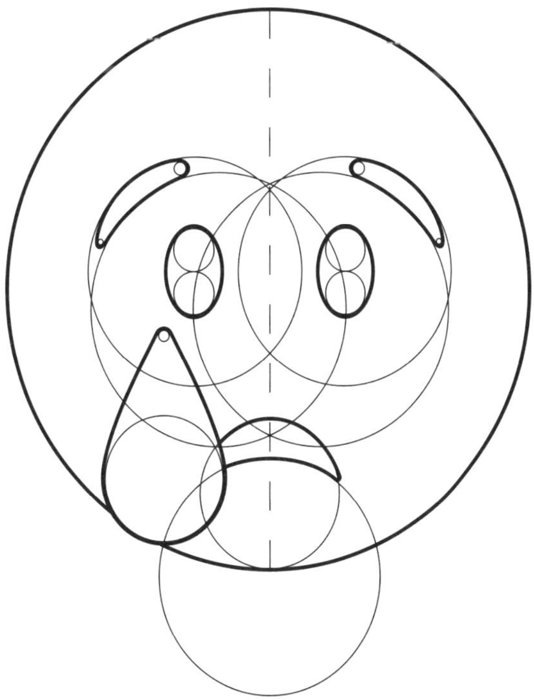

Fig. 303 **Kaila Ocampo** owner of Rainbowholic (Tokyo), see page 91

Fig. 304 **Hiromi Shirai** teacher, researcher

Fig. 305 **AR-Emoji created on the basis of Ocampo's photo** (Fig. 303)

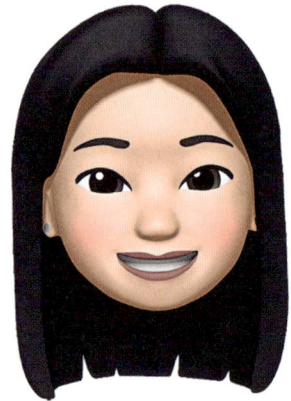

Fig. 306 **AR-Emoji created on the basis of Shirai's photo** (Fig. 304)

According to Freedman, the kawaii aesthetic is often characterized by a large head, the absence of a nose or mouth and large eyes (cf. Freedman 2020: 54). Such characteristics, as well as childishness and innocence, are characteristic of the kawaii aesthetic. To observe the kawaii aesthetic of the AR-Emojis, characters based on some of the interviewees were created for this chapter (Fig. 305, Fig. 306, Fig. 309, Fig. 310). At the top of the page are the photos used as a starting point and below are the AR-Emojis created with Apple iOS 17.4.1. As an AR-Emoji, the person depicted appears younger

photo by Hannah Smith

Fig. 307 **Ian Lynam** teacher, writer, designer, owner of Sailosaibin (Tokyo)

Fig. 308 **Lotta (Ayano Nakano)** artist

Fig. 309 **AR-Emoji created on the basis of Lynam's photo** (Fig. 307)

Fig. 310 **AR-Emoji created on the basis of Nakano's photo** (Fig. 308)

due to the rather low hairline, the smooth skin, the large eyes and the lack of wrinkles. The large eyes make the lower part of the face appear narrower, which supports the effect of the kawaii aesthetic. In addition, the faces, which tend to be visualized too broadly, suggest a large head. The lack of a neck in the AR-Emojis and the round, circular snub nose make the characters very different from the photo and are reminiscent of cartoons. Such features refer to the kawaii aesthetic, which in turn communicates in the sign process by associating the AR-Emojis with kawaii culture, see also pages 114–117 .

Friendly Signage

One of the most fascinating distinctions in Japanese visual communication, when viewed from a European perspective, is the extensive use of mascots and cute characters in public spaces. These elements can be found everywhere, for example, on official signs, government documents and public transportation. But the figures also provide information, give directions or make requests in pharmacies, on the subway, at the post office and in restaurants. They are not only used for reasons of politeness, but also facilitate communication with their immediate accessibility.

In what way is cuteness integrated into signage in Japan and what functions does it fulfill?

Stylized figures – called ›kyarakuta‹ or ›kyara‹ in Japanese – have established themselves in Japan as an everyday and useful means of communication (Wilde 2018: 14).

»*Living in Japan today means being surrounded by characters.*«

(Sadanobu, in: Wilde 2018: 14)

Significant are construction site signs with cute figures (Fig. 311) and signs with pictures of an apologizing construction worker (Fig. 312), who politely points out any inconvenience (see also page 141). In Japan, great care is taken not to disturb the well-being of fellow human beings and animals (cf.. Wilde 2018: 16, see also Fig. 316). Various figurative representations are employed in visual communication

Fig. 311 **illustration of construction site signs**

This illustration draws inspiration from the turtle construction site signs found in Kita Tokyo. These figures are interconnected by iron bars, allowing for the construction of corners as well. Primarily utilized as barriers in construction sites or dangerous areas, these constructions serve a vital purpose.

Fig. 312 **construction worker on a sign from Taito, Nishiasakusa, apologizing for the inconvenience caused during the construction work**

to provide support for the betterment of society. These are usually famous mascots, fabulous creatures, animals, anthropomorphized objects, children or cute people.

According to Packard et al., stylized figures evoke a special communicative disposition in people: this refers to a mirror-image intersubjective or social relationship that people – at least in many contemporary cultures – are inclined to interact with others, their faces, and bodies (cf. Packard et al. 2019: 22). This means that the interpreter communicates with the stylized representation as a kind of imaginary counterpart. This is supported by the personification of the figure by assigning it human attributes, such as a favorite color, hobbies or an entire life story (see for example Fig. 313). It seems that these

In Japan, there is a wide variety of motifs for construction site barriers. These barriers often feature images of animals, people or famous mascots such as Hello Kitty. The use of such cute motifs not only serves the purpose of fencing off and thus minimizing danger, but also of promoting a positive perception of construction sites.

fictional characters are seen as individuals who live in Japanese society and interact with others.

»Some countries have an unwritten rule: Cute mascots should not venture beyond the amusement park or sports stadium. But Japan is a land where these fuzzy creatures roam free: where no town is too small, no product too plain, no PR campaign too obscure to miss out on having its own mascot«

(Schauerte, in: Wilde 2018: 29)

According to Wilde, since the turn of the millennium almost no Japanese municipality, authority or office has managed without a representative kyara (ibid.). The figures are used on various documents, signs, for advertising purposes, on products, giveaways and often also as a full-body costume (›kigurumi‹). According to Sabine Frühstück, the use of mascots is intended, among other things, to soften the strict image of the police. Violence is abhorred in Japan and therefore organizations such as the

Fig. 313 ›Kanyan‹ mascot of a bus in Suginami, Tokyo

Many buses in Tokyo have little mascots next to the route description. One of the purposes of these mascots is to make it easier to identify the bus or route. This is particularly helpful for tourists, children or people with reading difficulties. The mascots often visualize local features or cultural aspects of the destinations.

The cute mascot shown on the left is the character ›Kanyan‹ from ›Kanto Bus‹, which has been around since 2014 (cf. Kanto Bus). It depicts a cat with a hat and wings. According to the company, the cat cannot fly, but dreams of being able to fly one day. Personal characteristics were assigned to the mascot in order to strengthen the figure's accessibility for the viewer.

Fig. 314 ›Pipo-kun‹ mascot in Suginami, Tokyo

Government agencies have official mascots in Japan. Each prefecture or city has its own character or characters. The mascot of the Tokyo Police Department (Fig. 314) is known as Pipo or Pipo-kun. According to Todd, the antenna means that Pipo is always informed about current happenings, while the large eyes enable him to recognize problems and the oversized ears alert him to calls for help (Todd 2017). Pipo is used for communicative purposes and is intended to convey a sympathetic image of the state authorities.

These and similar mascots are not only depicted on signs or documents, but are also often used as full-body costumes at events to create an emotional bond with the organization.

police have to be very careful with their potential for violence (Todd 2017).

Nittono defined kawaii as an emotion that makes a person feel unthreatened (Nittono 2016: 89). According to him, the perception of specific attributes such as the baby schema, a smile, roundness or colors leads to the positive, unthreatened and socially oriented emotion ›kawaii‹ (ibid.). Studies have shown that viewing images of human or animal infants activates the facial muscles more strongly, leading to smiling, and that this can even be transferred to inanimate objects (ibid. 90). Thus, kawaii mascots can have a positive effect on the recipient's state of mind simply by looking at them.

Mascots are not only omnipresent on signs in Japan. Their use extends to cultural areas such as art (see from page 76) as well as everyday life, for example in food (see from page 80), fashion (see from page 82) or stickers (see from page 90).

Fig. 315 ›Toaran‹ mascot in Taito, Tokyo

Toaran is the mascot of the Toden Arakawa Line in Tokyo. The image (Fig. 315) is from an information sign indicating the way to the elevator. The mascot is pointing with his hand in the direction of the elevator. Toaran is an anthropomorphized representation of a streetcar of the Toden Arakawa Line. The mascot is geometrically designed and integrates characteristic elements of the Toden Arakawa Line, especially the color green. The design of Toaran reflects typical features of kawaii culture, such as a broad face, large eyes and the stylized depiction of cheeks, with the lights of the car having been transformed into the cheeks of the face. The mascot is intended to create a positive association with the Toden Arakawa Line.

Toaran is available as a LINE sticker; see also page 95.

Fig. 316 image of an information board in Komabano Park, Tokyo

The girl with the cat comes from an information board in Komabano Park in Shibuya, Tokyo. The rules of the park are illustrated and described on it. These include, for example, the request to remove dog excrement and to refrain from feeding animals. The depiction on the left is meant to value life and not to harm or harass living creatures. It shows a girl stroking a cat lovingly. The depictions show distinctive kawaii faces; this can be seen in the shape of the girl's head and eyes and in the eyes of the cat. The round arc for the eye shape is used to signal contentment. Such a form of representation is often used for the visualization of satisfaction or for a smile. This is not only recognizable in the horizontal text-based emoji (Fig. 291), but also in the graphic emoji (Fig. 297) for a smile.

Fig. 317 ›luminous quake‹ acrylic on canvas

Socks the Ghostcat

LOTTA AYANO NAKANO
Artist

»I wanted to create a figure whose expression is conveyed through movement and background, even without a mouth. I project my own feelings onto this character.«

Nakano about her character Socks the Ghostcat (Nakano 2024)

Fig. 318 **Lotta**

Lotta is a Japanese artist known for her character ›Socks the Ghostcat‹ and her cartoon-like style. The characteristics of her paintings are revealed in a discreet color spectrum and a pronounced use of rounded forms.

›luminous quake‹
(Fig. 317) from
›Protect me‹, Dubai

›where do we go‹
(Fig. 319) from
›Once upon a time‹,
Shibuya, Tokyo

›Socks the Ghostcat‹ is a fusion of cat and ghost. The figure's head is characterized by cat-like ears, and the lack of legs gives the figure a ghostly appearance. The often floating figure was created by the artist Lotta in 2020 and acts as the main protagonist in almost all of the artist's works. The paintings, which are often in black and white, capture moments that are reminiscent of individual snippets from comics. Within this narrative framework, the protagonist figure encounters other figures, such as people or figures reminiscent of animals like rabbits (Fig. 317) or a dog made of balloons called ›Pufi‹ (Fig. 319).

The mascot-like character is a distinctive attribute of the artist's works. The element of the ghost is also of significance, as the artist has a fondness for Japanese ghosts and goblins, which are deeply rooted in Japanese culture (cf. Nakano 2024). Ghost figures have a prominent position in various cultural aspects such as literature, religion and art.

According to the artist, Socks the Ghostcat serves to express her own emotions. The lack of a mouth on the figure is reminiscent of horizontal, text-based emojis, which makes it clear that in Japanese culture a mouth is not necessary to convey emotions (see also page 44). By using round, cartoon-like figures and a strongly reduced use of color, the artist creates an atmosphere that invites the viewer to interpret stories. Each image appears like a frame of an animated movie. According to McCloud's formal aesthetic research, the reduced representation of the face makes it easier for the viewer to empathize with the story (see page 110).

In her works, the artist combines characteristics of the kawaii aesthetic, such as roundness, reduced facial expressions and the absence of a mouth, with elements from the cartoon, such as the narrative depiction of the characters and typical visual elements for the representation of movements, such as stars or splashes of water.

Fig. 319 ›where do we go‹ acrylic on canvas (1455x970mm)

Kawaii Food

In Tokyo, the world of mascots also extends to the culinary area. Meals become adorable kawaii creations, with food often presented in the form of cute characters. Sweets, which are characteristic of the kawaii culture, come in a dazzling variety of colors and shapes. Among the culinary kawaii creations, animal motifs are a particularly popular subject. Similar to the Purikura photos (see page 89), a lot of emphasis is placed on careful staging; the kawaii foods are not only photographed by consumers, but also carranged with various mascots.

By anthropomorphizing their food, restaurants and cafés that specialize in kawaii food create a kind of imaginary counterpart and evoke a special communicative disposition in people, see page 73. This refers to a mirror-image intersubjective or social relationship that people are prepared to adopt towards other people and means that the consumer communicates and sympathizes with the stylized representation[6] as a kind of imaginary counterpart. This confirms Liying's statement that the existence of something cute triggers a positive feeling, see page 84. Marcel Danesi made a similar observation about emojis when he said that the signs spread ›a positive mood‹ by being able to enhance the positive tone of an informal message (cf. Danesi 2017: 58).

Fig. 320 **illustration of a typical kawaii ice cream dish**

6   For the question of the right degree of anthropomorphism, see page 113.

Fig. 321 **sweet dish from ›Marine House‹ in Shibuya, Tokyo**

Kawaii Fashion in Harajuku

Fashion has become a strong means of expressing kawaii. The Harajuku quarter in Tokyo is considered an important area for the most extraordinary youth trends. The spread of kawaii culture and the diversity of fashions has led to a wide variety of styles. Takeshita Street is considered a central hub of kawaii culture and its various manifestations.

The expression of Kawaii is multifaceted and can be seen in various forms. For example, ›Yume Kawaii‹ is associated with a romantic dream world with lots of plush and fluffy elements. It is also characterized by pastel shades and cute accessories. ›Yami Kawaii‹, on the other hand, has a rebellious character and often addresses taboo topics such as mental illness, which are combined with the kawaii aesthetic. ›Yami‹ can be translated into English as ›darkness‹ and includes much stronger colors and a lot of black.

Kawaii fashion is characterized by its varied combinations. Individual styles are often mixed together to create a new style that becomes characteristic of a person or a specific group. Accessories play an important role and are often made and put together by the individual. The styles are so varied that an entire book could be filled with them. The following is just a small insight into the colorful world of kawaii fashion.

Some of the styles or trends presented in the following can be viewed critically. However, it is not the intention of this publication to criticize individuals or specific styles. Rather, the aim is to give a brief insight into the variety of styles and the respective people in order to understand the development and thus be able to establish a connection to the signs used in communication. In order to respect the privacy of the individuals, a critical examination of individual styles will be avoided.

The aim of these explanations is to develop an understanding of the formal background of the various visual signs in order to understand their creation and spread.

A personality with a particularly distinctive kawaii style is ›Rin Castles‹. She is a Harajuku fashion model, jewelry designer and a social media consultant. Rin Castles is her artist name. She models for the ›Sensational Kawaii‹ brand ›6%DOKIDOKI‹. Her unusual outfits contain the most diverse and colorful kawaii elements. Many of the clips and elements from her outfit are handmade by her or by friends in Japan.

According to Castles, her favorite color in USA is called ›hot pink‹, while in Japan it is called ›candy pink‹. See Shirai's statement on the different preferences for dolls in America and Japan on page 89.

Fig. 322 ›Rin Castles‹ in Takeshita Street

Fig. 323 **Liying in Harajuku**

HUANG LIYING
artist & graduate student

»To me, ›kawaii‹ is not just about the appearance of cuteness, but also about being fluffy like a stuffed animal, possessing the power to heal people. Seeing something kawaii naturally improves my mood. I believe it represents the small joys and happiness in everyday life.«

Liying represents an aesthetic fusion inspired by feminine grace with parallels to Kokeshi dolls. She unites traditional formal expression with modern elements. For example, her hairstyle has a traditional shape but is combined with the use of an eye-catching, modern color scheme. Through the integration of a feminine aesthetic with flashy purple accents, such as the tights, her appearance adopts a distinctively unique kawaii style.

Fig. 324 **illustration of a modern Kokeshi doll**

Fig. 325 **Miura in Harajuku**

In addition to the girlish cut and embellishments, her dress also includes floral elements reminiscent of kimono ornaments. By combining traditional shapes with modern elements, she bridges the gap between traditional elegance and modern expressiveness.

KAORI MIURA
cosplayer

Miura presents an equally feminine but very contrasting look compared to Liying. She dresses in the ›Jirai Kei[7] Harajuku style‹. This is a sweet, girlish fashion style that is combined with a dark aesthetic. The style is characterized by a high proportion of black in combination with an intense color such as red, purple or pink. Ruffles, blouses, bows and lacing inspired by ›Lolita style‹ are often used with a form of ›Namida Bukuro‹[8] make-up. Jirai Kei style can vary widely in appearance and has developed in different directions. It is characterized by a feminine and mysterious look.

7   ›Jirai‹ is a Japanese slang expression indicating something dangerous, particularly linked to stepping on landmines (j-fashion). In the Jirai Kei subculture, women are referred to as ›Jirai Josh‹, which means landmine girl, while men are referred to as ›Jirai Dashi‹, which can be translated as landmine boy (ibd.). The subculture often focuses on rebellious behaviour and taboo subjects. Due to its negative associations, the terms ›Yami Kawaii‹ or ›Dark Girl‹ are frequently used interchangeably with Jirai Kei, as these styles share similar or even identical elements (ibd.).

8   In a Namida Bukuro eye make-up, bags under the eyes are highlighted in pink or red, combined with black lines around the eyes and light-colored skin. To make the eyes appear larger, black circle lens contacts are often used.

Harajuku Decora King

Fig. 326 **various hair clips on Erunyan's hairstyle**

Fig. 327 **detail of Erunyan's outfit showing the gloomy bear**

ERUNYAN
Visual Kei Singer

»The expression of Kawaii is unlimited, free and far-reaching. What was once considered cool can be transformed into a feeling of kawaii.«

(Erunyan 2024)

Erunyan is a Japanese visual kei singer from the band ›Shingeki no Awake‹. Due to his appearance, he is also known as the ›Harajuku Decora King‹.

Erunyan embodies kawaii culture through his appearance and behavior. His style aligns with the Japanese ›Decora‹ fashion, popular in Harajuku, known for its bright colors and plethora of accessories. Erunyan's numerous accessories, including hair clips featuring sweets, rainbows, stars, and characters like Mickey Mouse and Waniyama-san (Fig. 326), reference kawaii culture, comics, and manga. Although Decora generally features positive and colorful elements, it can also incorporate darker ones, such as the ›Gloomy Bear‹ in Erunyan's outfit (Fig. 327). This character, designed in the typical kawaii style with round shapes, pastel colors, and subtle expressions, contrasts with blood details, reflecting a broader aesthetic seen in other styles (see also page 85). Staging is crucial in kawaii culture, represented not only through appearance and behavior but also through a specific image aesthetic.

In Japan, the audience at concerts often perform a kind of choreography with movements and gestures to create a pleasant atmosphere for the artist. Popular movements include turning the palms of raised hands (Fig. 329) and forming various patterns in the air. The choreography is rehearsed in advance by the fans so that it is performed in synchrony and coordinated with the music.

Fig. 328 **Erunyan in Harajuku, Tokyo**

Fig. 329 **illustration of a popular movement**

Kawaii Aesthetic in Purikura Images

The kawaii image aesthetic form Purikura is very popular in Japan. The photos are usually taken as group pictures in booths and can be edited and decorated with many different elements (Fig. 330). The aesthetics of these photos include many characteristics of kawaii culture and are particularly popular among young people. As a pastime, Purikura is celebrated as a shared experience.

The photos taken with Purikura photo booths are heavily edited and users add numerous decorative elements. The editing makes the people depicted appear much younger with enlarged eyes, high foreheads and smooth skin. These photo booths are particularly popular with Burikko[9] girls.

According to Shirai, the Japanese aesthetic sense has focused on the acceptance of immaturity and incompleteness, asymmetry and imbalance (Shirai 2019). According to her, the preference for childlike faces stems from the preference for neoteny [imperfect state of development]. In Japanese culture, children are seen as better beings because of their purity and chastity. Development into adulthood seems to be more of a necessary evil in Japan (see Sato in: Shirai 2019). The heroes in Japanese manga are young, usually children or teenagers. In American or European comics, on the other hand, they are more adult, mature and sexy. Something similar can also be observed with dolls: While Barbie embodies an adult and tall woman, the Japanese counterpart – the ›Rika-chan doll‹ – is childlike and immature (Shirai 2005: 56). According to Shirai, harmony and conflict avoidance are of great importance in Japanese culture. For this reason, kawaii is not only used to avoid conflict, but also as an expression of politeness and respect towards others. In Europe, on the other hand, kawaii is perceived more as an infantile practice.

9   Burriko is a slang term for an imitation childlike behavior that is often combined with the kawaii aesthetic.

Fig. 330 **illustration depicting the process of making Purikuraphotos**

Kawaii-themed stationery is particularly popular in Japan. The stores themselves (Fig. 337) and the products are rich in detail and include a variety of items such as stickers, stamps, gift cards and postcards in the kawaii aesthetic. In addition to stickers, stamps are particularly popular as they are deeply rooted in Japanese culture.

Stamps have a long tradition in Japan and are used for official signatures, among other things. Each train station has its own individual stamp, which is based on typical features of the station or its surroundings. The stamp of Shimbashi Station (Fig. 332), for example, shows the former roof of the station. The lettering of the station is combined with the roof to form a pictorial sign. The stamp of Akihabara Station (Fig. 331), on the other hand, shows the Mansei Bridge, whereby the corresponding character is transformed into conductor tracks with connection points, which refers to the electronics. Akihabara is known for its electronics trade. The stamp of Higashi-Jūjō Station (Fig. 333) shows the platform of the station in conjunction with a camera, indicating that the location is popular with railroad photographers. Each station in Tokyo has its own unique stamp that can be used at the station.

The Kawaii lifestyle store ›Rainbowholic‹ has taken up this tradition and developed its own kawaii stamps that represent different areas of the store in a funny way. Ocampo, the owner of the store (see Fig. 303), places particular emphasis on elements of kawaii culture, many of which can be found in her store. As at the train stations, the owner has set up a stamping station where the stamps can be used. One of her stamps (Fig. 335) shows a kawaii local character ›Kitanyan‹ (where, according to Ocampo, ›kita‹ being the name of the city and ›nyan‹ being the Japanese equivalent of ›meow‹) of Jujo Ginza Shotengai shopping street, where Rainbowholic is located. Fig. 334 contains an anthropomorphized locomotive and Fig. 336 modified the famous local food ›Takoyaki‹ into mascots. Ocampo uses the stamps to create a kawaii representation of her store.

Fig. 331 **stamp from Akihabara Station**	Fig. 332 **stamp from Shimbashi Station**	Fig. 333 **stamp from Higashi-Jūjō Station**

Fig. 337 ›Rainbowholic‹ storefront in Kita, Tokyo

Fig. 334 **Rainbowholic stamp by tazdaunicorn**

Fig. 335 **Rainbowholic stamp by tazdaunicorn**

Fig. 336 **Rainbowholic stamp by chichilittle**

The Influence of Kawaii Culture on (Emoji-)Sticker

The use of stickers is very widespread and an incredible formal variety of different stickers has emerged. The presence of the kawaii aesthetic is characteristic of the formal design.

Fig. 338 (according to Smileysnetwork, edited by D.E.)

■ [187 px]
■ [29 px]
■ [23 px]

Kaoanis belong to an early form of sticker. The term ›kaoani‹ is a combination of the words ›kao‹ [face] and ›ani‹ [animation]. It refers to an animated variant of graphic, mostly floating faces from Japan. They can embody numerous figures such as animals or food. According to Trautsch and Wu, these are image personifications that are created through a combination – such as BaoZi dumplings and human faces (cf. Trautsch/Wu 2012: 61).

Stickers can combine different elements such as images or letters. For example, the laughing kaoani (Fig. 340) contains Japanese characters that form an onomatopoeia of laughter. The giggling kaoani (Fig. 338) also contains characters that complement the illustration. Such combinations are reminiscent of the use of signs in comics. Cartoon-like representations are not only used for pictures, but also for words in order to visually clarify the content (see, for example, Fig. 378 or Fig. 379).

With their broad heads, personification of food and typical facial expressions, kaoanis embody the kawaii aesthetic. In most cases, stickers are animated and available as ›GIF‹ (Graphics Interchange Format) files. GIF files with a small number of individual

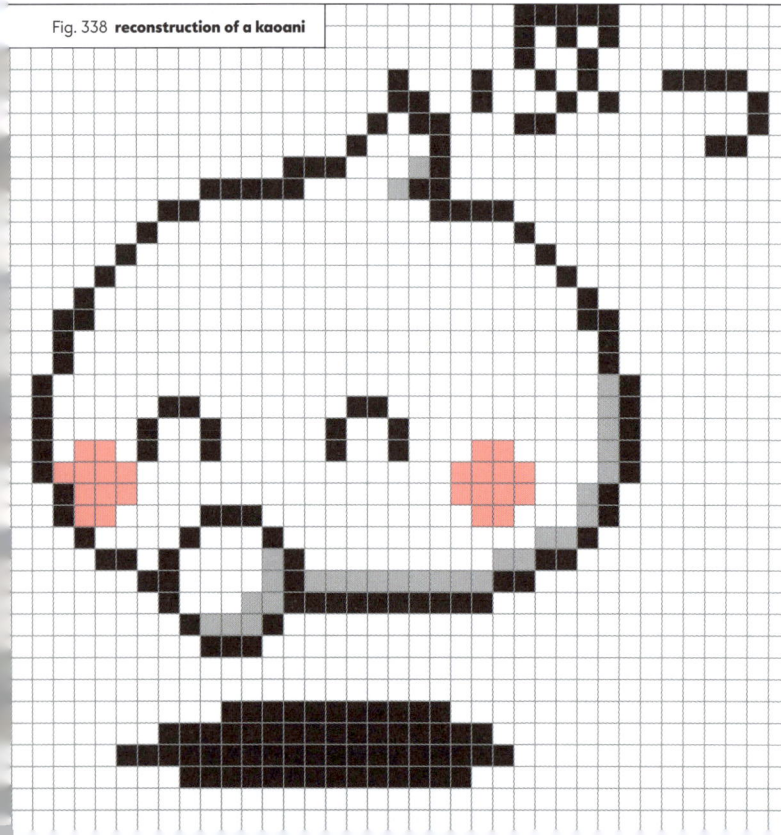

Fig. 338 **reconstruction of a kaoani**

Fig. 339

Fig. 340

images appear hectic, which was particularly characteristic of the earlier stickers (Fig. 338–Fig. 340). The stickers shown on this page were particularly popular in chat rooms in Japan in the early 2000s, around the same time as the stickers featured on page 58.

Nowadays, much more detailed character sets are used. The instant messaging services ›LINE‹ and ›KakaoTalk‹, for example, offer a formal variety of emojis and stickers. Both providers have their own emojis, which can be integrated into text messages if the user communicates within the platform. In addition, the platforms offer a significant number of different sticker packs. Pictorial signs that can be used within the text tend to have a reduced design, as they have to function in the smallest of spaces (Fig. 344–Fig. 355, Fig. 365–Fig. 376).

Well-known characters from KakaoTalk are the ›Kakao Friends‹ (Fig. 341–Fig. 361). Image personifications are also recognizable among them, with ›Apeach‹, for example, representing a personified peach with frequently hyperbolic expressions (cf. Kakao Friends a). This also includes the radish in a rabbit costume called ›Muzi‹ (cf. ibid.). It contains typical Kawaii elements or expressions, such as the dreamy eyes in Fig. 342. Kawaii eyes are characterized by the use of multiple light reflections. The cat ›Neo‹ also contains various kawaii elements, such as the typical reddening of the face, which is shown in the form of hatched lines (Fig. 348) or as a solid surface (Fig. 355).
The platform offers the use of other character sets, such as ›Baby Choonsik‹ (cf. Kakao Friends b). This also belongs to the Kakao Friends and shows a baby cat in a wide variety of situations, such as eating (Fig. 356), celebrating (Fig. 357) or driving a toy car (Fig. 358).
Some stickers contain Korean characters (Fig. 358, Fig. 359), as the service comes from Korea. The stickers can be seen as a graphical evolution of text-based emojis, which are composed of the Korean alphabet ›Hangul‹ – called ›geurim mal‹ [›picture words‹] or ›Korean emoticons‹ (see Karpinska et al. 2020: 67, see also Enzmann 2023: 77).

The phonetic sign for laughter – which resembles a mirrored ›F‹ – corresponds to the German equivalent ›haha‹ and is considered the Korean equivalent of ›LOL‹ (cf. Karpinska et al. 2020: 78). The iterated use is used to potentiate the statement. According to Karpinska et al., ignorance of hangul can lead to misinterpretations of Korean text-based emojis. In the aforementioned study, it is explained that analyzing the form is not enough to interpret Korean text-based emojis; the culture in which they were created and sometimes even the meaning of the individual elements must also be taken into account (cf. ibid.: 79).

As with the mascots already discussed (see pages 74–75), the Kakao Friends are assigned human characteristics such as friendships or experiences and adventures (cf. Kakao Friends a). For example, according to the company, ›Angmond‹ likes chocolate and is lazy, while ›Cob and Bbanya‹ form a curious duo who pretend to be detectives (cf. Kakao Friends c).

LINE also has numerous different characters, such as a rabbit Cony (Fig. 363) and a bear Brown (Fig. 362), who appear as a couple (Fig. 364). While Brown is always depicted with restrained facial expressions, Cony uses exaggerated emotions like those used by the Kaoanis or in comics. As with KakaoTalk, Cony and Brown are also available as stickers (Fig. 362– Fig. 364), which are sent as individual files, and as picture characters (Fig. 365– Fig. 376), which are integrated into the text.

Furthermore, the provider offers a very large number of different sticker sets, such as the already themed mascot ›Toaran‹ (see page 75). The special thing about LINE is that it enables designers to make their own stickers available to the community. One example of such a sticker set is the ›Shahimi shark energetic‹ by designer Yi-Ling. The sticker set shows a cute shark in a wide variety of activities, such as eating onigiri (Fig. 380), consuming media (Fig. 382) and experiencing a wide range of different emotions, such as joy about something (Fig. 381).

KAKAO FRIENDS (KakaoTalk 10.8.3)

Fig. 341 **Apeach**	Fig. 342 **Muzi**	Fig. 343 **Neo**

Fig. 344	Fig. 345	Fig. 346	Fig. 347	Fig. 348	Fig. 349

Fig. 350	Fig. 351	Fig. 352	Fig. 353	Fig. 354	Fig. 355

BABY CHOONSIK by Kakao Friends (KakaoTalk 10.8.3)

Fig. 356	Fig. 357	Fig. 358

HELLO NINIZ by Miniz (KakaoTalk 10.8.3)

Fig. 359 **Penda Jr.**	Fig. 360 **Angmond**	Fig. 361 **Cob & Bbanya**

BROWN & CONY © LY CORPORATION (LINE b)

Fig. 362 **Brown**

Fig. 363 **Cony**

Fig. 364

Fig. 365

Fig. 366

Fig. 367

Fig. 368

Fig. 369

Fig. 370

Fig. 371

Fig. 372

Fig. 373

Fig. 374

Fig. 375

Fig. 376

TOARAN © TOEI TRANSPORTATION (LINE a)

Fig. 377

Fig. 378

Fig. 379

SHAHIMI SHARK ENERGETIC ©YI-LING (LINE d)

Fig. 380

Fig. 381

Fig. 382

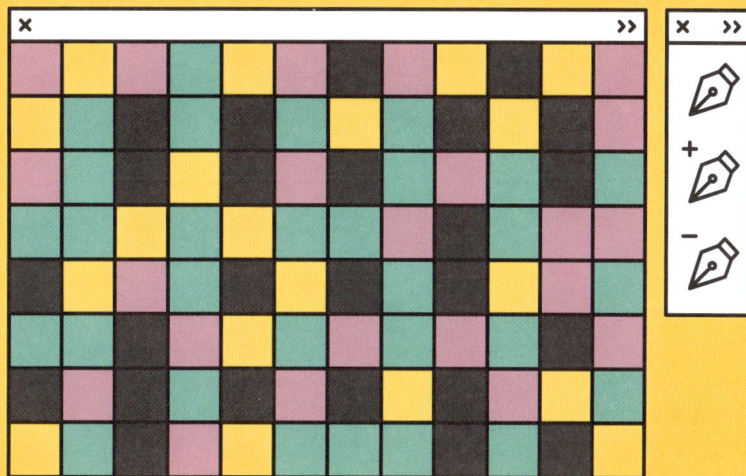

Creative Variety of Emojis

The emergence and spread of emojis is perceived ambivalently and provokes controversial reactions. In addition to the frequently mentioned points of criticism such as the accusation of infantilization, the association with childishness and regression, the visual design level is also criticized by designers. Despite the ongoing discussions, some designers are actively engaging with this issue and developing remarkable projects that use the potential of emojis constructively. This chapter focuses on such approaches and shows how emojis are used in visual communication.

How are emojis used in visual communication?

What creative potential do emojis offer designers?

How is formal diversity used?

Until now, the use of emojis has been tied to the technical possibilities.[10] As designers, we have countless options for using different fonts and the associated expression. The formal variety of emojis has so far been limited on smartphones due to technical restrictions. Although it is possible to design your own picture characters and use them as stickers, it is not possible to replace the existing emoji keyboard with your own or new character sets. In most cases, stickers are sent as individual image files and cannot be integrated into the text like emojis on all platforms, which limits their use.

Another option for using your own emojis is to design a font. Although this can be used on many relevant media, it cannot be used on the communication medium on which emojis are mainly used – the smartphone. Despite the technical hurdles and limitations, there are initiating projects that deal with the formal diversity of emojis and contribute to the creative variety of emojis. Some of these projects are presented in this chapter. Due to the current technical possibilities mentioned, a basic distinction is made between emoji-fonts and (emoji-)stickers. This distinction can overlap in practice if, for example, emojis from a font are used

10   More recent developments promise the use of custom emoji combinations and a wider formal variety of emojis (see page 62 f.).

as stickers, as is the case with the OpenMoji project (see pages 130–137). Stickers, such as the 1000 Emoji Project by Dan Woodger, can also be integrated into the text using platforms that make this possible, such as LINE (see pages 164–168).

Despite some technical exceptions, a fundamental distinction is made below between the two groups mentioned. This is based on the current possibilities for designing emojis, where either a new emoji can be designed as a glyph and thus part of a font, or an emoji is created as a sticker and thus as an image file. Projects that have been created with different intentions are presented and discussed in the two categories mentioned. The aim of the publication is not to create a complete collection of existing emoji projects, but to highlight the potential of emojis in visual communication. For this reason, projects that were conceived from different backgrounds or with different formal elaboration are thematized in order to demonstrate the diversity of the resulting projects.

Before concrete design projects are presented, a brief theoretical introduction to emojis is given. This is intended to create a theoretical foundation in order to better understand, locate and comprehend the different design approaches from a theoretical perspective. The basic questions of why emojis are signs and what sign processes taking place through emojis look like according to semiotic understanding will be clarified. I mainly refer to the semiotics of Charles Sanders Peirce, as well as existing studies on emojis.

In addition to discussing the basic semiotic principles, the role played by the aesthetics and imagery of the signs in the communication process with emojis will be addressed. What aesthetic potential do the characters have? What influence does the design of the emojis have on the sign process? Is there a so-called ›immediate understanding of the image‹ that ensures that emojis are usually referred to as a ›universal language‹ in journalistic articles (Lobo 2017; Giannoulis/Wilde 2020: 2)? Research agrees that emojis are not a universal language that is free from cultural coding, contextual ambiguities or countless opportunities for misunderstanding (cf. Wilde 2020: 171). Nevertheless, the signs are said to have a so-called ›universality‹ that is rarely questioned (cf. ibid.: 174). How does such an immediate understanding of the image and the only apparent universality that goes with it come about? To what extent do emojis deserve the classification ›image‹ when they are used like words and sentences? In order to investigate the immediate understanding of the image, the work

refers to Wilde's research on emojis in this area as well as to findings from image theory and cognitive semiotics.

The existence of the aesthetic qualities, their influence and the impact on communication, as well as the meaning of the characters are discussed on the basis of messages from the Textmoji case study. This is done on the basis of semiotic studies, in relation to kawaii aesthetics and with the aid of various image and comic theories. I explore the question of the extent to which identification and abstraction are related and what effects the formal-aesthetic properties of the signs have on the sign process and the meaning of the emojis. The focus is on the medium of the image and its advantages. Does the sign itself create an existence through its pictorial constitution – a kind of coexistence – that communicates in the sense of an imagined counterpart?

The intention of the chapter is to show the creative potential of emojis in visual communication and to demonstrate the creative variations of the characters. Emojis have become an integral part of our communication, and the future will show how the formal diversity of emojis will develop. As designers, we have the opportunity to become active ourselves and develop new emojis that can make our communication even more individual and expressive.

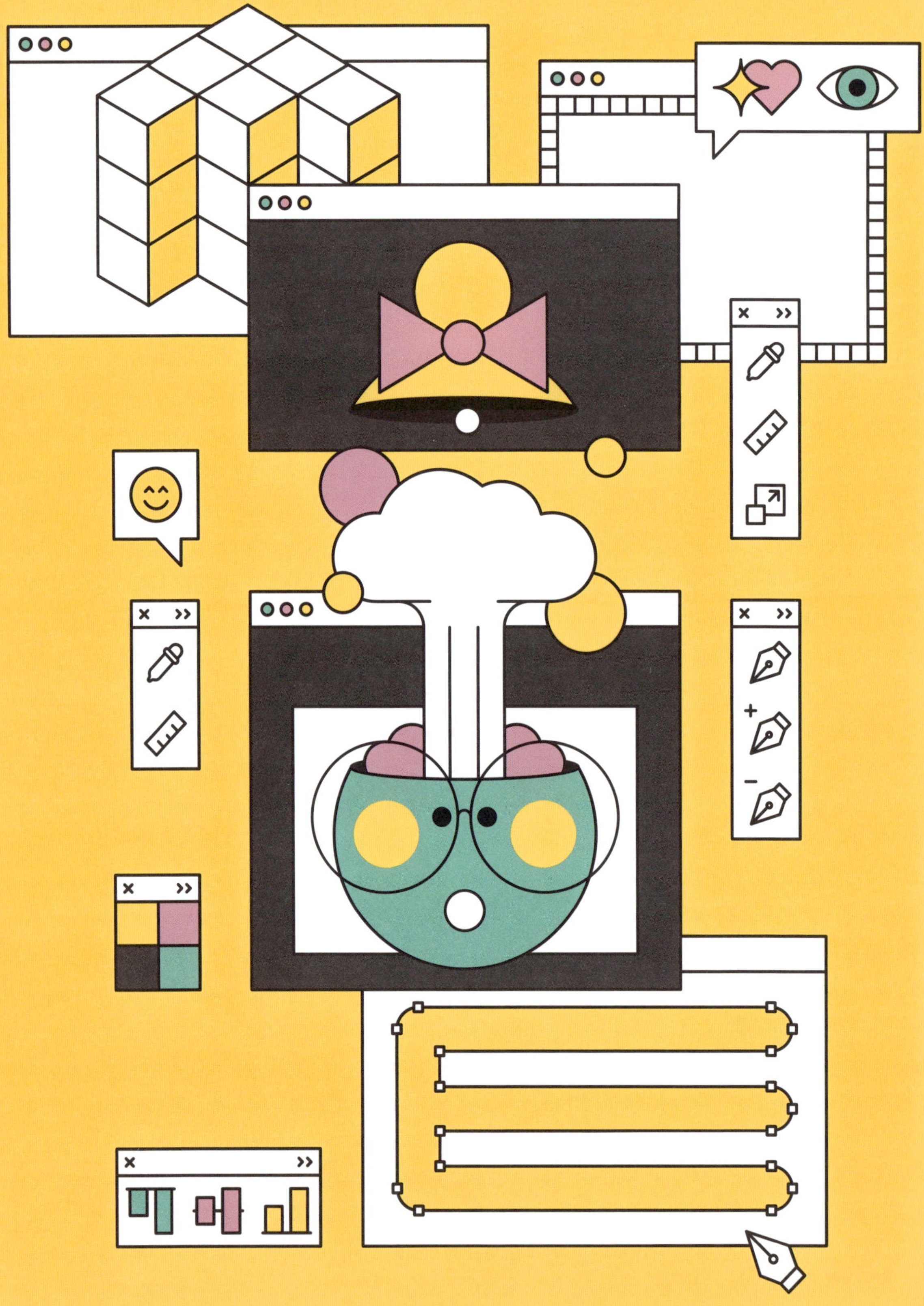

Theoretical Introduction

Emojization has changed the way we communicate, and the ubiquity of the emoji aesthetic has had a formative influence on our perception and use of signs. In recent years, a wide variety of projects have been created with emojis. This subchapter looks at this development from a theoretical and design perspective. The functions of emojis are very different and the variability of meanings, the context-dependent, polyfunctional and ambiguous character of the signs is fascinating. Research into the functions of emojis and attempts to structure and classify the signs come mainly from the field of linguistics. But what opportunities does the rise of friendly characters offer to designers?

What do the sign processes with emojis look like?

What influence do the formal aspects have on the effect and meaning of the characters?

What is the relationship between form and content?

And how are abstraction and identification connected?

The use of emojis is becoming more and more important in our writing behavior and is thus influencing the way we communicate. Digital communication systems have changed the use of writing. Private communication and entertainment now take place in the same media as work-oriented interactions. Such a mixture changes the use of writing and the attitude of users towards it.

The integration of pictographical elements was previously only tolerated in informal, personal, mostly handwritten interactions. It must be taken into account that the communicative output of society has increased enormously since the emergence of the internet. Communicating, commenting on content and sharing everyday life digitally has become the norm. Purely textual communication would be extremely exhausting.

Due to the increasing presence and use of emojis, a certain internalization of the signs is to be expected, which in turn has an influence on the perception of such signs. The transformation process currently taking place in visual communication is an important discourse for designers. What possibilities do emojis offer for design projects?

To what extent does the omnipresence of emojis change our perception of other characters? Are we in the process of redefining design values? To what extent can Paula Scher's statement ›more is more‹ be applied to the design and use of emojis? Can this change be interpreted as a creative paradigm shift, or does it rather indicate an infantile, regressive development that potentially signals a linguistic decline?
These and similar questions are explored in the following from a theoretical and design perspective.

»He who loves practice without theory is like the sailor who boards ship without a rudder and compass and never knows where he may cast.«

(Leonardo da Vinci, in: Helmann 2017: 10)

Before looking at how emojis are used in design projects and how their formal diversity is realized, a theoretical examination of the phenomenon of Emojization is carried out. Concepts and principles from various scientific disciplines such as semiotics, linguistics, image theory and comic theory are used to enable an interdisciplinary view of the phenomenon.

The semiotic Potential of Emojis

In general usage, it seems completely plausible to refer to emojis as signs. But what exactly makes an emoji a sign? To delve into this, it is essential to understand the nature of signs themselves and how a sign process that happens with emojis works.

What is a sign?

What does a sign process that takes place with emojis look like according to semiotic understanding?

Semiotics is not a unified science and contains different perspectives, currents and tendencies (cf. Nöth 2000: 3). Nevertheless, a fundamental distinction can be made between two semiotic directions: Linguistic-structuralist semiotics and semiotics with a general orientation towards sign theory. Ferdinand de Saussure (1857-1913) is considered the founder of the linguistic-structuralist direction. De Saussure was primarily concerned with linguistic signs and distinguished between two levels of the sign: the idea and the image of sound, also known as the signified and the signifier (cf. Nöth 2000: 74). According to de Saussure, the sign is constituted by a correlation between signified and signifier. The arrows in the following diagram by de Saussure (Fig. 383) indicate a mutual influence. In the case of a graphic emoji, the signifier is the image of a yellow smiling face. Possible signifieds are, for example, ›smiling‹, ›being happy‹ or ›Acid House‹ (Fig. 384). The sign integrates both – image and meaning(s). While de Saussure concentrated primarily on linguistic signs, Charles Sanders Peirce (1839-1914) developed a more philosophical approach that deals with all types of signs and sign systems. He is regarded as the founder of the second main current, general semiotics based on sign theory. Peirce provided the most complex description and explanation of what a sign is and how it works (cf. Friedrich/Schweppenhäuser 2010: 30). He gives several definitions of the sign in different places, which are based on the idea of a triadic relation (cf. Nöth 2000: 62). According to Peirce, a sign always has three references: A ›medium‹ refers to an ›object‹ and is interpreted by a third party, the ›interpretant‹, as standing in this relationship (cf. Schönrich 1999: 9).

In semiotics, this tripartite nature is arranged in the form of a triangle using various terms, some of which differ greatly in terms of content (see Enzmann 2023: 115).
Peirce called the medium ›representamen‹ or simply ›sign (in itself)‹. However, he was of the opinion that the word ›medium‹ can replace the term sign, as the sign stands as a mediator between an object and interpretant (cf. Nöth 2000: 467). In this work, the term ›medium‹ is used. Those who interpret the sign are called ›interpreters‹.

Fig. 383 **Saussure's model of the sign**	Fig. 384	Fig. 385 **the semiotic triangle** (Walther 1974: 54; see also Eco 1977: 30)

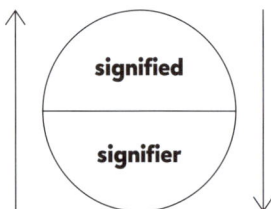

signified
signifier

(according to Saussure 1967: 76/78; cf. Enzmann 2023: 107)

smiling
being happy
Acid House
...

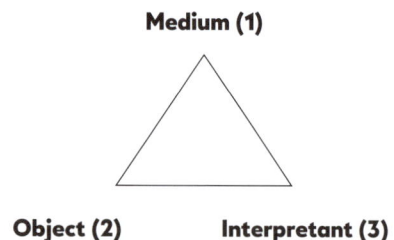

Medium (1)

Object (2)   Interpretant (3)

The relationship between these three correlates – and thus the semiotic triangle – forms the basis of Peirce's semiotics and is a precondition for the formation of a semiotically valid sign process – also known as ›semiosis‹. It is therefore not a dyadic process, as with de Saussure, but a triadic one.

Since Peirce did not limit his studies to linguistic signs, his method is suitable for analyzing a phenomenon such as emojis and the sign processes generated by the signs.
A graphic emoji is used as an example. The medium is the expression of the sign, in the case of the emoji, the graphic form. The sign can be interpreted in different ways. If it is interpreted as a smiling face, for example, it refers to a smiling face (Fig. 387). If, on the other hand, it is interpreted to mean that a person is happy, it refers to an emotion or a state

of mind of the sender (Fig. 388). An emoji can also be interpreted as a sign for acid house (Fig. 389, see also page 33) and thus stands for a certain music culture or attitude to life. This changes the reference object and thus also the semiotic nature of the sign. There are further distinctions to be made in order to analyze the semioticity. Peirce subdivides the three references into further trichotomies, denoting sub-types of sign classes. This is usually presented in the form of a table (Fig. 386) (cf. Nöth 2000: 66)

Peirce's semiotics is based on the three ›universal categories‹ ›firstness‹, ›secondness‹ and ›thirdness‹. These form the fundament of his ›phenomenology of universal categories‹, which is a theory of experience (Peirce 2000b: 17). Peirce understands ›phenomenon‹ to mean everything that is present in one way or another at one time (cf. Peirce 1983: 40): According to him, there is no more than these three kinds of elements to be found in a phenomenon (cf. Peirce 2000b: 109). For a more detailed explanation of universal categories, see Enzmann 2023: 110-113.

Fig. 386 the triadic relation within the types of sign classes and their numerically reduced representation

Categories	Sign References					M	O	I
	Medium (M)	**Object (O)**	**Interpretant (I)**			**M**	**O**	**I**
Firstness	1.1 Qualisign	2.1 Icon	3.1 Rheme		1	1.1	2.1	3.1
Secondness	1.2 Sinsign	2.2 Index	3.2 Dicisign		2	1.2	2.2	3.2
Thirdness	1.3 Legisign	2.3 Symbol	3.3 Argument		3	1.3	2.3	3.3

(cf. Enzmann 2023b: 181; also Peirce 2000b: 48; Nöth 2000: 66; Walther 1974: 56)

Fig. 387 interpreted as an icon	Fig. 388 interpreted as an index	Fig. 389 interpreted as a symbol

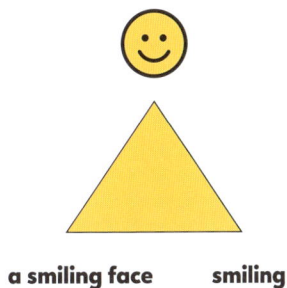

a smiling face   smiling

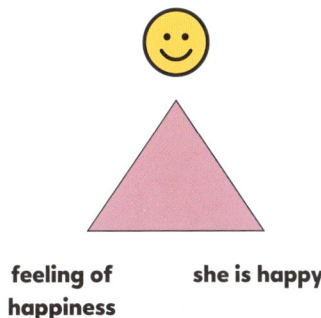

feeling of   she is happy
happiness

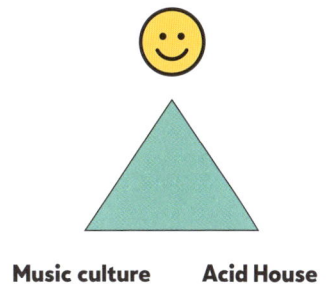

Music culture   Acid House

The nine constituents are not complete signs on their own; only the combination with one sign type from each of the other sign references results in a complete sign. According to Peirce, the object reference is the most important reference for the classification of signs into sign classes. For this reason, it is described in more detail below.

The object reference is divided into three sign types: Icon (2.1), Index (2.2) and Symbol (2.3).[11] An icon (2.1) refers to its object on the basis of qualities that it has in common with this object, or on the basis of an analogy (cf. Peirce 2000c: 375). By resembling its object, the medium refers to the denoted object on the basis of its qualities. In turn, the medium itself forms a kind of existence, see page 115.

Like its object, an index (2.2) has an individual existence. Peirce distinguishes between symptoms and subindices (also called hyposemes) (Peirce 1983: 65/157 f.). The former refer to an object in that they are really influenced by this object. There is a causal connection to the object, such as smoke, which is a sign of fire, or a footprint, which indicates a person. A subindex, on the other hand, only functions in the presence of the indexed object, such as a finger pointing to an object or a signpost (cf. Eco 1977: 61; Peirce 1983: 65). A subindex becomes a sign through its spatial location.

A symbol (2.3) is a sign that establishes a connection to a certain object on the basis of a law or an agreement (cf. Peirce 1983: 125). A symbol is used when the users are certain that it will be understood in a certain way (cf. ibid.: 66). It is a sign that is linked to the meaning by convention. A symbol has no direct connection with the object it designates; it has been chosen arbitrarily and interpreted as connected with the object ›by force of law‹ (cf. Nagl 1992: 44). According to Walther, it does not refer to a specific, individual, local or temporal thing or event, but to a type of object, a category or a ›general object‹ to which the principles of arbitrariness

and conventionality apply (cf. Walther 1974: 65).
The Textmoji case study was designed to investigate the sign process with emojis.[12] The case study is a qualitative study in which users were asked to explain the background of their message and the emojis used. The message displayed on the smartphone is the sender's message and the text in the thought bubble is the translation that was created as part of the case study. It is a kind of meta-level to explain what emojis are intended to convey.

The context of the dialog in the illustrated message (Fig. 390) is as follows: The sender and the recipient agree to meet. The recipient is unable to attend the meeting and suggests an alternative date in the following week. The sender then replies with the message shown.

The message contains a text-based and a graphic emoji. The text-based emoji refers to the meeting that did not take place and the graphic emoji refers to the upcoming meeting. Both emojis depict a facial expression that acts as a kind of personal commentary on the preceding statement.

The sender explains the use of the almost outdated text-based emoji by the fact that it appears less negative to the sender than its graphic counterpart due to its form, especially in combination with the graphic emoji, which the sender uses as reinforcement. According to him, the latter reinforces the ›(pre)joy about the upcoming meeting‹. According to the descriptive framework, they can be categorized in the group ☺, as they convey the sender's feelings.

What does it look like in Peirce's sense? Since the character constellation :(represents a facial expression, the text-based emoji is originally iconically motivated in its object reference. Although it consists of the arbitrary characters colon and bracket, it is recognized iconically as a facial expression, i.e. the character combination ›resembles‹ the facial expression. The convention stipulates that character constellations can represent facial ex-

11 For a detailed explanation of the individual sign types and the generation of Peirce's ten sign classes, see Enzmann 2023a: 106-171. In the study, a possible derivation of subclasses is considered, which in turn can be divided into the existing sign classes as subclasses.

12 The original messages and the corresponding metabens were written in German by the respective authors and translated by the author for the book. For further messages and their classification into sign classes, see Enzmann 2023: 144-163.

pressions rotated by 90°. A person who is not familiar with this rule is unlikely to understand the sign, which gives the sign a symbolic aspect. However, by knowing about the 90° rotated constellations, it is possible to decode such signs – even if they are unknown to the recipients – making it possible to decode vertical text-based emojis purely by their iconic reference. If the rule is known, the object reference takes place iconically by recognizing a smiling facial expression. With graphic emoji, the iconic aspect is more obvious than with text-based emoji. In contrast to text-based emojis, no rules are required to decode the facial expression. That means the object reference in emojis is iconic, in that a negative and a positive facial expression are recognized. The emojis resemble their objects (facial expressions) in some ways. Once the facial expression is recognized, it is in turn associated with the intended emotional state of the sender. In the case of :(, this is ›disappointment that the meeting did not happen‹. Facial expressions are in some way connected with the emotional life, namely with emotions or states of mind. This is because an emotion can be the cause of a corresponding facial expression in a FTF situation. In such a case, a facial expression can arise through causality and can therefore be read as a kind of symptom: The medium (facial expression) is connected to its object (emotion), it is influenced by it. Since facial expressions are expressions for emotions, a facial expression in an FTF situation can function as an indication of a certain emotion for an interpreter.

An emoji is always deliberately selected and used. If an emoji is used to convey a certain emotional state, the sign functions as an indication of the intended emotional state of the user. While the facial expression represents the real, original or genuine index, the emoji is a degenerated index of an emotional state with an enclosed icon. As Schönrich discovered during an exchange, it is a kind of offset sign relationship: emojis are similar to a face, the face in turn is an indexical sign for, in this case, disappointment. It does not matter whether the sender really feels the state, because an emoji cannot be causal. Emojis are always used deliberately.

To summarize: If an emoji stands for a state of mind of the sender, it is an index, because it stands for an actual existing event, in this case for the intended emotional state of the sender. However, if an emoji stands for (any) smiling facial expression, it is an icon. Since emojis are always used consciously and are not causally related to their objects, both emojis in Fig. 390 can be classified in the second sub-category of indices, the sub-indices, which include an object-pointing finger or a signpost.

Fig. 390 **example from the Textmoji case study**

The context of the next message (Fig. 391) is as follows: Two female students are chatting about a term paper. The recipient writes a long message with several questions to the sender. The sender is still busy with another activity and only wants to deal with the questions once this has been completed and writes the message shown.

The sender paraphrases the three emojis as »paint my nails«. They thus take on a reference function and can be categorized in the group ⊗. The question about the iterated use of the graphic emojis was justified by the fact that the sender wanted to signal that it could take a little longer. The iteration of the signs therefore does not serve as reinforcement, but represents a longer period of time. The sender thus makes use of the language of comics, in which, according to McCloud, time in comics is conveyed through space (cf. McCloud 2001: 108 f.). According to him, our eyes are trained by photography and naturalistic art to see a single moment in each self-contained image (cf. McCloud 2001: 104). By repeating the same action, a longer window of time is depicted.

By generally referring to the action of ›painting nails‹, the emojis are iconic.[13]

The background to the next message (Fig. 392) is as follows: The sender is in the same area as the receiver on day X. The sender would like to meet the receiver. The two agree that the receiver will contact the sender as soon as the receiver can foresee when a meeting is possible so that the place and time can be determined. The recipient does not get in touch within the agreed timeframe. This prompts the sender to write the message shown (Fig. 392). The sender chooses the ›Crying-Face‹ emoji to signal his disappointment and at the same time – as can be seen from the meta-level – to make the recipient feel guilty. In that the emoji stands for the sender's perceived disappointment, it is comparable to the emojis in Fig. 390, but differs in that, according to the sender, it appeals to the receiver's sense of guilt. The ›Crying-Face‹ emoji therefore stands for disappointment and at the same time signals that

the sender does not agree with the (non-)action of the recipient. In the object reference, the sign contains an indexical reference by indicating the sender's state of mind, like the emojis in Fig. 390.[14] It can also be categorized in the group ⊚.

The context of Fig. 393 is as follows: Sender and receiver are planning to meet up later in the week. They discover during their exchange that their appointments overlap inconveniently. Because of this, the receiver reschedules and informs the sender that the meeting can take place next Thursday. In response, the the sender writes the message shown to the receiver. The message contains the emoji ›Folded Hands‹. If the sign is interpreted in the way the name suggests, it would be an icon because it is an image of the gesture ›folded hands‹. An icon refers to its object based on characteristics it has in common with the object. It should be noted that the emoji is used differently across cultures. The pictured gesture means ›please‹ or ›thank you‹ in Japanese contexts. In addition, the gesture is used in Thailand as a traditional greeting – also called ›wai‹. The same sign, however, is also commonly used for praying hands or for a ›high-five‹.

The sender used the emoji indeed as a ›high-five‹ here, as is clear from the the meta-level. A high five primarily signals a success. If the sign is interpreted accordingly, it refers to its object ›success‹ merely symbolically because ›success‹ shares no features with folded hands. The sign must instead be learned to understand it accordingly. In the case of Fig. 393, it represents the successful scheduling of the joint appointment.

An emoji can be classified differently depending on how it appears and its intended purpose. It is clear that the semioticity of emojis can change when they are used, in contrast to when they are viewed on their own. The analysis reveals that the actual semioticity of emojis only become apparent in the context of the message, i.e. emojis must be analyzed in their actual use.

13   The emoji is often associated with a sexual context. In this case, the emoji is used symbolically.

14   For an analysis of the division into subclasses of the two messages, taking into account the different intentions, see Enzmann 2023a: 166–171.

Fig. 391 **example from the Textmoji case study**

Fig. 392 **example from the Textmoji case study**

Fig. 393 **example from the Textmoji case study**

It can be stated that an emoji can be iconic, index-ical or symbolic, depending on how it is used. But what enables us to recognize a facial expression in the most rudimentary forms?

According to Blanke, the concept of similarity is often used; visual representations are essentially based on similarity to the represented object (cf. Blanke 2003: 9; Packard et al. 2019: 21). How-ever, this assertion is treated very critically in image theory research (Scholz 2009: 21; Blanke 2003: 9–25). The main argument against it is that a re-presentation that bears little or no resemblance to what is depicted can still be an image. For example, a speech bubble bears no resemblance to any ob-ject. Nevertheless, we would call the speech bubble an image – and if we think about what it is sup-posed to represent, an image of sound created by speaking. It is a visual element that is often used in comics and functions as a frame to isolate mes-sages, to assign them to a speaking person and to indicate a dialog. It is impossible to identify a simi-larity between speech bubble and sound.

The comic contains many such ways of represen-ting the invisible in the form of images, such as stars and circles for dizziness, clouds for speed or light-ning for pain (cf. McCloud 2001: 137).

Emojis also contain such elements, such as the cloud for speed (Fig. 394). The same object – the cloud – can be represented in the form of a thought bubble (Fig. 395) and, in addition to speed, can also stand for thoughts, daydreaming or thinking in general. Possibilities for representing movement can be found in the form of parallel lines (Fig. 398, Fig. 399). Emotional states can be conveyed, for example, by means of an emoji with two hearts as eyes (Fig. 397), which can stand for being in love, or by a jag-ged speech bubble (Fig. 396), which can be used for an angry statement.

»Now, if pictures can, through their rendering, re-present invisible concerns such as emotions and the other senses then the distinction between pic-tures and other types of icons like language which specialize in the invisible may seem a bit blurry.«

(McCloud 2006: 127)

The theory of similarity is also untenable from a se-miotic point of view, because it would mean that a medium is only an image if it refers iconically to its object. However, the previous explanations show that a pictorial sign can refer symbolically to an ob-ject in the same way as a written sign.

In comparison with an iconic use, semioticity in-creases when a sign is used symbolically.

It remains unclear how we are able to recognize a face in the most rudimentary forms such as a bracket and a colon. Research based purely on the meaning of the signs seems to reach its limits at this point. Because an emoji can mean exactly the same thing as a word – yet we still recognize a fa-cial expression in an emoji that stands for joy, such as the smiling face in Fig. 390, while the correspon-ding written counterpart seems to refer directly to the emotion ›joy‹. With the emoji, a kind of detour via an icon is recognizable. This ›detour‹ – or the included icon – includes further information that in-fluences the impact of the signs.

The following considerations are based on Wilde's (2020) image-theoretical studies on emojis. Based on cognitive semiotics, Wilde defines perception as the process in which a sensory stimulus is associ-ated with a repertoire of known types and classi-fied as an element of this repertoire (cf. Wilde 2018: 95 f.). Iconic types can be associated with a ›cogni-tive type‹ – called ›encyclopaedic type‹ by Blanke (cf. Blanke 2003: 36). This makes it possible to pro-duce an image object that corresponds to the type according to certain criteria (cf. ibid.: 47-70). Accor-ding to Blanke and Wilde, a process of recognizing relevant cognitive types takes place before cultural codings or connotations (cf. Wilde 2020: 17/186 f.).

In order to be able to interpret something, some-thing must first be recognized in a medium. In order to recognize a facial expression, we make use of cognitive types. According to Wilde, these are not directly linked to the meaning of the signs, but are inherent in the form of the sign – in the medium. Ac-cording to Wilde, once the face is recognized, a re-levant cognitive type is available that enables us to decode signs of the same kind (cf. Wilde 2020: 182).

Frutiger made similar observations in typography, recognizing a kind of skeletal form in letters:

»It can be assumed that readers remember the outlines of syllables and words in a kind of skeletal form and that the details determining the type style are taken in as the ›resonance‹, which does not disturb the reading process so long as the typeface as a whole has been designed in accordance with the basic rules.« (Frutiger 1989: 200 f.)

According to Frutiger, the character is modeled in the resonance zone and the artistic is expressed (cf. ibid.). Using the letter ›a‹, he shows what a common skeleton can look like (Fig. 400). The same principle can also be applied to the graphic emojis (Fig. 401). In order to better understand the principle of the image recognition according to cognitive semiotics, McCloud's abstraction model, applied to emojis (Fig. 402), is added to the following explanations according to Wilde and Blanke.

Fig. 394

Fig. 395

Fig. 396

Fig. 397

Fig. 398

Fig. 399

Fig. 400

Fig. 401

Fig. 394 ›**dashing away**‹
Fig. 395 ›**thought balloon**‹
Fig. 396 ›**right anger bubble**‹
Fig. 397 ›**smiling face with heart-eyes**‹
Fig. 398 ›**beating heart**‹
Fig. 399 ›**waving hand**‹

Fig. 400 **a common skeleton**
(according to Frutiger 2004: 200)**.**

Fig. 401 **skeleton of the emoji ›grinning face‹** (according to ibid., edited by D. E., f. l. t. r.: Apple iOS 13.3, Facebook 4.0, WhatsApp 2.19.352, Samsung One UI 2.5)

Iconic Categorization Threshold

Blanke and Wilde explain the process of image recognition with the ›iconic categorization threshold‹ (Blanke 2003: 91-106; Wilde 2018: 94-112). The decisive factor here is the recognition of relevant cognitive types, which we base our recognition of images on.

How are abstraction and identification connected?

According to Wilde, the main difference between looking at a word and a pictorial sign is that something is always recognized in a pictorial sign (cf. Wilde 2019). Although what is recognized in the picture may not be the meaning of the sign, the recognition of the cognitive type gives the impression of guessing the meaning of the pictorial sign. With an unknown word, it is difficult, often even impossible, to guess its meaning. Consequently, according to Wilde, image recognition often involves ›pre-attentive intelligibility‹ (cf. Wilde 2018: 94). A large part of the recognition takes place without

one	a few	thousands/millions

Fig. 402 **abstraction model according to McCloud** (2001: 39, 57; edited by D. E. with emojis from Apple iOS 16.3.1; cf. Enzmann 2023a: 184)

THE RELEVANCE CRITERIA

1. The number of iconically relevant properties:
The more details a representation contains, the more likely it is that the categorization threshold will be exceeded (cf. Wilde 2018: 101). The photo contains a large number of iconically relevant properties, and the concept of similarity can be used here: The more similar a representation is to what is depicted, the more likely it is to be recognized as such.

2. The degree of iconic relevance of these properties:
For example, eyes and mouth are particularly relevant for the representation of the iconic type ›face‹, whereas nose and ears are less so (cf. Blanke 2003: 93). According to Blanke, there is a kind of qualitative weighting of characteristics. A characteristic is all the more concise – iconically highly relevant – the more it can be distinguished from other types in the repertoire (cf. ibid.). This can be seen in the previously explained model (Fig. 402):

While the AR-Emoji contains many iconically irrelevant properties for the iconic type ›face‹, the horizontal text-based emoji ^_^ only has the most rudimentary ones – eyes and a mouth. With this relevance criterion, it becomes more problematic to work with the concept of similarity. This is because what the iconically relevant characteristics are for a certain type, or in other words, what is considered typical for a certain type, can vary depending on the culture (cf. Wilde 2018: 101). For example, in Japanese culture, it is common for interlocutors to focus more on the eyes of the other person in order to infer emotions, as facial expressions are traditionally used with restraint in Japan, see page 44. This led to the development of a wide variety of horizontal text-based emojis with different representations for the eyes. This means that the eyes are relevant for the representation of emotions in Japan, while in other countries the mouth may be more relevant for the representation of emotions.

conscious attention. Blanke and Wilde explain a process of image or object recognition with the term ›categorization threshold‹ (cf. Blanke 2003: 91–106; Wilde 2018: 94–112).

They distinguish between the ›iconic categorization threshold‹ and the ›object categorization threshold‹.[15] In order to recognize an image, it must be above the iconic categorization threshold and below the object categorization threshold of the type. The decisive factor in categorizing the iconic threshold is the recognition of relevant cognitive types, which we rely on when recognizing images. At least one characteristic of an image must be identified that corresponds to a feature of the iconic type (cf. ibid.). The iconic categorization thresh-

15   In contrast to the iconic categorization threshold, the object categorization threshold includes, for example, certain materials that an object must have in order to be recognized as such (cf. Wilde 2018: 100).

old can be exceeded to different degrees, as is the case with a photo of a face and an emoji: both exceed the iconic categorization threshold for the type ›face‹ – but to different degrees. To illustrate this, McCloud's model of abstraction, applied to emojis, is used. The photo exceeds the iconic categorization threshold by a large margin, while the text-based emojis only just exceed the threshold.

The word ›face‹ lies below the iconic categorization threshold. According to McCloud, the description of a face, such as ›two eyes, a nose and a mouth‹, would be even further below the categorization threshold (cf. McCloud 2001: 57).

A so-called ›degree of iconicity‹ can be determined. According to Blanke and Wilde, who refer to Morris' degrees of iconicity, this depends on three different relevance criteria (cf. Blanke 2003: 96; Wilde 2018: 101).

| (nearly) all | ICONIC CATEGORIZATION THRESHOLD |

∧_∧   :-)   Face   Two eyes, a nose and a mouth

3. The (cognitive) accessibility of the iconic type:

This criterion makes it clear that similarity alone is not relevant for images. According to Blanke, the recognition of a type in formally weakly iconically relevant signs is not only due to the form, but also to the structure of the repertoire (cf. Blanke 2003: 95). He speaks of different degrees of accessibility, in that familiar objects are recognized more easily than unfamiliar objects by means of weakly iconically relevant signs. Wilde calls this strongly culture-dependent level ›ethnoperceptive‹, as it refers to the relevance of an object within a cultural area (cf. Wilde 2018: 101). It is thus essentially based on our experience (cf. Blanke 2003: 36). The authors identify a further, ›ideoperceptive‹ level of accessibility, namely that in the current situational context (cf. ibid.: 36/94). This enables the identification of a cognitive type even in abstract forms. For example, a point in the sky, without recognizing the shape of the bird can be identified as a bird (cf. ibid.: 37). This happens because of the experience and knowledge that

birds exist, can fly and move differently from airplanes. Here we cannot speak of a similarity between the point and the bird.

If no ›intrinsic iconic categorization‹ is possible by the first two criteria mentioned, the authors speak of an ›extrinsic categorization‹ (cf. Wilde 2018: 107; Blanke 2003: 97).

A kind of ethnoperceptual level can also be observed in vertical text-based emojis: By knowing the rule that in a CMC punctuation marks can represent faces, it is possible to decode characters of such type. The cognitive type 'face' is associated with the iconically relevant properties of eyes and mouth.

Graphic emojis, which represent a facial expression, are reduced to basic shapes (see page 69), sometimes hyperbolic facial expressions. Such forms of expression can also be found in comics. In the following, McCloud uses the terms ›cartoon‹ for the form of pictorial representation – the style – and ›comic‹ for a medium that often uses this form of representation (cf. McCloud 2001: 29). In his formal-aesthetic studies, McCloud found that the more cartoon-like a face is, the more people it represents (cf. ibid.: 39). McCloud believes that when we look at a photograph or a realistic drawing, we see the face of another person, but when we look at a cartoon, we see ourselves (cf. ibid.: 44). He believes that this, along with other factors such as the universality, simplicity and childlike appearance of many cartoon characters, is the cause of the fascination that cartoons exert on children.

»The cartoon is a vacuum into which our identity and awareness are pulled... an empty shell that we inhabit which enables us to travel in another realm. We don't just observe the cartoon, we become it!«

(McCloud 2006: 36)

Our brain forces us to recognize a face in two dots and a line. This phenomenon, also known as ›pareidolia‹, enables us to recognize familiar objects like a face when we look at them (cf. Li 2016: 34). The brain tries to complete fragments and relate them to familiar shapes. Recognition depends on the relevance criteria, see page 110 f. When looking at objects, people search for familiar shapes, so that the recognition of a human expression is used specifically in product design, for example. A cute face can awaken the protective instinct, so that anthropomorphic objects appear familiar to us.

The hypothesis of the ›Uncanny Valley‹ (Fig. 403) according to Masahiro Mori states that the degree of anthropomorphization plays a decisive role here (cf. Plamper 2012: 37). Text-based emojis are not very close to human likeness, so they can be classified between industrial robotics and stuffed animals. Graphic emojis, on the other hand, already contain more human-like attributes, making them

comparable to a stuffed animal, while animated AR-Emojis should be higher on the vertical scale. In contrast, the AR-Emojis presented by Samsung as part of the Galaxy S9, see page 60, appear to be somewhat closer to – or even in – the Uncanny Valley. According to the Uncanny Valley graphic, familiarity decreases as soon as the stylized shape is too human-like (Fig. 403). This creates a kind of acceptance gap, known as the Uncanny Valley. However, certain human-like attributes are necessary to create familiarity. The question of the right degree of anthropomorphism is crucial for the familiarity of the form. In the case of emojis, we can also speak of the degree of stylization – or cartoon aesthetics.

According to Packard et al., cartoons evoke a special communicative disposition in people. By this he means a mirror-image intersubjective or social relationship that people in many contemporary cultures are prepared to adopt towards other people, their faces and bodies (cf. Packard et al. 2019: 22). This means that the interpreter communicates with the stylized representation as a kind of ›imaginary counterpart‹ (ibid., see also pages 114–115).

As can be seen from the model of abstraction (Fig. 402), cartoonization achieves optimal identification with the imagined counterpart. According to the Uncanny Valley (Fig. 403), a certain human likeness or a certain richness of detail, provided the depictions are not too human-like, enables familiarity and immersion in a world full of sensual stimuli (cf. McCloud 2001: 50–53). A formal richness of detail can trigger a positive feeling and set graphic emojis apart from the written word as surface appearances. On the one hand, abstraction is required to allow optimal identification and, on the other, details seem to enable us to immerse ourselves in a world of sensual stimuli and create familiarity, which is responsible for the ›positive mood‹ (see page 69).

There are various degrees of abstraction in the emoji character set. The perspective of representation also varies. Some of the graphic emojis are so detailed that it is difficult or even impossible to

Uncanny Valley

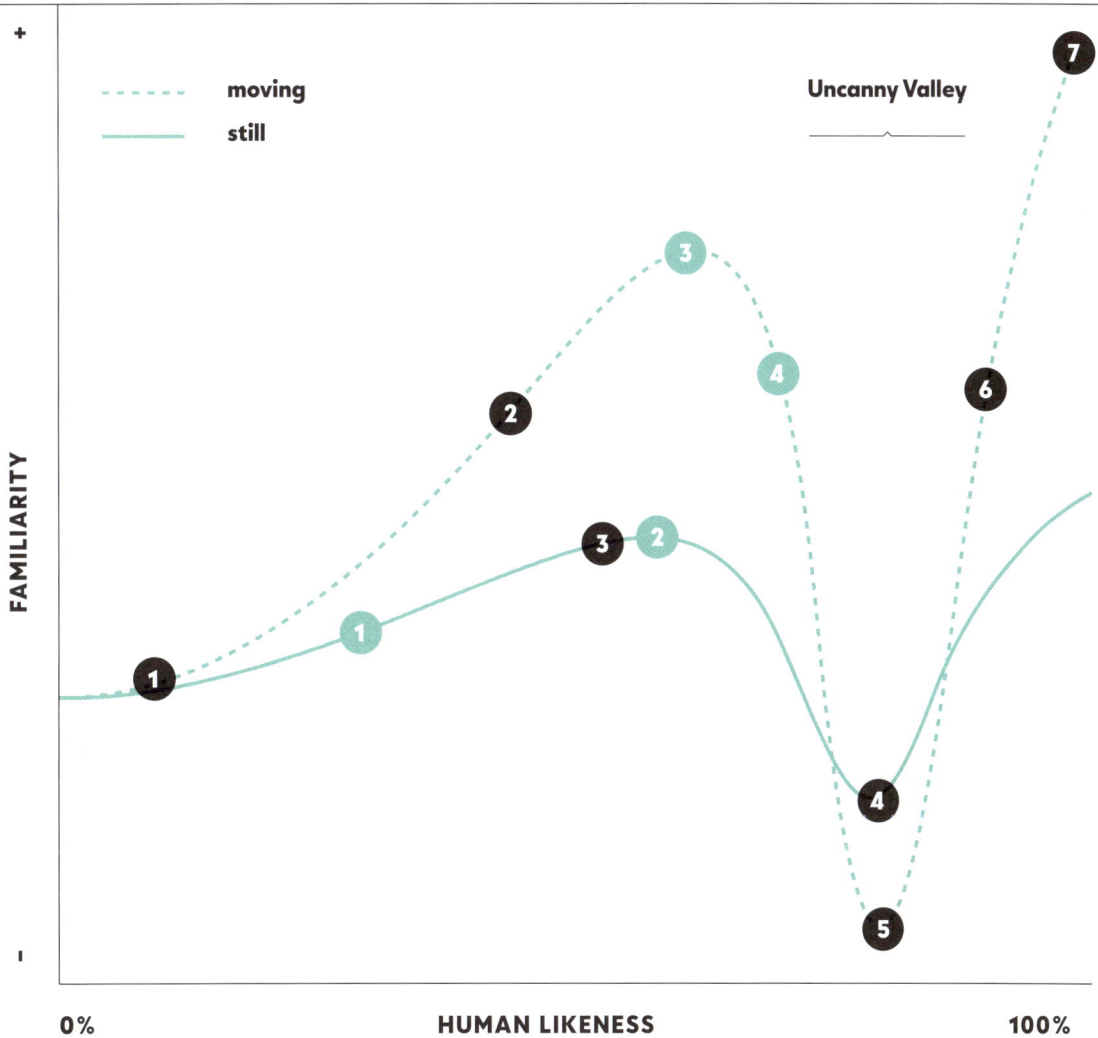

moving (dashed)
still (solid)

Uncanny Valley

FAMILIARITY

0%   HUMAN LIKENESS   100%

1	industrial robot	4	corpse	1	text-based face expression emoji
2	humanoid robot	5	zombie	2	graphic face expression emoji
3	stuffed animal	6	bunraku puppet	3	animated AR-Emoji
		7	healthy person	4	AR-Emoji (Samsung Galaxy S6)

Fig. 403 **Uncanny Valley according to Masahiro Mori** (Plamper 2012: 37, edited by D. E.)

fully recognize the characters in the small display space, as is the case with some animals, mythical creatures, food or activities (Fig. 416–Fig. 421).

According to McCloud, our idea of the ›I‹ belongs to the world of thought, since it is an idea (cf. McCloud 2001: 74). He believes that the cartoon belongs to the world of thought because it emphasizes the idea of form over the material world.

Thus, according to McCloud, cartoonists can depict the outside of the world through realism and its inside through the cartoon (cf. ibid.: 48 f.). The combination of realistic backgrounds and highly stylized figures enables readers to immerse themselves in a world full of sensual stimuli behind the mask of a character (ibid.: 51). According to McCloud, Japanese illustrators use the objectifying power of naturalistic drawings to consciously separate certain figures from the readers, while the identification figures are cartoon-like (cf. ibid.: 52).

Something similar can also be observed with graphic emojis. Graphic emojis, which are used like a kind of mask to project an emotional or mood state (e.g. Fig. 404–Fig. 409), require a high level of identification and are constructed with reduced geometric shapes and depicted with a clear perspective. Others, on the other hand – such as animals, food or activities (Fig. 416–Fig. 421), which require less or no identification – are much more detailed.

When looking at the degree of abstraction of emojis, it can be seen that the character set uses different degrees. Cartoonization is needed for optimal identification, while the objectifying power of naturalistic drawings is used to create sensual stimuli. In pictorial signs, for example, the frontal representation of the face and generally the visualization of eyes, nose and mouth is unusual, see page 30. Emoji designers, however, seem to use precisely these forms of representation for those characters with which users can and should identify. In addition to the frontal view, the side view is also available for some animals (Fig. 410–Fig. 415).

According to Müller, frontal eye contact iconographically stands for closeness and identification, while the profile view adopts a dismissive, distancing perspective (cf. Müller 2003: 84). The frontal representation seems to intensify the imaginary counterpart according to Packard et al. Apple uses the frontal display for the AR-Emojis, which can be used by users to directly imitate facial expressions. Identification is therefore highly desirable.

APPLE IOS 17.4 (Emojipedia g)		SAMSUNG ONE UI 2.5 (Emojipedia h)		FACEBOOK 4.0 (Emojipedia i)	
Fig. 404	Fig. 405	Fig. 406	Fig. 407	Fig. 408	Fig. 409
Fig. 410	Fig. 411	Fig. 412	Fig. 413	Fig. 414	Fig. 415
Fig. 416	Fig. 417	Fig. 418	Fig. 419	Fig. 420	Fig. 421

It can be established that colors and shapes can be responsible for conveying a feeling or a mood (see page 68). In addition, the reduction in the sense of cartoonization and the frontal view allow optimal identification with the character. In contrast, richness of detail and realism create an immersion in a world full of sensual stimuli. The right degree of anthropomorphization plays an important role here, as it can create familiarity. The formal investigation revealed that the graphic emojis use the potential of abstraction and realistic representations in different ways. From a design perspective, this gives them a certain formal imbalance with regard to the entire character set.

The representation of the characters varies depending on the operating system and device brand. Discussions about their design are ongoing and have intensified with the increasing level of detail of the characters (see page 59). To what extent do emojis create their own identity through their aesthetic properties?

According to the sender of Fig. 390, the shape of the text-based emoji :(weakens the intensity of the sign, while the graphic emoji has a more intense impact. The formal aesthetic attributes of the emojis are therefore essential selection criteria for the use of an emoji. How can such a selection be understood through the autonomy thesis?

The autonomy thesis – also known as the autoreflexivity or self-reflexivity thesis – argues that the aesthetic sign only has a secondary referential function and that attention is particularly focused on the medium (cf. ibid.: 426 f.). According to Nöth, this does not assert the referentiality of the aesthetic sign, but emphasizes that aestheticity does not lie in the referential function of the sign. In that the medium itself conveys itself in its sensual representation, the aesthetic sign exhibits a strong autonomy from the referential function or object of the sign (cf. Nöth 2000: 426 f.). The autonomy thesis thus confirms what Packard et al. have already established with cartoons, namely that an emoji – in contrast to a word – has a direct existential relationship in the sense of a communicating imaginary counterpart to the acting person. Such an imaginary counterpart can be described as coexistence, which in turn can be the basis for further discourse. For example, in his lecture on the imagery of emojis at the ›Emojisierung‹ symposium, Wilde explained the Twitter discussion as to whether the emojis for the three monkeys (Fig. 422–Fig. 424) are one or three emojis (Wilde 2019; 2020: 190 ff.).

APPLE IOS 17.4 (Emojipedia g)

Fig. 422

Fig. 423

Fig. 424

Fig. 404 **grinning face with smiling eyes**
Fig. 405 **face with spiral eyes**
Fig. 406 **star-struck**
Fig. 407 **face exhaling**
Fig. 408 **face-holding-back-tears**
Fig. 409 **nauseated-face**
Fig. 410 **tiger face**

Fig. 411 **tiger**
Fig. 412 **cat face**
Fig. 413 **cat**
Fig. 414 **dog face**
Fig. 415 **dog**
Fig. 416 **dragon**
Fig. 417 **people wrestling**

Fig. 418 **pot of food**
Fig. 419 **horse racing**
Fig. 420 **t-rex**
Fig. 421 **woman fairy**
Fig. 422 **see no evil monkey**
Fig. 423 **hear no evil monkey**
Fig. 424 **speak no evil monkey**

By assuming that a monkey exists – at least one, perhaps even three – Wilde speaks of the naturalization or resemantization of the third sign space. By this he means the idea of the existence of a space in which the emojis live and postulates that this emoji is not only seen as a sign for monkeys, which can be used in very different ways. In contrast, the yellow graphic emojis, which represent a face, are not spoken of as disembodied heads or as spheres, but as signs for emotions (cf. ibid.).

The graphic emojis form an optimal identification surface through cartoonization and can therefore represent a high number of individuals, see page 110. According to McCloud's cartoon concept, they are more cartoonish than the three monkeys and contain fewer details. Can it be assumed that a higher degree of cartoonization creates an optimal identification surface for the viewer, but that this makes the emoji less coexistent?

Based on the message in Fig. 390 , it was possible to determine that the text-based and graphic emoji have different degrees of iconicity, see page 110. They exceed the iconic categorization threshold for the cognitive type ›face‹ to varying degrees. A text-based and a graphic emoji, as well as an AR-Emoji, are able to refer to the same object. By possessing formal characteristics of the kawaii aesthetic (see page 70), AR-Emojis refer to cultural values, which in turn communicate in the sign process. Can this be attributed to coexistence?

In order to investigate this, it is helpful to consider the infantilization and regression critique. A frequently emerging discourse regarding emoji communication that could be related to aesthetics is the infantilization and regression critique. The use of emojis is described as infantile, regressive or unprofessional (Seargeant 2019: 11/14). To what extent can this be viewed from a semiotic and design perspective?

The attribution of infantility or regression may be due to the kawaii aesthetic, in which the childlike is associated with various characteristics already explained. By being seen as belonging to a style such as the kawaii aesthetic or the cartoon, emojis are given the identity represented by the style that accompanies the communication. The use of the emojis in Fig. 390 is a suitable example to demonstrate this. The sender is of the opinion that the text-based emoji has a less intense impact than the graphic emoji. By using the standard linguistic sign system, text-based emoji are associated with writing, while graphic emojis are associated with images. Why emojis are seen as regressive could be due to the mixing of visual and written communication. This is reminiscent of the early days of learning to read. Something similar can also be observed with comics. For example, comics were and still are sometimes regarded as reading for children or young people and the combination of words and images is seen as inferior or superficial (cf. McCloud 2001: 149).

A possible aversion to image communication could also stem from the fact that images were the basis for the development of written languages. Johannes Bergerhausen explained the origins of writing in his lecture at the ›Emojisierung‹ symposium (Bergerhausen 2019). According to him, the Sumerians developed cuneiform writing around 3300 BC – the oldest writing system known to date (see Bergerhausen 2014: 7/13). The pictorially constituted starting point is recognizable in some signs (Fig. 429, Fig. 430). The development from image to written language can be seen as a development and progress of human beings. Vilém Flusser suggests that if literate culture is viewed in its entirety as a single line extending over three thousand years, it can be recognized as a loop that begins with images and ultimately returns to them (cf. Flusser 2002: 141).

Fig. 425	Fig. 426	Fig. 427	Fig. 428

According to Bergerhausen, the Latin letter ›A‹ (Fig. 428) (via the Greek alpha) derives from the Phoenician letter ›Aleph‹ (Fig. 425), which means ›cattle‹ in Phoenician' (cf.. Bergerhausen/Helmig 2020: 25). If the sign ›Aleph‹ (Fig. 425) is rotated by 180 degrees, the bull's head (Fig. 426) is recognizable.

Should such a return be seen as a regression? According to Hartmann and Bauer, the more abstract the code that a culture uses, the more highly valued it is (cf. Hartmann/Bauer 2006: 15). From this perspective, the thesis of infantilization or regression is obvious. However, the discourse must examine how images are used. Do they merely fulfill an image function or do they go beyond this?

The examples from the ›Textmoji‹ case study show that emojis can be much more than simple images (cf. Enzmann 2023a: 224). Society has not only developed a reading competence, but also a ›visual literacy‹ that allows images to be used and understood beyond their illustrative function. According to Frutiger, information through pictorial signs has led to a change in reading in recent decades (cf. Frutiger 2004: 348). As Giesecke noted, standard language has become part of our nature and its highly artificial character is often no longer noticed. He calls this process the ›renaturalization of language‹ (Giesecke 1991). Despite the internalization of language, we find it easier to look at a picture than to understand a spoken message (cf. Frutiger 2004: 224). This in turn could be due to the degree of iconicity: What is seen is brought into relation with something similar, something familiar; this creates the referential connection of the iconicity thesis.

In summary, it can be stated: The autonomy thesis asserts that the aesthetic exhibits an autonomy that does not lie in the referential function of the sign and thus forms a kind of coexistence. The iconicity thesis, on the other hand, claims that the aesthetic manifests itself in the fact that the image contains similar characteristics to the depicted, which in turn means that the aesthetic has a particularly referential relationship to its object. This seems contradictory, although examples of both theses can be found in emojis. Are these two theses compatible in the case of emojis?

Different degrees of abstraction were identified in the emojis. The more detailed and naturalistic emojis are designed, the more they are able to produce sensual stimuli and the more difficult it is for multiple actors to identify them (Fig. 402). The further a sign crosses the categorization threshold, the more iconic it is and the more coexistent it becomes. It corresponds to McCloud's view that when you look at a photograph you see someone else, but when you look at a cartoon you see yourself. This means, as Morris already stated, that optimal iconicity can lead to the autoreflexivity of the sign, in that the icon has characteristics in common with an object, but through its representation is also a sign of itself (cf. Nöth 2000: 428; 2009: 44). It must be emphasized that a pure autoreflexivity is impossible: an autoreflexivity can only exist as a ›concurrent self-reference‹ (cf. Nöth 2008: 12). Aesthetics is therefore part of the sign process. Accordingly, the aesthetic qualities of a sign can form a coexistence through their iconic nature. However, according to Nöth, coexistence in the sense of a self-referentiality of signs is always only a reference to one aspect or part of this sign (cf. Nöth 2008: 5).

Coexistence is capable of influencing the effect and interpretation of the sign, which is formed through the aesthetic manifestation. I describe this process as dynamic and extremely individual, because aesthetics can have very different impacts on the individual, which in turn depends on individual cultural, social and situational factors.

In conclusion, it can be said that the further an emoji crosses the iconic categorization threshold and thus becomes more autonomous and coexistent, the more its form can become content.

In the following, this observation is examined and compared using specific design projects.

Fig. 429 **development of the cuneiform sign ox** (Bergerhausen 2014: 32)	Fig. 430 **development of the cuneiform sign bird** (ibid.)

Emoji-Fonts

The integration of emojis into the Unicode system provoked numerous controversies (see page 59). In addition to the need to include the characters in a standard to enable their world-wide use, it caused unease to place the pictorial signs on an equal footing with our writing system developed over decades, as they were seen as a destruction of the typeface. But isn't it the task of designers to give visual elements a suitable form and to develop optimal design solutions for such challenges? Which projects are rising to this challenge?

Projects featured in this subchapter:

Diglû Font
Emphase

OpenMoji
HfG Schwäbisch Gmünd

GT Maru
Grilli Type

Variable Emojis
Hannah Witte

When designing emojis as glyphs, the question arises as to a suitable degree of abstraction for the pictorial signs.[16] Emojis that are integrated into a font interact hand in hand with the corresponding letters. As Daniel Utz pointed out, letters have a specific ductus, while the complexity of pictorial signs can vary greatly (see also pages 130–137).

How can pictorial signs be integrated into a font? How are more complex pictorial signs designed so that they function like letters in the smallest of spaces? What design principles underlie a font with pictorial signs? How do pictorial signs work when different weights are used? What criteria are used to select the motifs? What possibilities arise from the integration of pictorial signs as glyphs in fonts? The projects presented in this subchapter have tackled these and similar challenges and achieved different approaches and results.

The Diglû font is the result of research into the complex question of how pictorial signs can be used in science communication. The focus is on conveying knowledge, reducing to the essentials and applying stringent design principles. In some cases, the communication functions of pictorial and written characters merge.

The second project – the OpenMoji character set – pursues the goal of creating a uniform pictorial system from a formal perspective that is freely accessible and can be used by everyone. The result is an impressive collection of uniform pictorial signs that is being continuously expanded.

The third project – GT Maru – is a cultural fusion of different ways of using signs, inspired by a trip to Japan. It illustrates how different cultural approaches to visual communication can serve as inspiration for one's own projects. In the last project of this subchapter, the focus is not necessarily on the result, but on the underlying thought processes. The project addresses the political and cultural dimensions of emoji communication and is an attempt to explore and test new typographic possibilities.

The fourth project – Variable Emojis – is a thought experiment that attempts to use technical possibilities for cultural diversity.

The projects presented serve to shed light on the possibilities of designing emojis as glyphs and to address different approaches and aims.

16   The degree of abstraction of the signs and their influence on the communication process is explained in more detail on pages 102–115.

Diglû Font

EMPHASE Swiss Graphic Design Lab

»*Pictograms serve as compact carriers of knowledge and operate in a field of tension between the reduction of complexity and the preservation of diversity. They are conceived in our design process in a similar way to infographics.*«

Fabienne Kilchör & Sébastien Fasel

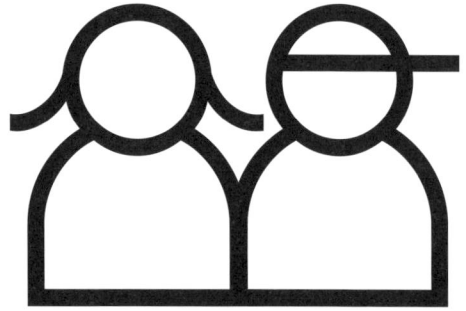

Fig. 431 **Diglû people** [E4C6, E612 in Diglû light]

The standardized pictorial font was originally developed for data analysis and visual representation of archaeological findings and features. The creators recognized the potential of a font with pictorial signs and expanded it to include over 1500 signs for various applications, like architecture, health, environment, science, etc. Today, the project has developed into a comprehensive sign system for the visual communication.

Typeface design
Fabienne Kilchör

Pictorial signs and website design
Sébastien Fasel
Fabienne Kilchör
Alice Laurent
Deborah Steffen

www.diglu.ch

Fig. 432 **Diglû accumulations** surfaces, motifs, patterns

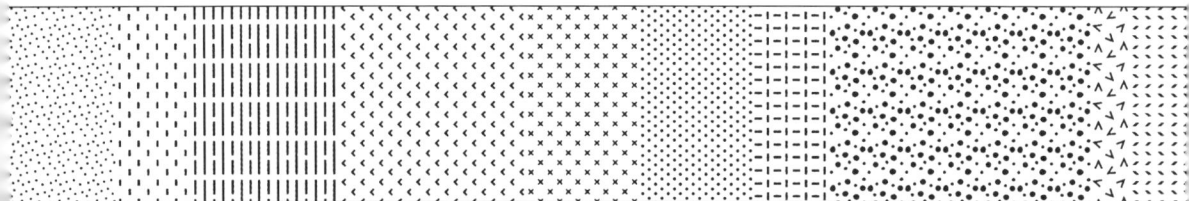

Diglû[17] was created as part of Fabienne Kilchör's practice-oriented research project and was developed in collaboration with the Swiss National Science Foundation (SNSF), the University of Bern and the Bern University of the Arts. The aim of the project is to improve the analysis of archaeological findings and features as well as the transfer of scientific knowledge (cf. Kilchör 2020: 1). Complex issues are to be communicated more simply or large data sets are to be presented in such a way that an overview is possible (cf. ibid.: 12). The interdisciplinary approach combined methods from archaeology, data visualization and information design. One part of the research result is the conception of the Diglû font, which can be used to communicate complex topics more directly and simply. Pictorial signs serve as a visual method of representing archaeological data and are presen-

Fig. 433 **the weave weight represented in different degrees of abstraction**
Drawing: Nicole Gäumann

ted in reduced complexity and minimal size so that they can be used within the text (cf. ibid.: 70). The abstraction process can be seen in the drawing and the pictorial sign of the weave weight (see Fig. 433). During the development of the sign system, a geometric font was created that contains numerous pictorial signs and different patterns. Diagrams, maps and texts are simplified by the integration of pictorial signs, and the more than thirty available patterns (see Fig. 432) can be used, for example, to visualize different ground conditions on plans or in diagrams. The font is based on solid design principles, some of these are explained on the following (Fig. 435–Fig. 450). The font is available in different weights, from hairline to heavy (Fig. 434).

17   In Babylonian, the name of the scripture means to see, to look up, to look at, to make visible (cf. Kilchör 2020: 5).

Fig. 434 **from hairline to heavy** (Kilchör 2020: 101)

In order to design the pictorial and text signs as an inherent system, they were based on a geometric grid with basic elements (Fig. 435 and Fig. 436). Such a systematic structure facilitates the construction of a large character set and gives the signs visual continuity.

»The use of the grid as an ordering system is the expression of a certain mental attitude inasmuch as it shows that the designer conceives his work in terms that are constructive and oriented to the future.«

(Müller-Brockmann 1996: 10).

In his work, Müller-Brockmann shows how the use of grids simplifies design decisions and thus also design processes. In his opinion, a mathematical way of thinking ensures clarity, objectivity, transparency and a functional and aesthetic result (ibid.).

Diglû is an excellent example of how solid design principles can be used to create a new pictorial system. The creators have opted for a sans serif font, as this provides the objectivity and neutrality required in science (cf. Kilchör 2020: 80). The design language of Diglû is based on the ›Swiss International Style‹ and the ›Futura‹, ›Avenir Next‹ and ›Euclid Flex‹ typefaces (ibid.: 80 ff.). The large circular shapes of the fonts are characterized by large punches (Fig. 435), which makes them easier to read in small font sizes (ibid.). The high ascenders and descenders characterize the appearance and are important for legibility (Fig. 437). This is because the pronounced k and p lengths help the eye to find fixation and rest points when reading a continuous text (ibid.). Defining a standard width and a minimum and maximum extension (Fig. 437) is advantageous when used in tables or on maps, for example.

caps height

x-height

baseline

descender

According to Frutiger, information with text, in contrast to visual language, has the disadvantage that a different number of letters is required for the individual statements (cf. Frutiger 1980: 84). This makes it difficult to use uniform widths. From a formal point of view, this is a clear argument for the use of pictorial signs. The design principles of the Diglû are characterized by their field of application in archaeology. For example, the ends of strokes on pointed objects can also be conical (Fig. 438). In some cases, an archaeological find is defined by its function rather than its form (cf. ibid.: 84). Therefore, additional signs such as arrows for directions and movements are introduced (Fig. 443). Lines can indicate fragments (Fig. 449) or a punching (Fig. 450). Additional information on decoration, materiality or size can be marked with different diacritics (Fig. 446, Fig. 448). This means that each basic shape can

be supplemented with specific features. This saves space and reduces the number of signs required. Neurath had already applied this principle to the isotype, for example by adding a cogwheel or a hammer to the worker's picogram, turning it into an industrial worker (ibid.: 87) (see Fig. 43). Connections between individual characters are also possible using conjunctions[18] (Fig. 444).

When developing the design principles, the designers drew up a list of criteria containing over sixty items, such as degree of abstraction or relevance (ibid.: 76). Based on numerous design principles, a fascinating system of signs has been created that offers an incredible variety of communicative applications, see page 127.

18   The principle goes back to the idea of Charles Bliss, who developed pasigraphy (Blissymbols) in the 1940s.

BASIC PRINCIPLES OF THE FONT DESIGN

Fig. 435 **font characteristics**
the font is constructed on the basic shapes of square, circle and triangle (cf. Kilchör 2020: 80)

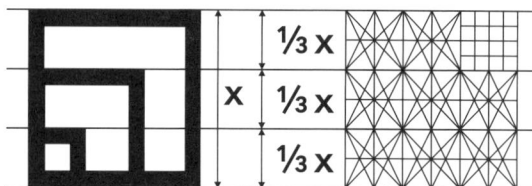

Fig. 436 **the grid on which the pictorial signs of the font are based**
the three-part fine-mesh auxiliary construction offers numerous application options (ibid.: 82)

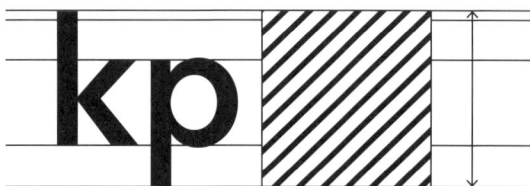

Fig. 437 **vertical extension**
high ascenders and descenders characterize the font (ibid.: 81)

Fig. 438 **stroke end**
inspired by a sans serif linear antiqua (ibid.: 84)

Fig. 439 **horizontal extension**
definition of a standard width and a minimum and maximum extension (ibid.: 81)

Fig. 440 **font styles**
the letter H in ultralight, light, medium, bold, extrabold, black and the pictorial sign in regular

Fig. 441 **stroke thickness**
the character is shaped by uniform line widths (ibid.: 84)

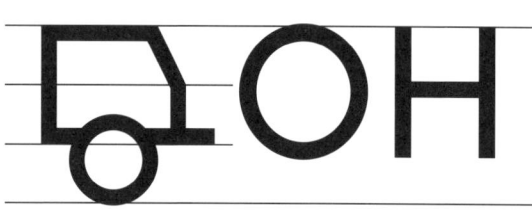

Fig. 442 **type anatomy**
the baseline for the font has been lowered slightly to achieve a visual balance (ibid.)

For more details on the visual characteristics
and design principles, see Kilchör 2020: 79-98.

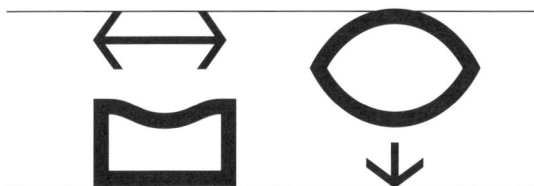

Fig. 443 movement
visualization of the movement using the friction block
and plunger tools (ibid.: 91)

Fig. 444 conjunctors
two pictorial signs can be combined with a line (ibid.: 89)

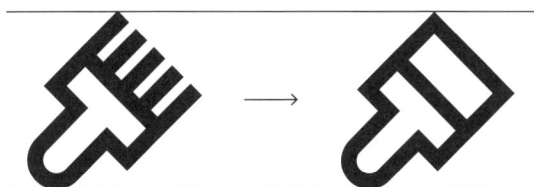

Fig. 445 abstraction level
various degrees of abstraction are available so that the signs
function in the smallest possible space, see page 128 (ibid.: 92)

Fig. 446 diacritics
individual expansion of the found signs by diacritics (ibid.: 88)

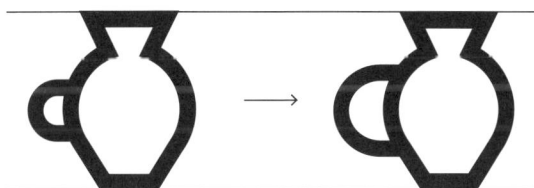

Fig. 447 hyperbole
special characteristic can be emphasized by exaggeration,
see page 128 (ibid.: 93)

Fig. 448 material
different materialities are abbreviated with letters (ibid.: 88)

Fig. 449 fragment
incomplete finds are marked with a dashed line (ibid.: 83)

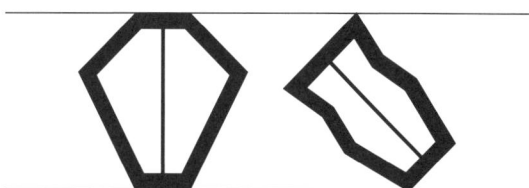

Fig. 450 punching
fine lines represent punchings in vessels or small finds
and a solid line indicates a punching (ibid.: 87)

Fig. 451 **the sign for the wheel model** [uniE1C4] **on the grid** (ibid.: 95)

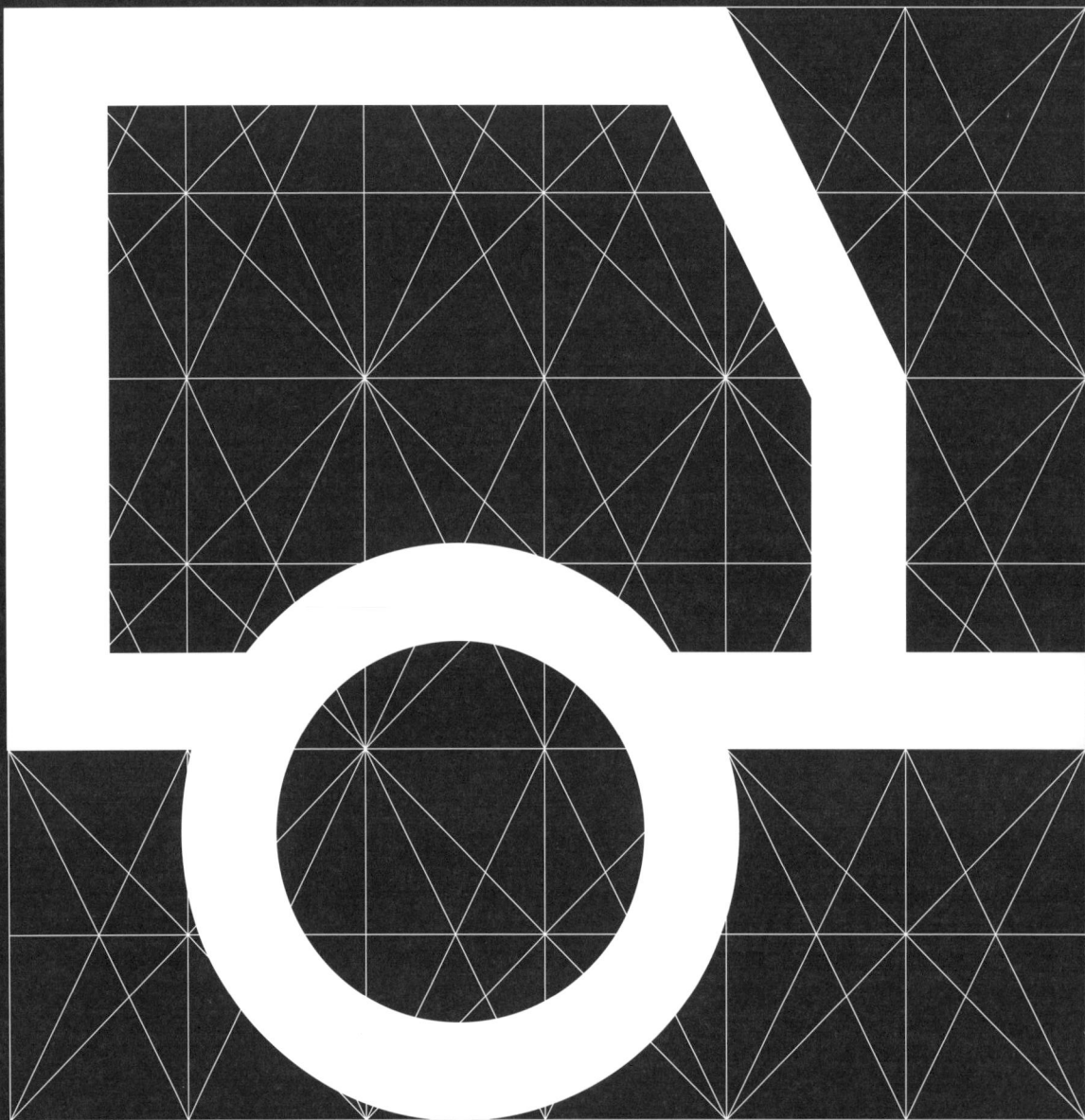

The signs have intentionally not been given names so that they can be used in various ways in different areas of application. However, they can be assigned to certain categories.

Fig. 452	Fig. 453	Fig. 454	Fig. 455	Fig. 456	Fig. 457
Fig. 458	Fig. 459	Fig. 460	Fig. 461	Fig. 462	Fig. 463
Fig. 464	Fig. 465	Fig. 466	Fig. 467	Fig. 468	Fig. 469
Fig. 470	Fig. 471	Fig. 472	Fig. 473	Fig. 474	Fig. 475
Fig. 476	Fig. 477	Fig. 478	Fig. 479	Fig. 480	Fig. 481
Fig. 482	Fig. 483	Fig. 484	Fig. 485	Fig. 486	Fig. 487
Fig. 488	Fig. 489	Fig. 490	Fig. 491	Fig. 492	Fig. 493
Fig. 494	Fig. 495	Fig. 496	Fig. 497	Fig. 498	Fig. 499

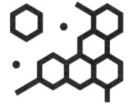

Fig. 500 **hyperbole** (Kilchör 2020: 93)

Fig. 501 **abstraction** (Kilchör 2020: 92)

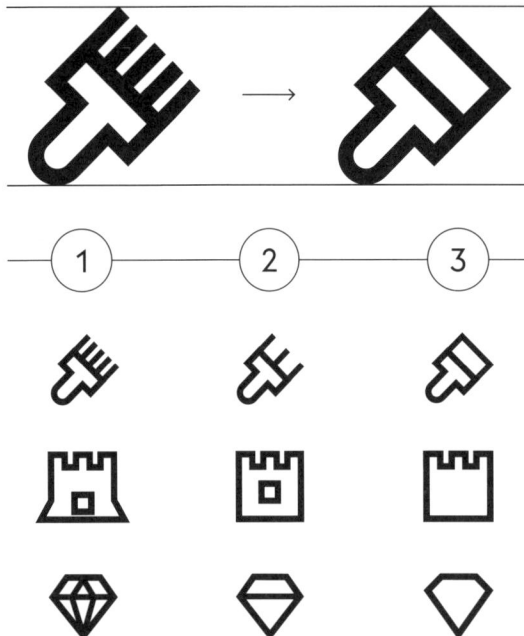

In the sign set, function-specific elements, such as the handle of a drinking vessel, are deliberately emphasized by exaggeration to distinguish them from a large vessel (Fig. 500). This crystallizes characteristic qualities and visually reduces and simplifies secondary information (cf. Kilchör 2020: 93).

However, in order for the signs to function in the smallest of spaces, they must not contain too many details. In keeping them as minimalist as possible, the drawing system is based on a modular construction kit of curves and straight lines derived from the three basic geometric shapes of triangle, square and circle (cf. ibid.: 95). These in turn are based on a three-part fine-meshed grid construction (Fig. 451). Different sizes of representation also require different degrees of abstraction. Elements are omitted or abstracted so that the hallmarks do not run when reduced in size (Fig. 501). In doing so, the signs cross the iconic categorization threshold to varying degrees, see 110. Depending on the degree of abstraction, the pictorial signs include more or less detail. Such an inductive design process of omitting details can be seen, for example, in the sign for resin (Fig. 501). The sign depicts a brush with bristles in the most detailed version, while the second level of abstraction contains fewer bristles and the bristles are combined into a box in the third level of abstraction.

Although the pictorial signs contain pictorial elements, the standardized signs are not universal, and their use in archaeology in particular must be learned. The fact that the brush can stand for resin or the diamond for a shiny surface cannot be recognized purely by the shape of the pictorial sign. We have learned through a fully developed language and social interactions what meaning and function a brush can have. According to Kilchör, pictograms are defined by their symbolic character and not, like a found drawing for example, by their claim to represent reality (cf. ibid.: 92).

In order to seamlessly integrate the pictorial signs into the text, the designers opted out of utilizing one of the most crucial features of emojis – color. The Diglû characters are specifically designed within the Diglû font in different font styles (see Fig. 504–Fig. 506).

Fig. 502 **Diglû regular 71 pt**

thx 🫶

Fig. 503 **Diglû hairline 71 pt**

thx 🫶

Fig. 504 **Diglû bold to hairline 23 pt**

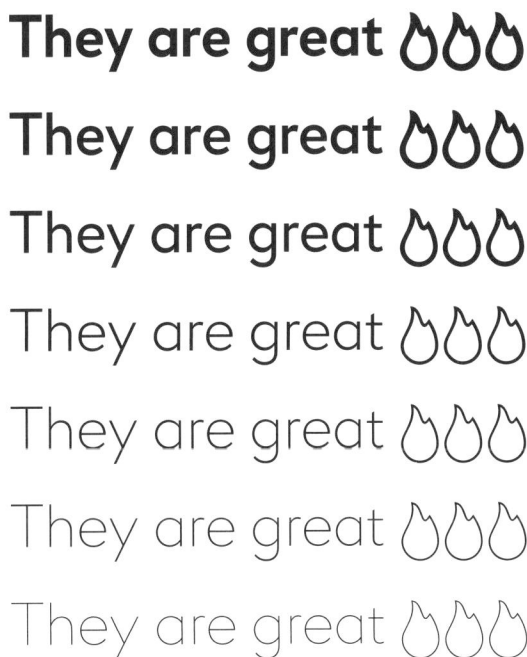

They are great 🔥🔥🔥

They are great 🔥🔥🔥

They are great 🔥🔥🔥

They are great 🔥🔥🔥

They are great 🔥🔥🔥

They are great 🔥🔥🔥

They are great 🔥🔥🔥

Fig. 505 **Diglû bold to hairline 14 pt**

oh and I also fancy a burger or schnippo 🐋 **I kiss you lovingly**

oh and I also fancy a burger or schnippo 🐋 **I kiss you lovingly**

oh and I also fancy a burger or schnippo 🐋 I kiss you lovingly

oh and I also fancy a burger or schnippo 🐋 I kiss you lovingly

oh and I also fancy a burger or schnippo 🐋 I kiss you lovingly

oh and I also fancy a burger or schnippo 🐋 I kiss you lovingly

oh and I also fancy a burger or schnippo 🐋 I kiss you lovingly

Fig. 506 **Diglû bold to light with italic 7 pt**

Well, you'll have to put up with this ugly design 🕯 until tomorrow

Well, you'll have to put up with this ugly design 🕯 until tomorrow

Well, you'll have to put up with this ugly design 🕯 until tomorrow

Well, you'll have to put up with this ugly design 🕯 until tomorrow

Well, you'll have to put up with this ugly design 🕯 until tomorrow

Well, you'll have to put up with this ugly design 🕯 until tomorrow

Well, you'll have to put up with this ugly design 🕯 until tomorrow

Well, you'll have to put up with this ugly design 🕯 until tomorrow

The text examples illustrated on this page to show the font with the pictorial signs in use are taken from the Textmoji case study (Enzmann 2023: 144–163, see also pages 105–107).

The examples (Fig. 502–Fig. 506) demonstrate how the pictorial signs harmonize inside the text and also function in the different font sizes and in the various font weights.

OpenMoji

HFG SCHWÄBISCH GMÜND

Fig. 507 **person raising hand** by Johanna Wellnitz

»For us, emoji are much more than colorful images decorating fun short messages. We think they are rather part of an important and exciting development: the return of pictorial symbols to written communication. For the first time in history, it is possible to communicate with a combination of letters and icons. Now it becomes feasible to say things and convey meanings that were previously impossible.«

Daniel Utz & Benedikt Groß

Daniel Utz and Benedikt Groß at HfG Schwäbisch Gmünd initiated this project. In collaboration with students from the field of interaction and communication design, they developed an extensive emoji set as part of an interdisciplinary course.

The project OpenMoji was created at the beginning of 2018 in response to the fundamental question of why designers leave the design of the emojis that characterize our daily communication to the big companies of this world (cf. HfG Gmünd 2018).

Fig. 508 **custom font**

ABCDEFGHIJKLMNOPQRSTUVWXYZ
1234567890 $£¥€!#?

Openmoji can be understood as a positive rebellion against the increasingly globally prevailing standard aesthetics of emojis. With remarkable endurance, the creators are constantly engaged in the continuous expansion of the character set with the aim of making the emojis accessible for everyone. A style guide ensures a consistent design of the character set and makes sure that the emojis fit perfectly together. It also allows everyone to make a contribution to the design of emojis. So far, over 4000 freely usable emojis and a custom Font (see Fig. 508) to contain typographic elements have been created.

OpenMoji is proving to be a promising project for implementing a coherent emoji set. The open source project creates a unique platform that is essential for promoting the creative diversity of emojis.

Fig. 509 **rabbit face** by Sofie Ascherl with **hole** by Laura Humpfer

THE GRID

The grid contains four shapes for size orientation and forms the base for the placement of emojis (cf. OpenMoji 2024a).

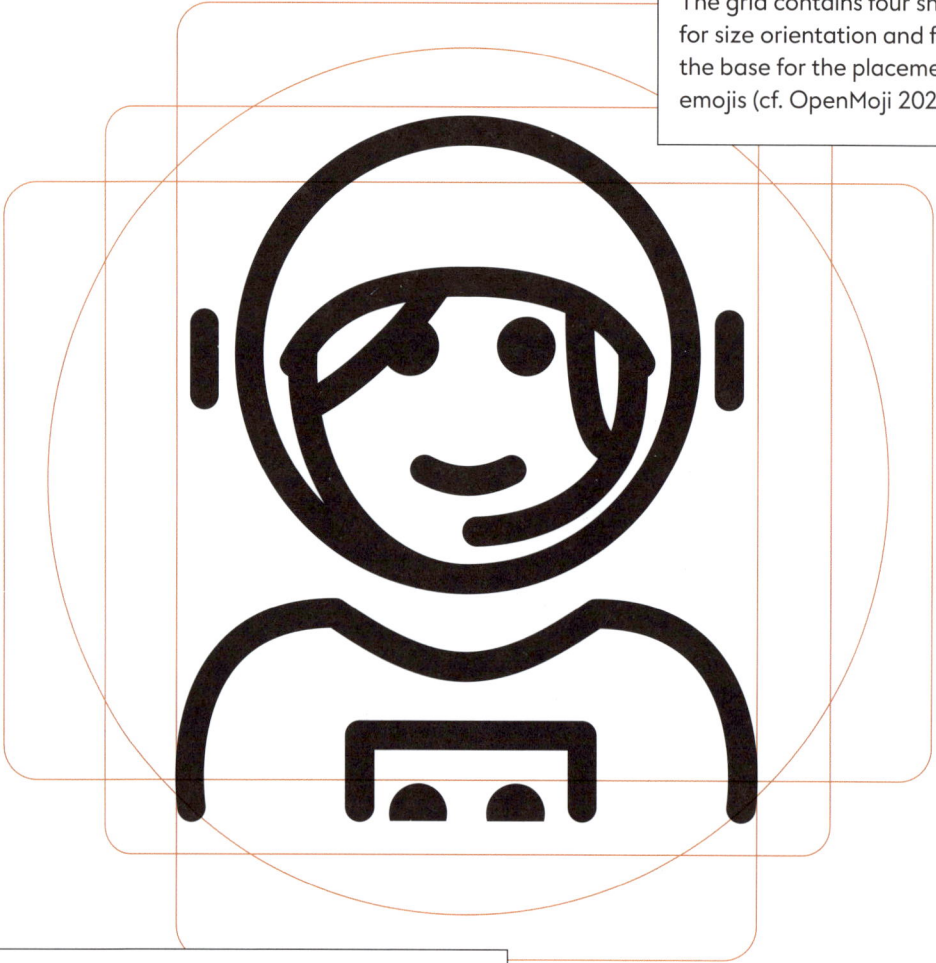

EXTRACT FROM THE STYLE GUIDE

Fig. 510 **woman astronaut** by Lisa Thiel

Fig. 511 **deciduous tree** by Hilda Kalyoncu

Fig. 512 **church** by Martin Wehl

Fig. 513 **articulated lorry** by Ronja Bäurlen

Fig. 514 **example bust**

BUST

The facial structure is elliptical, lacking a distinct neck, yet featuring a gap between the head and shoulders. The eyes are positioned centrally within the head. To achieve a neutral expression, the mouth should be aligned with the midpoint of the eyes (ibid.).

round caps   round edges   centered contour

Fig. 515 **contour**

CONTOUR

The stroke attributes include a standardized weight, along with rounded corners and ends. The utilization of open contours results in the characteristic and appealing appearance of Open-Moji (see Fig. 518), making them well-suited for overlapping lines or perspectives (ibid.).

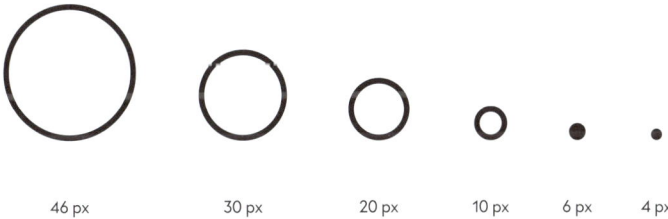

46 px   30 px   20 px   10 px   6 px   4 px

Fig. 516 **basic circles**

BASIC CIRCLES

The uniform size of circles contributes to a uniform appearance across the entire set. Segments of the basic circles can also be applied for creating rounded corners or undulating forms. These fundamental circles find application in various contexts (see Fig. 517; ibid.).

Fig. 517 **example application basic circles**

Fig. 518 **open contour**

#92D3F5	#61B2E4	Fig. 519 **ice**	

author
Evelyn Soos

unicode
1F9CA

category
food-drink

#EA5A47	#D22F27	Fig. 520 **strawberry**	

author
Liz Bravo

unicode
1F353

category
food-drink

#B1CC33	#5C9E31	Fig. 521 **green apple**	

author
Marius Schnabel

unicode
1F34F

category
food-drink

#F1B31C	#FCEA2B	Fig. 522 **mango**	

author
Ricarda Krejci

unicode
1F96D

category
food-drink

| Fig. 523 **peach** | #E67A94 | | #FFA7C0 |

author
Marius Schnabel

unicode
1F351

category
food-drink

| Fig. 524 **eggplant** | #B399C8 | | #8967AA |

author
Marius Schnabel

unicode
1F346

category
food-drink

| Fig. 525 **tangerine** | #F4AA41 | | #E27022 |

author
Liz Bravo

unicode
1F34A

category
food-drink

| Fig. 526 **coconut** | #A57939 | | #6A462F |

author
Marius Schnabel

unicode
1F965

category
food-drink

The idea for the project arose during a lunch meeting between Professors Utz and Gross. They were discussing an open source library for pictorial signs that could be used and expanded by students. The conversation shifted to emojis, as they cannot be freely used in projects.

With this in mind, they initiated a course for the fourth semester at HfG Schwäbisch Gmünd, which focused on the design of emojis as a project topic. In the initial phase of the course, students explored the creative diversity of emojis. From simple pixel icons to more intricate vector drawings, they delved into the topic and experimented with various levels of abstraction and motifs.

The students learned about the possibilities and limitations of pictographic representations. According to an interview with Utz (April 17, 2024), individual letters can be derived from one another when designing a font, while pictorial signs encompass varying degrees of detail depending on the depicted subject areas. Utz further noted that achieving a uniform design for a comprehensive set of pictorial signs poses a greater challenge compared to letters (ibid.).[19] This is because fonts possess a distinct character and are less intricate than emojis and pictorial signs. Added to this is the difficulty of finding a conclusion when selecting motifs.

In the previously discussed course at the HfG Schwäbisch Gmünd, small exercises were used to first create pixel icons and then vector drawings. The students were given a list of pictorial signs with a wide range of different levels of detail. Using this list, the students designed a uniform sign system. The result was a great formal variety with different designs ranging from black and white to color, flat, linear, strongly constructed or free-form.

The various drafts were then tested in short messages and prepared for voting among the students. In a second phase of the course, the designs with the most votes were transformed into a final design by the students. The tasks were distributed differently by forming groups. The group responsible for the guidelines took on the task of standardizing the drafts. An example of this is the idea of using two different colors for the shading, which originated from one of the drafts and was subsequently formed into a rule by the responsible group: The primary colors, see page 134 f. are mainly used. The lighter colors are used as the default color and the darker ones for shading. The secondary colors shown on the page 135 are used only in special cases (cf. OpenMoji).

The system was gradually expanded in workshops. Originally a pure project of the HfG Schwäbisch Gmünd, it also integrated external contributions after publication, which means that OpenMoji now contains signs from designers from different parts of the world. For example, students from the University of Chile initiated the Guemil Project, within which they designed pictorial signs for emergencies such as earthquakes, floods (Fig. 541), structural fires (Fig. 543) and tsunamis. Some of their characters were adapted to the OpenMoji style guide. Through this and other projects on various topics such as climate change, horticulture and medicine, the standard set of emojis based on Unicode has been expanded to include custom emojis.

OpenMoji continued to spread and was even used in American comics, a TV quiz show and school textbooks (ibid.). They were also used to train an AI to test the design possibilities of the characters. According to Utz, this resulted in a strange output, but it was perfectly integrated into the OpenMoji system. In addition, experiments were carried out on how emojis can be automatically grouped according to subject areas, making OpenMoji not only a library for picture characters, but also a field of experimentation for various purposes.

The use of the creative variety and the associated expression is currently limited by the technical possibilities, so that mainly the pre-installed emojis or stickers are used. However, it can be observed that more and more fonts containing emojis are being designed.

---

19   For his font ›Netto‹, Utz designed a series of pictorial signs to match the font, which also include emojis. In the design, Utz derived the pictorial signs from the letters, which are now also included in different font styles. He developed a fascinating, inherent system that even makes use of the possibility of variable picture characters.

Fig. 527

Fig. 528

Fig. 529

Fig. 530

Fig. 534

Fig. 531

Fig. 532

Fig. 533

Fig. 535

Fig. 536

Fig. 537

Fig. 538

Fig. 541

Fig. 542

Fig. 539

Fig. 540

Fig. 543

The emojis are categorized into main categories, each of which is further organized into subcategories. A small selection of emojis from six of the twelve categories is shown.

smileys-emotion

Fig. 527 **face holding back tears** by Liz Bravo
Fig. 528 **squinting face with tongue** by Mariella Steeb
Fig. 529 **shushing face** by Emily Jäger
Fig. 530 **face with tears of joy** by Emily Jäger
Fig. 534 **revolving hearts** by Laura Humpfer

food-drink

Fig. 531 **spaghetti** by Liz Bravo
Fig. 532 **hamburger** by Miriam Vollmeier
Fig. 533 **bubble tea** by Liz Bravo

activities

Fig. 535 **japanese dolls** by Liz Bravo

objects

Fig. 536 **trumpet** by Sina Schulz
Fig. 537 **camera** by Sina Schulz

animals-nature

Fig. 538 **tiger face** by Sofie Ascherl
Fig. 539 **panda** by Sofie Ascherl
Fig. 540 **cat face** by Sofie Ascherl

extras-openmoji

Fig. 541 **flood** by Guemil Project
Fig. 542 **nuclear protection** by Robin Kurz
Fig. 543 **structural fire** by Guemil Project

(OpenMoji 2024b)

GT Maru from Grilli Type

THIERRY BLANCPAIN
Graphic designer & typographer

»GT Maru is based on ideas stemming from two completely different writing systems: the Japanese and Latin. Throughout the design process, I kept trying to strike the perfect balance between the typeface as a functional tool, but also as an expression of joy.«

(Blancpain, in: Murphy 2021)

Fig. 544 **Thierry Blancpain** (photo by Ben Barry)

The ›GT Maru‹ typeface was created after a trip to Japan, during which Thierry Blancpain was inspired by the friendly signs. Blancpain is together with Noël Leu, founder of the Type Foundry Grilli Type. They are known for creating a fascinating visual world in which they present their typefaces (see for example Fig. 545).

Typeface design
Thierry Blancpain
(2017–2021)

Emojis design
Grilli Type
with Anya Danilova

**Production of
GT Maru Mega**
Huw Williams with
quality control by
Christoph Koeberlin

**Website design
and artwork**
Grilli Type

Website developed
Grilli Type
and Sensor Station

Animations
Josh Schaub
and Grilli Type

Grilli Type started as a project during their time at Bern University of the Arts, when Leu and Blancpain were studying visual communication. As part of a student-led course, they had the idea of creating a publishing house and an associated type foundry so that the book publisher could use the typefaces. Originally conceived as a platform for art students, Grilli Type has since developed into one of the most well-known and leading foundries in the industry, known for presenting their typefaces in a complex visual world to convey a feeling for the use of type. Grilli Type is also characterized by taking inspiration from their surroundings or new developments to create their own typefaces. One of these experiences gave rise to the GT Maru font. During a trip to Japan, the Japanese approach to the design of warning signs got Blancpain reflecting. In Europe, signs are presented with the most reduced pictograms and clear geometric shapes possible. Japanese signs are usually much more complex and often give the impression of entering into a dialog with the viewer, see also page 73.

»The choreography of bright colors and faces-in-places creates an atmosphere that seems more welcoming.« (Blancpain, in: GT Maru 2024)

Significant differences can also be seen in construction signage. While in Switzerland construction site barriers are shown in the signal color red and with strict geometric shapes (Fig. 547), in Japan metal poles are combined with friendly and cute characters (Fig. 549), see also page 72.

Construction signage often features a construction worker apologizing for the inconvenience caused by the construction work. Another difference is the production of the signs:

»Many signs in Japan are still painted by brush. The letters often showcase rounded terminals and a natural flow that is specific to sign painting.«

(Blancpain, in: GT Maru 2024)

Hand-painted signs are rarely seen in Switzerland (cf. GT Maru 2024). Instead, most signs are printed in strict sans serif fonts (see Fig. 546). These observations inspired Blancpain to combine the two very different sources of inspiration and create a typeface inspired by the friendliness of Japan, but communicating in a casual and functional way.

In the four years that followed his journey to Japan, Blancpain dedicated himself to the exploration of round letters. The GT Maru family is the result of this creative exploration of roundness – known as ›maru‹ in Japanese (cf. GT Maru 2024). Blancpain investigated the question of how he could transfer this rounding, which is found in Japanese characters with brush writing, to the completely different Latin alphabet.

The Japanese writing system is moreover characterized by the block-like design of the characters, while Latin letters usually vary in height and width (cf. GT Maru 2024).

Fig. 545 **illustration by Grilli Type for the presentation of GT Maru** (GT Maru 2024)

According to Blancpain, in order to harmonize the two systems, the letters of the Latin alphabet drawn by Japanese designers for Japanese-language fonts have extremely short ascenders and descenders (see Fig. 548) (cf. GT Maru 2024). Blancpain used these two formal characteristics – the roundness and block-like appearance of the letters – in the design of the GT Maru. This resulted in the compact and friendly nature of the font (cf. ibid.). The font GT Maru Mono, which is part of the family, exploits the square aesthetic by making the width of the individual letters correspond to the height.

Fig. 546 **illustration by Grilli Type of a typical typeface construction in Switzerland** (GT Maru 2024)

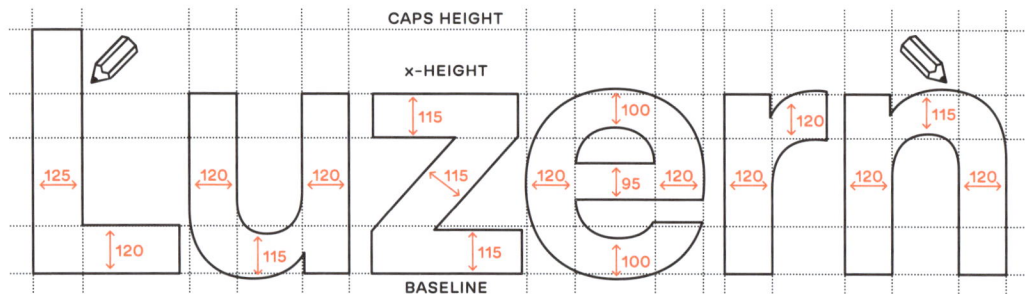

Fig. 547 **illustration by Grilli Type of typical construction signage in Switzerland** (GT Maru 2024)

Blancpain also designed GT Maru Mega (Fig. 550), which takes the liberty of freeing itself from the strict rules. The font uses the variable technology of fonts to adapt the font weight to individual needs. It makes use of the variable possibilities of font design by allowing letters to be expanded and deflated again (cf. GT Maru 2024). The font style is mainly suitable for headlines or bold applications.

The two emoji fonts (GT Maru Emoji) complete the family and support the friendly character of the font, see pages 142–145.

Fig. 548 **illustration by Grilli Type of the GT Maru typeface construction** (GT Maru 2024)

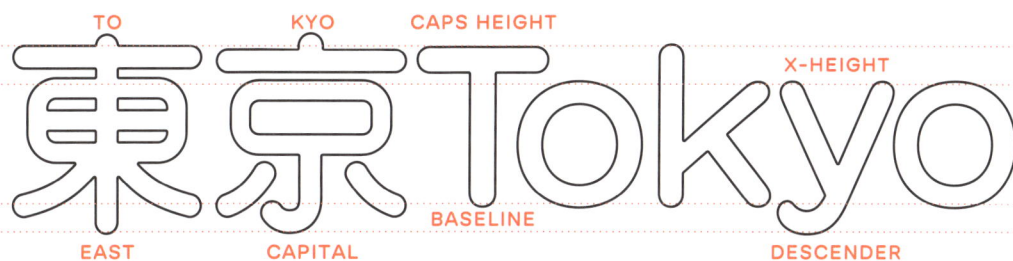

Fig. 549 **illustration by Grilli Type of construction signage in Japan** (GT Maru 2024)

Fig. 550 **lemon in combination with GT Maru Mega**

Fig. 551 nerd face

Fig. 552 doughnut

Fig. 553 pizza

Fig. 554 cherry

Fig. 555 umbrella

Fig. 556 rabbit

Fig. 557 banana

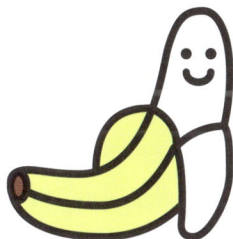

Fig. 558 octopus

Fig. 559 partying face

Fig. 560 japan

Fig. 561 fuji

Fig. 562 yen

Fig. 563 **GT Maru light with beer emoji color**

Kanpai

The emoji character set contains 450 emojis, each available in color and black and white. They have a linear structure and adopt the characteristic features of the GT Maru letters such as rounded line ends, geometric shapes and the friendly nature.

In contrast to conventional emojis, the GT Maru emojis have a nose and a cartoon-like outline, which gives them a unique character.

The design of the eyes and mouths is hugely inspired by the kawaii aesthetic. For example, the pleading face (Fig. 571) uses the eyes, which often also stand for desire or dreams (see page 114). But the minimalist representation of the mouth using a segment of a circle and two small dots as eyes are also characteristic of the Kawaii aesthetic. One of the most typical features of Kawaii, however, is the anthropomorphization of objects or food, see page 80. This is also practised in the GT Maru emoji, for example by giving a cloud (Fig. 581) a face or anthropomorphizing numerous foods (e.g. Fig. 552 f.)

Fig. 564	Fig. 565	Fig. 566	Fig. 567	Fig. 568	Fig. 569

Fig. 570 **smiling face with hearts**	Fig. 571	Fig. 572	Fig. 573	Fig. 574

Fig. 575	Fig. 576 **rainbow**	Fig. 577

Fig. 578	Fig. 579	Fig. 580		Fig. 581

Fig. 582 **GT Maru Mega outline with yellow heart emoji color**

Arigato ♡

Typical elements from comics such as an exaggeratedly wide mouth (Fig. 574) or hyperbolic expressions (Fig. 577) are also included in the character set. The motifs of the GT Maru Emoji are based on the already coded emojis and add a few more, such as the balaclava helmet emoji (Fig. 573) .
The Japanese influence is also evident in the representation of numerous typical Japanese motifs, such as the yen (Fig. 562), the Japanese flag (Fig. 560) or Mount Fuji (Fig. 561).

The skillful blending of cute and geometric elements follows the concept of font construction and leads to an appealing and systematically structured result. The GT Maru is an ensemble of soft, friendly characters paired with a constructive, rigorous system. Blancpain thus proves that the two contrasting characteristics can be harmonized.

The font demonstrates how enriching different cultural influences can be for creative processes.

Fig. 583 **mouse face**

Fig. 584

Fig. 585

Fig. 586

Fig. 587

Fig. 588

Fig. 589

Fig. 590

Fig. 591

Fig. 592

Fig. 593 **party popper**

Fig. 594

Fig. 595

Fig. 596

Fig. 564 **folded hands**
Fig. 565 **pinched fingers**
Fig. 566 **crossed fingers**
Fig. 567 **ok hand**
Fig. 568 **oncoming fist**
Fig. 569 **waving hand**
Fig. 571 **pleading face**
Fig. 572 **facepalm**
Fig. 573 **balaclava helmet**
Fig. 574 **grimacing face**
Fig. 575 **smiling face with open hands**
Fig. 577 **loudly crying face**
Fig. 578 **sun with face**
Fig. 579 **sweat droplets**
Fig. 580 **droplet**
Fig. 581 **cloud**
Fig. 584 **monkey face**
Fig. 585 **tiger face**
Fig. 586 **pig face**
Fig. 587 **frog**
Fig. 588 **panda**
Fig. 589 **chicken**
Fig. 590 **evolving hearts**
Fig. 591 **collision**
Fig. 592 **heart with arrow**
Fig. 594 **skull**
Fig. 595 **beating heart**
Fig. 596 **ogre**
(GT Maru 2024)

Variable Emojis

HANNAH WITTE
Designer

»It's really quite striking how much common emojis reduce physical and cultural diversity to a few standardized representations of people. Variable Emojis is an experiment to find a way for more anti-discriminatory representation options.«

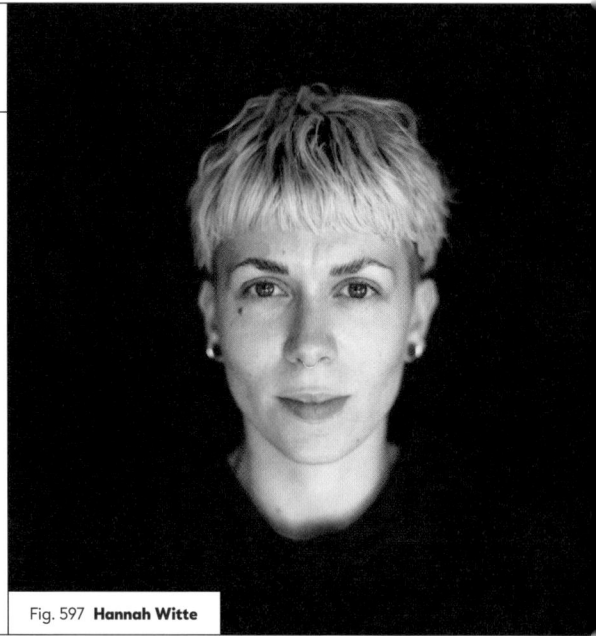

Fig. 597 **Hannah Witte**

Witte is known for her work on gender-sensitive use of language and typography. With her variable emojis, she is committed to overcoming stereotypical representations in the emoji character set by using the possibilities of variable fonts.

Emoji design
Hannah Witte

Design Partizipa City
Nike Dieterich

Adviser for the Partizipa City Emojis
Shorouk El Hariry

The Variable Emojis project was created as part of a university course at the Folkwang University of the Arts in Essen, where students explored the possibilities of variable fonts.
The technology inspired Witte to develop the idea of an emoji font that allows individual customization. It is her response to the fact that emoji representations often use stereotypes, which can be potentially discriminating.

With the coding and spread of graphic emojis, discourses on the diversity of characters are increasingly coming to the fore. The topic was discussed particularly frequently after the emergence of more detailed emojis representing gender or certain culturally specific characteristics. The further they cross the iconic categorization threshold, the more material for discussion was created, see page 110.

According to Freedman, emojis can reflect social, economic or political conditions and trends (cf. Freedman 2020: 53). She notes that until 2016, the only female workers in the emoji character set were either in the entertainment or service industries, such as dancers, receptionists and Playboy bunnies. Emojis of female professionals in jobs requiring university degrees were only added in Unicode 11.0 – still after the addition of different skin tones (Unicode 8.0 in 2015) and homosexual couples (Unicode 6.0 in 2010). According to Freedman, this shows that the advancement of the female gender often comes later than progress in multiculturalism (cf. ibid.).
Furthermore, emojis show how Japanese popular culture is changing global communication and reflecting the spirit of different populations and places (cf. ibid.).

Fig. 598 **Katrin Friedrich**

Fig. 599 **Michael Shitembi**

Fig. 600 **Fares Abubakr**

Fig. 601 **Zahra Habibi**

The variable emojis were used in 2021 as playing cards for ›Partizipa City‹ (Fig. 598–Fig. 601). It is a simulation game by the Institute for Applied Cultural Research Göttingen (ifak) on structural racism and discriminatory behavior in everyday life (cf. ifak). In the fictitious Partizipa City, the players take on different roles of people from a wide range of backgrounds and milieus. They are confronted with racist statements or actions in the form of short role plays. The game manoeuvres the players into concrete situations in order to reflect on their own behaviour and to sensitize them to possible unconscious behaviour that can be perceived as discriminatory or racist. There is a particular focus on anti-Muslim racism (cf. ibid.).

The aim of the game is to reflect on the understanding of racism and to question it critically in order to be aware of discriminatory behavior in everyday life and to be able to react prepared in concrete situations.

The game was designed by Nike Dieterich with illustrations by Witte. Shorouk El Hariry advised on the icon development.

Fig. 602 **Emojis created with the existing parameters**

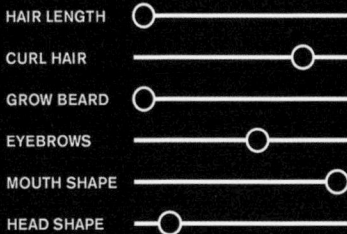

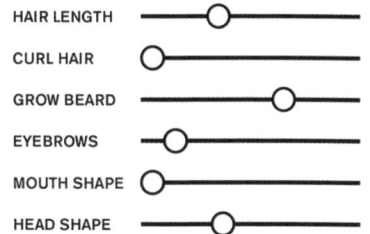

Emojis are therefore an important tool for observing and analyzing cultural competence in the digital age:

»Emoji culture is becoming a placeholder for people to distil their identities and politics into distinctive — but at times, reductive — icons.«

(Crystal Abidin & Joel Gn, in: Giannoulis/Wilde 2020: 5)

According to Anatol Stefanowitsch (2017), cultural struggles are bubbling behind the seemingly innocent facades of the colorful little images.

With her project, Witte has taken up this discourse and programmed a variable font with a website where the variable emojis can be tried out (Fig. 602). Because of the technical possibilities at the time, the font was designed exclusively in black and white and with six different parameters.

The project does not serve as a finished application for the use of a comprehensive tool for the deployment of emojis. It serves as a thought experiment to question the use of emojis and to test the technical possibilities[20] for future character tools with emojis.

20 However, the idea of using the technology of variable fonts for emojis need not be forgotten. Recently, we have seen the increased emergence of fonts with emojis. The technology of variable fonts could be used, for example, to adapt the individual emojis to the font styles.

The use of emojis in fonts is a great way to use pictorial signs that harmonize with a font to achieve an aesthetically pleasing result.[21]
The Diglû project demonstrates how a complex and aesthetically pleasing system can be created for numerous applications in visual communication. In addition, the project – as well as the GT Maru – shows how pictorial signs can interact harmoniously with characters. While the focus of the Diglû concept is on conveying information and knowledge, the GT Maru combines different culturally anchored writing practices.
With a different starting point and different approaches, both projects show in different ways that pictorial signs can offer added value as an integral part of fonts. While both projects focus on the harmonious integration of pictorial and written characters, the OpenMoji project creates a comprehensive library of pictorial signs for free use. The creators of OpenMoji are dedicated to the formal diversity of characters by focusing on the graphical standardization and reduction of emojis. Their goal is to create a pool of branch-independent and standardized characters that everyone can contribute to and use. Variable emojis are an interesting approach to using technical possibilities that can serve as inspiration for future emoji applications.

The inherent problem in a character system consisting of images is that certain characters are missing. Often, an emoji that is currently required is not available in the character set. The question arises as to which criteria should be used to encode characters. Where does coding begin and where does it end? A seemingly endless discussion during development is the expansion of the character set. One of the best-known examples was the introduction of the hijab emoji into the Unicode standard in 2017, which caused a worldwide stir. A consortium decides whether an emoji will be included in Unicode and thus enable cross-platform and cross-device compatibility (see page 59).

Through their global use, emojis have become an important and powerful tool for communication, reflecting socially relevant topics such as equality, cultural diversity and gender stereotypes. Do emojis therefore serve to raise awareness and contribute to more open and diverse communication or do they reinforce existing stereotypes? To what extent can the creative diversity of the characters be used to expand individual expression and enrich our communication?

Recent developments such as Genmoji or Emoji-Kitchen show a constantly growing demand for new characters and character combinations (see page 62). The need for individual expression has continued to increase in the course of emojization. How can designers use the creative diversity of emojis to contribute to a more individual and personal way of expression?

In addition to the emergence of emoji-fonts, stickers are becoming increasingly widespread, see also pages 94–95. The resulting formal diversity is fascinating. The following subchapter focuses on a number of projects that contribute to the diversity of emojis in terms of form and content in the form of stickers. Projects by designers from different backgrounds are presented, and their creations address important topics such as the representation of different cultures in the emoji character set (see pages 156–163), the availability of the formal diversity of emojis (see pagse 164–168) and typographic stickers that can take on similar functions to emoji stickers by blurring the boundaries between typography and image (see pages 152–155).
The focus is on the projects that have been developed to enrich the creative diversity of emojis. Selected projects are presented and the associated topics explained. The aim of the following subchapter is to highlight projects that are relevant in the context of the emojization.
These presented projects offer a fascinating insight into the dynamic development, cultural significance, creative variety, and usage of emojis in visual communication.

---

21   Another interesting project in which emojis have been harmoniously integrated into a font is ›Show Me the Mono‹. This monospace typeface was designed by Rob Keller from ›Mota Italic‹ and was launched at the end of the year 2021.

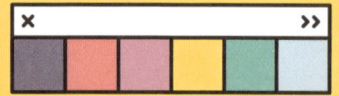

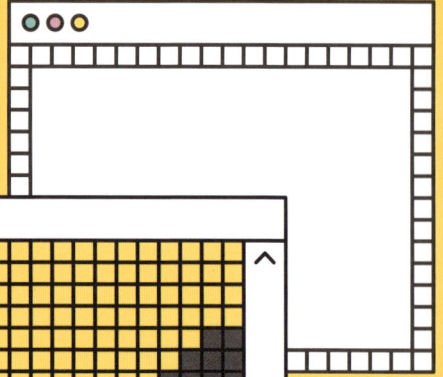

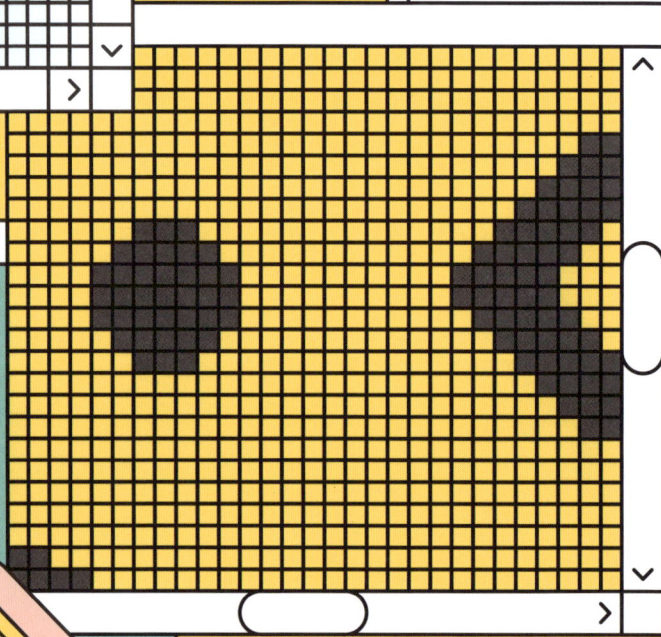

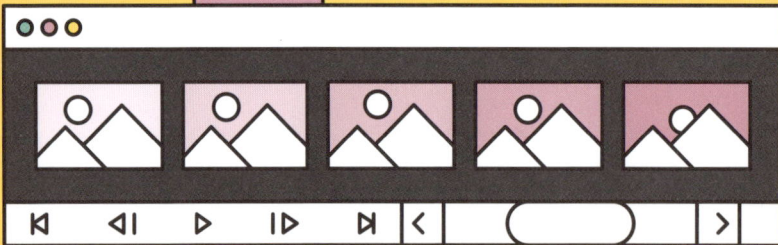

(Emoji-)Stickers

The technical restrictions on the use of emojis and the limitation of available pictorial signs have resulted in further interesting developments. The implementation of character sets as image files opens up new design possibilities that free themselves from the corset of the Unicode standard and also allow other degrees of abstraction than the design of emojis as part of a font.

Projects featured in this subchapter:

Kinetic Typography
Mat Voyce

Zouzoukwa
O'Plérou Grebet

1000 Emoji Project
Dan Woodger

The use of stickers on most platforms means that emojis cannot fulfill the same range of functions as when the pictorial signs are integrated directly into the text. On the other hand, the use of stickers as image files opens up new creative possibilities that are conditioned by the formats used.

There is currently a remarkable variety of stickers (see pages 94–95), which are used to varying degrees depending on the platform. These stickers are often animated and are used as GIF files. The formal diversity is extremely broad. This sub-chapter introduces three designers who have created projects with very different intentions.

The first project shows how visual constellations can be created on a typographic basis, some of which take on the functions of emojis, for example by representing emotions using typographic design elements. What is interesting here is the mixture of pictorial and textual elements.

The second project, Zouzoukwa, responds to the limitations of the emoji character set. It serves as an example of how restrictions can be used productively to develop one's own project ideas. There are other similar projects that focus on the limitations of the character set and make a valuable contribution, by designing emojis that are not included. From a formal perspective, the Zouzoukwa emojis exceed the iconic categorization threshold further than the emojis, which are used as glyphs. This leads to the signs becoming more coexistent (see

pages 114–115). The project uses the form to convey cultural characteristics. For Aichler, abstraction implied cultural neutrality (see page 32). With the African emojis, it can be observed that the details establish a connection to African culture and thus create an emotional bond. The richness of detail is used to convey sensual stimuli (see pages 110–115).

The third project, the 1000 Emoji Project, shows how an artistic approach can lead to the use of a visual variety of emoji stickers. It demonstrates the need for differently designed character sets. The project was made possible by the LINE platform, which allows for a wide formal variety of different stickers. In addition, it is possible to use the pictorial signs integrated in the text within the instant messaging service, which allows them to use the range of functions of the standardized emojis within the platform.

The projects presented in this sub-chapter provide an insight into the diversity of sticker development. The formal diversity of the pictorial signs used shows the creative range and provides indications that emoji communication is not only about conveying information, but that its use also includes other important aspects, which are related to the formal properties of signs and thus also to the autonomy thesis (see pages 114–115).

Kinetic Typography

MAT VOYCE

Type Designer & Animator

»I like to give font and type designs a little bit of character.«

Voyce specializes in 2D typography animation, known for his pioneering style in illustrative kinetic typography. Under his hand, a lettering develops into a unique identity.

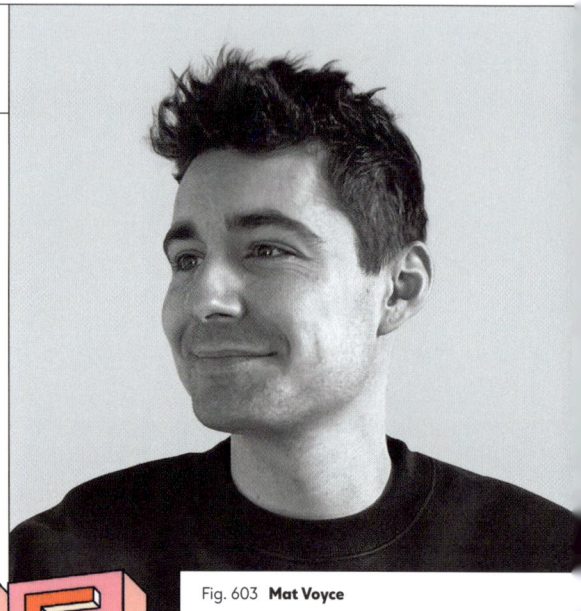

Fig. 603 **Mat Voyce**

Fig. 604 The animated lettering ›alive‹ is one of the many typefaces he created for personal use. He makes many of his colorful typographic creations available for free personal use on various platforms.

Fig. 605 The artwork was created as part of ›36 Days of Type‹. The project was first launched in 2014 by graphic designers Nina Sans and Rafa Goicoechea (36 Days of Type 2023). They started the project as a personal challenge. Since then, the project has achieved a wide reach and participants design a letter or number every day for 36 days and share their creations on social media (ibd.).

Fig. 604 **animated lettering ›alive‹**

Voyce is known for his graphic and kinetic style. Through the use of bold and bright colors and clear graphic shapes, combined with a unique animation style, he has developed an individual form of visual expression. His creations are mostly realized in the form of animated GIFs, stickers or videos.

In Voyce's animated visual elements, the question of a clear demarcation between image and text becomes seemingly impossible to answer, see Fig. 605. Such a fusion of pictographic and typographic elements into a coherent interplay casts a new light on the infantilization and regression discourse that repeatedly arises in emoji communication. Voyce's works show that not only emojis are taking on an increasing pictorial character, but that typography itself is also undergoing an aesthetic transformation: Where does something start to be a picture and where does it finish? To what extent does reading competence differ from visual competence, which enables us to use and understand images beyond their mere iconic function?

According to Peirce's semiotics, there is no clear boundary between image and text. The signs are classified as icons, indices or symbols depending on how they are interpreted. A letter, such as the letter ›B‹ reproduced on the right with graphic elements,

Fig. 605 **36 Days of Type** letter B

is in itself a symbol – it must be learned in order to be understood. However, because the individual elements together represent the letter, it can be interpreted iconically, because the sum of the individual images resembles the letter ›B‹. A similarity is created between the arrangement of the elements and the letter.

According to the iconic categorization threshold of cognitive semiotics, the individual elements of

Fig. 605, such as the basketball or the books, exceed the iconic categorization threshold, while the combination of elements – the letter ›B‹ – lies below the iconic categorization threshold of the iconic type, see also page 110. The typographic arrangements presented on this double page turn out to be more multilayered than initially assumed. Although a lettering undoubtedly falls below the iconic categorization threshold, elements are revealed that go beyond it. One

Fig. 606

Fig. 609

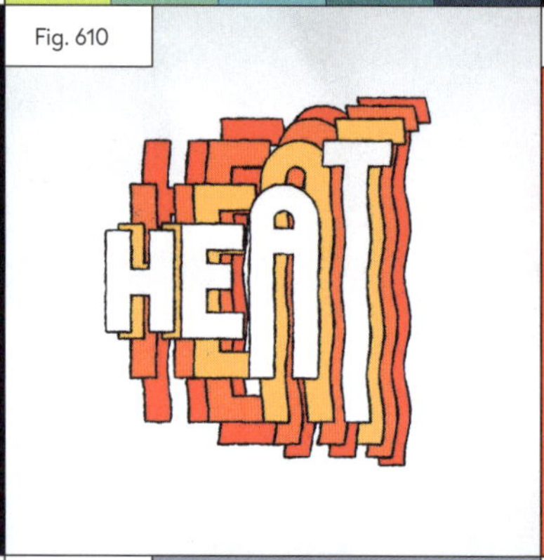

Fig. 612

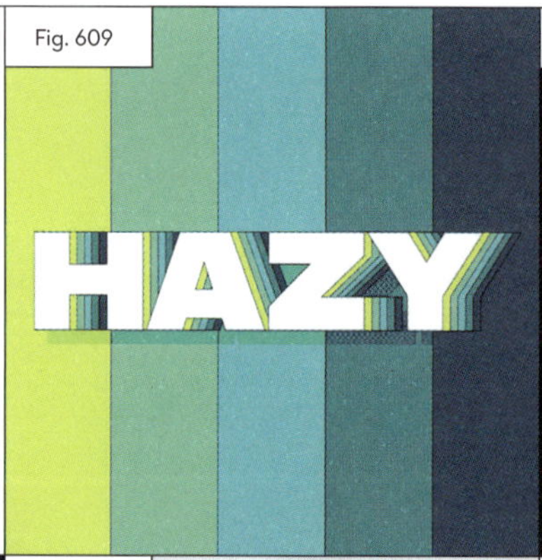

Fig. 607

Fig. 610

Fig. 613

Fig. 608

Fig. 611

Fig. 614

exemplary feature is the use of lines of movement in the lettering ›Heat‹, which reminds us of the flames of a fire. Similarly, the wavy line in Fig. 615 crosses the boundary of the categorization threshold, while the underlying typography is below it. These subtle contrasts lend the typographic compositions a fascinating dimension that goes beyond clear categorization. In a constantly evolving visual world, the artist impressively presents the diverse expressive possibilities of typography and blurs the boundaries between type and image. An examination of his work shows the importance of considering the formal-aesthetic development of Emojization.

Fig. 606–Fig. 615: The figures on this page were all created as personal projects by Voyce. He makes his image-text constellations freely available for personal use on social media. His stickers can be added to photos or videos in your own stories on the social platforms.

Fig. 615

Zouzoukwa

O'PLÉROU GREBET
Artist & Designer

»I wanted to create a project to promote African cultures to change the image the Western media have of Africa: hunger, poverty and wars. I wanted to show a different and positive side «

(Grebet, in: Ratcliffe 2019)

Fig. 616 **O'Plérou Grebet** (photo by Tidiane Berté)

In 2018, O'Plérou Grebet realized that African culture was insufficiently represented in the emoji character set. He created an emoji every day that displayed a cultural element of Africa and published it on Instagram.

Emoji design
O'Plérou Grebet

Year
From 2018 until today

Suggestions for new emojis
People from all over the world

With this project, Grebet is focusing on a crucial aspect of emoji proliferation: the diversity and expansion of the existing emoji set. The more pictorial the emojis become, the more pressing the question of which characters should be coded and for what reasons, see also page 59. Simultaneously, the increasing use and integration of emojis require the representation of a wider range of topics.

Grebet observed as an arts student at the Institute of Sciences and Communication Techniques in Abidjan, that African culture is underrepresented in the emoji character set and that it misses emojis to express itself. He chose to break free from the tight corset of Unicode and create his own emojis that authentically reflect his individual experiences from the African culture. In 2018, he created an emoji every day and published it on Instagram.

He gave the project the name ›Zouzoukwa‹, which means ›image‹ in the regional Bété language (cf. Hawgood 2019), and the first emoji he published was a traditional African dish called foutou (Fig. 617) – a bowl of mashed plantains and cassava (cf. Ratcliffe 2019).

He subsequently developed numerous emojis that include various cultural aspects such as architecture, cuisine, music, fashion, means of transportation, sports and facets of African culture and tradition. He published the Emojis on a monochrome background (see Fig. 622–Fig. 633), creating a colorful gradient. In this way, he visually supported the intention of the project, namely the promotion of cultural diversity.

This project is not only an important contribution to the diversity of emojis, but also to the representation of culture diversity in the emoji character set.

Fig. 617 **foutou**

Fig. 618 **libation**

Fig. 619 **khamsa**

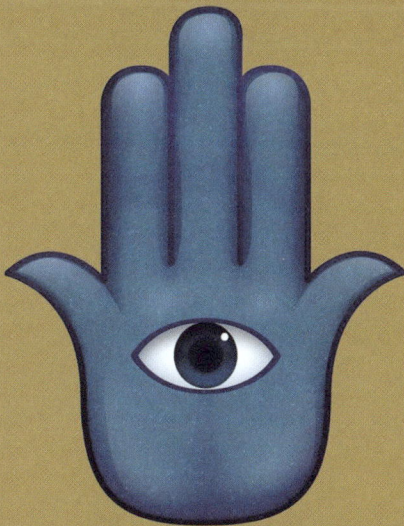

Fig. 620 **garba fork**

Fig. 621 **Zaouli**

Fig. 622 **stone circles of Senegambia**

Fig. 623 **tomb of Askia**

Fig. 624 **Meroe pyramids**

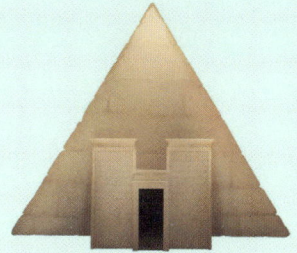

Fig. 625 **kaftan**

Fig. 626 **habesha kemis**

Fig. 627 **gandoura**

Fig. 628 **traditional mill**

Fig. 629 **tbiga**

Fig. 630 **mehraz**

Fig. 631 **ogene double bells**

Fig. 632 **begena**

Fig. 633 **brekete**

Greber was inspired for his emojis by his own life and his experiences with African culture. He created emojis of typical African dishes, such as akassa (Fig. 638), which is made from maize and wrapped in banana leaves. He also illustrated elements of African flora and fauna in an impressive way, such as the Traveler's Tree (Fig. 635). Furthermore, he also included typical gestures, such as pulling down the eyelid with one finger (Fig. 646), which means something like ›I told you so‹.

»People like to see the elements of their own daily life in their phone. And it's funny to have expressions that really correspond with the ones you use yourself.«

(Grebet, in: Brown 2019)

Grebet draws his emojis digitally and, unlike other emoji character sets, his creations are very detailed. They contain the finest color gradations and have an almost realistic character. This supports the project's intention of depicting the reality of African culture and distancing itself from the negative image of Africa that is often portrayed by the media. To underline this in terms of color, Grebet uses bold and bright colors for his emojis.

After Grebet had published an emoji every day for a year, he made an app available in which his creations can be used as stickers on various communication platforms such as WhatsApp. The emojis are divided into different categories, such as people, food, instruments, activities, etc.
In 2021, two emojis created by Gebert, ›libation‹ (Fig. 618) and ›khamsa‹ (Fig. 619), were even included in Unicode. Libation is a religious offering to gods or the deceased. The emoji was included with the name ›Pouring Liquid‹ and, according to Emojipedia, can be used both for ritual libations or to honor the deceased by pouring a drink in memory of a person, as well as to represent the act of pouring (cf. Emojipedia f). The Khamsa emoji was added to Unicode with the name ›Hamsa‹ and is often used to protect against angry looks. It is also known as the Hand of Fatima and, according to Emojipedia, stands for luck, protection, guidance,

feminine power, and faith, among other meanings (cf. Emojipedia g).
The project became very well received and Grebet's emojis were widely used, so that even after a year he did not finish designing more emojis.

»People reach out to tell me what they think I should design, or what they think is missing. Those interactions are some of the aspects I like best about what I do.«

(Grebet, in: Hawgood 2019)

Inspired by the many inputs from people all over the world and the positive reactions, the project continues to grow. Grebet is constantly creating new emojis that represent African culture and is inspired by people to develop new motifs.
The variety of emojis created through Grebet's consistent and patient way of working makes the project an important part of the discourse on the diversity of emojis.
The project shows that emojis are more than just little colorful pictures that embellish our messages. They represent personal attributes that shape an identity, which are relevant for interpersonal communication.

»Emoji really represents the voice of the people.«

(Lee, in: YouTube 2020)

With his work, Grebet builds a bridge between art, respectful cultural interaction and life in the digital age. The project is a wonderful example of how cultural diversity can be conveyed in a positive and constructive way.

»I think [Zouzoukwa designs] became popular because they fill a gap in digital communication for Africans. My work helps us to communicate more clearly, using emojis that represent how we live and what we want to say.«

(Grebet, in: Ratcliffe 2019)

The Zouzoukwa emojis have found a way to represent African culture in a friendly and positive way and make it a little more visible to other countries.

Fig. 634 **krar**

Fig. 635 **traveler's tree**

The emojis shown on this, the previous and following two pages are just a small selection of the more than 350 emojis that have been created and are constantly being added to. The characters can be used with the free Zouzoukwa app, in which they are grouped into 16 categories.

Fig. 636 **akoumin**

Fig. 637 **agouti**

Fig. 638 **akassa**

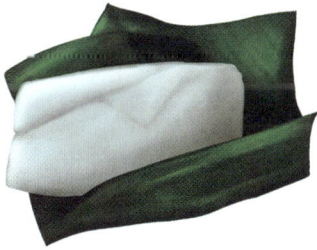

Fig. 639 **rabouz**

Fig. 640 **heliconia**

Fig. 641 **belgha**

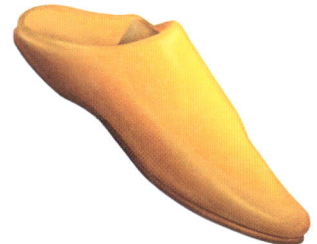

Fig. 642 **henna**

Fig. 643 **mbira**

Fig. 644 **pinasse**

Fig. 645 **chekeré**

Fig. 646 **gesture which means something like ›I told you so‹**

Fig. 647 **làmb/njom**

Fig. 648 **malabary**

Fig. 649 **komian**

Fig. 650 **bandji**

Fig. 651 **shields and spears**

Fig. 652 **fang mask (ngil)**

1000 Emoji Project

DAN WOODGER

Illustrator & animation director

»I feel proud that so many people are using my drawings to communicate with one another – it's quite a surreal thought actually!«

(Woodger 2024a)

Fig. 653 **Dan Woodger**

Woodger is specializes in illustration and animation. He is known for his humorous and cartoonish style. In 2014, he designed 1000 Emojis for social messaging app ›LINE‹ with which people from all over the world can communicate. In an unbelievable deadline of ten weeks, he created 100 stickers every week. Woodger is one of the rare few who have been able to communicate with millions of people via LINE using his unique visual language.

Client
LINE

Art Direction
Jenny Yoo

Illustration
Dan Woodger

LINE is a messaging platform that is characterized by the fact that a large variety of different emojis can be used, see also pages 94–95. In contrast to conventional platforms, LINE enables the integration of formally different emojis directly into the text flow and gives them a status comparable to that of standard emojis as long as they are used within the platform.

LINE has collaborated with various artists to expand its emoji library into a comprehensive ›emoji encyclopedia‹ with over 10,000 emojis (cf. Cartwright 2014). Woodger's emojis were the first to be integrated into LINE's standard emoji keyboard. In order to implement the project within the incredible deadline of ten weeks, the artistic director and Woodger developed an efficient system. Based on a list created by the art director, Woodger delivered 100 emojis each week. This list contained 60 predefined motifs based on a specific theme, as well as the opportunity for Woodger to develop 40 of her own emojis (cf. ibid.).

Woodger followed a strict approach when designing the characters. He worked on a predefined 3x5 grid in Din A3 format and sketched an emoji in each box (cf. ibid.). Originally, all emojis were drawn by hand and then digitally colored and refined. This process is similar to Woodger's usual workflow for other projects. However, for this project, he had to focus specifically on simplifying the designs and employing thicker lines, necessitated by their small size for seamless integration into text messages. The result is a humorous and wide-ranging character set that has Woodger's visual signature.

The emojis shown on this and the following pages are a small selection of Woodger's many stickers available on LINE.

The stickers function as representations that embody a variety of topics that can be import-ant in interpersonal interactions. As a rule, they are characterized by a humorous and sometimes hyper-bolic nature that is strongly resembling cartoons.

Fig. 654 **kiss boy**

Fig. 655 **huff**

Fig. 656 **eyes shut**

Fig. 657 **oh no**

Fig. 658 **tiger face**

Fig. 659 **mischievous**

Fig. 660 **ugh**

Fig. 661 **doh**

Fig. 662 **rave girl**

Fig. 663 **rainbow vomit**

Fig. 664 **iritated**

Fig. 665 **phew**

Fig. 666 **mime**

Fig. 667 **gramps**

Fig. 668 **doctor**

Fig. 669 **surgeon**

Fig. 670 **vetriloquist**

Fig. 671 **farmer**

Fig. 672 **grandma**

Fig. 673 **detective**

Fig. 674 **fisherman**

Fig. 675 **worker**

Fig. 676 **spray can**

Fig. 677 **student**

Fig. 678 **librarian**

Fig. 679 **rave girl hat**

Fig. 680 **burglar**

Fig. 681 **bike cop**

The emojis cover different topics such as professions, facial expressions, animals, food and objects. The stickers include a diverse range of elements used in classic emojis as well as in comics. For example, the squinted eyes (Fig. 656) are reminiscent of text-based emojis such as >_<, while the angry eyes (Fig. 664) are reminiscent of the ò_ó or Fig. 657 of x_x. Typical emoji motifs such as the kissing emoji (Fig. 654) can also be found in the character set. By using elements such as the depiction of a cloud, the emojis draw on representations from comics. The cloud is used in various ways, including the visualization of a puff of air (Fig. 665), which can signal relief when a stressful event comes to an end, for example. However, the same object –

the cloud – can also be used to express feelings of anger or frustration (Fig. 655) by indicating that the mood has darkened.

The depictions of the eyes and mouth are also strongly reminiscent of cartoonish depictions, such as in Fig. 659 or Fig. 661. Woodger employs a variety of geometric shapes for the eyes, complemented by hyperbolic expressions typical of cartoons. Furthermore, the prominent black outlines, a signature feature of Woodger's style, further reinforce the cartoon aesthetic.

Woodger's emojis go a step beyond the classic emojis and almost develop a narrative character. These multi-layered depictions make it possible to convey emotions and actions in a multi-faceted way.

Fig. 682 **working too hard**

Fig. 683 **boom box**

Fig. 684 **light bulb**

Fig. 685 **dinghy**

Fig. 686 **rainbow peace**

Fig. 687 **skateboard**

Fig. 688 **crab**

Fig. 689 **dragon**

Fig. 690 **meh cat**

Fig. 691 **cool dog**

Fig. 692 **argh**

Fig. 693 **ice cream**

Fig. 694 **ice lolly**

Fig. 695 **slushie**

Fig. 696 **oh no no**

Fig. 697 **heart hands**

Fig. 698 **muscle arm**

The projects presented in this subchapter do not fully represent the variety of available stickers and emoji-related projects. It is not the intention of this book to create a complete collection of emoji projects, but rather to show different approaches and intentions of emoji projects in order to demonstrate the directions in which the distribution of different emoji character sets can develop and the potential this can offer for designers. In addition to the projects presented here, there are numerous other interesting works that deal with the (formal) diversity of emojis.[22] The projects presented in this subchapter show different approaches in which the formal diversity of emojis is of considerable importance.

Voyce's kinetic typographic stickers impressively illustrate how typography can be used as a medium to convey emotions and show that they can be just as expressive as pictorial signs. Through the fascinating fusion of text and image, his creations transcend the conventional boundaries of typographic and pictorial elements. As Paula Scheer noted:

»Words have meaning, and type has spirit«

(Scheer, in: Pentagram 2023)

The Zouzoukwa project by Grebet shows the relevance of cultural representation in the emoji character set. In addition, it illuminates the limitations and infinity of the emoji character set. The project has found a way to free itself from the limitations of Unicode. However, the emergence of this and similar projects once again raises questions.
In contrast to a character set made up of letters, an image character set can be extended endlessly. The degree of abstraction is an important factor here. The more figurative the emojis become, the more the question arises as to which characters should be included in the set and which should not. For example, if the character for ›dog‹ indicates a specific breed, it prompts the question as to why other breeds are not also depicted. The question arises as to which criteria should be used to encode characters. Where does the coding begin and where does it end? Which details are important for a pictorial character set and which can be omitted? What role does the degree of abstraction play?

The 1000 Emoji project by Woodger shows how an artist's visual language can be transported into an emoji character set and become a means of communication accessible to billions of people.

Historical reconstruction has shown that emojis have evolved from the medium of writing to the medium of images. In the process, the pictorial aspect became an important part of the communication process. The emergence of the formal diversity of stickers shows the strong need of users to be able to use different means of expression. It shows that messages are not just about conveying information, but that stickers and emojis, through their aesthetic manifestation, also have communicative attributes that play an important role in the interpersonal communication process (cf. Enzmann 2023: 227). The visual language of emojis and stickers can therefore contribute to a more nuanced, personal and individual way of expression. It shows that different visual languages are important in communication so that people can identify with them.

In this context, the question arises as to what potential these extended means of expression offer designers. How can emojis become part of a visual identity? And how can the rise of digital stickers be used for visual language?

The next chapter is dedicated to these questions. It shows how emojis can be used as part of a visual identity in different ways. The first subchapter explains how emojis can be integrated into corporate design, and the second part shows how they can serve as a visual language. Here, not only the emojis themselves or their technical applications are discussed, but also the aesthetics involved and how they are used by designers.

22   Jessica Walsh and her team at ›&walsh‹, for example, designed a pack of emojis in response to frustrations with the limitations of the current emoji set (cf. &walsh). The Designer Emojis draw inspiration from the unique experiences of a designer. The project offers a humorous and entertaining reflection on life as a designer.

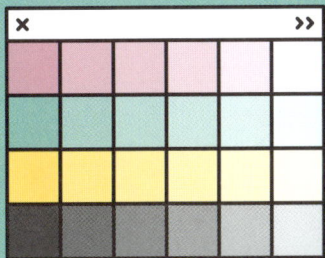

Emojis in Visual Identity

Emojis have become part of the visual expression repertoire of billions of people and have taken a solid place in our everyday lives. This chapter examines the influence of the emergence, spread and formal diversity of emojis on the design of visual identities. The focus of the chapter is on illuminating the creative potential of emojis in visual communication with regard to visual identities for designers and visualizing it using practical examples.

How can emojis become part of a visual identity?

How can I use the potential of emojis for my work?

What exactly is understood by the term ›visual identity‹? In the following, I refer to Martin Lorenz's definition of the term visual identity, in which he refers to a visual language:

»Visual Identity: A visual language used by a company, organization, institution, but also product, campaign, person, or event to be regognized, remembered, and identified.«

(Lorenz 2021: 4)

I do not use the terms ›visual identity‹ and ›visual language‹ synonymously. A visual language consists of concrete visual elements and their rules of application, which are used for communication and creation and can form the basis of a visual identity. A visual language is like creating a toolbox with which something can be communicated using visual elements and rules. Such a language can be used in different contexts, for example in a book or on a website. A visual language is the prerequisite for creating a visual identity and serves to make a brand or a person recognizable and unique.

A visual language can be formed and expressed through the combination of different visual elements (Fig. 699). This includes the use and handling of photos, illustrations, icons, pictograms, typography, colors, shapes, patterns, a specific animation style or the use of a grid that runs through the entire visual identity. The weighting and combination of the individual elements is crucial. All of this can contribute to the creation of a visual language. As designers, it is our challenge to define and apply rules in order to form a visual language that can lead to the creation of a visual identity. It is up to the designer to decide how the rules are defined and applied and where the system allows or even makes it necessary to break out, which in turn can become part of the visual identity.

The definition and application of the rules can be described as the creation of a ›visual system‹ (cf. Lorenz 2021: 4). Nowadays, people are increasingly talking about ›flexible visual systems‹, as the application possibilities have become more complex due to the emergence of CMC and, above all, social media. New communication channels and communication platforms have been created to which visual identities must react flexibly. Consumers have become part of communication by sharing content, commenting on it and influencing others with it (cf. Lorenz 2021: 8).

»We need contemporary visual languages to be able to solve contemporary communications problems.«

(Lorenz 2021: 8)

This chapter focuses on the question of how the rise and spread of emojis can be used for visual identities. The focus is on how they are employed as part of a visual language. The chapter is divided into two sub-chapters. The first subchapter focuses on how emojis can function as an integral part of a brand. It presents projects that use emojis as part of brand communication, making them part of the brand's visual identity. It shows how emojis can be used as a communication tool, serve as a source of inspiration and convey values and be integral part of a subbrand.

The second subchapter discusses how the emergence and increased use of digital (emoji) stickers can be used for design projects. Stickers are seen as part of a visual language. They do not necessa-rily have to be part of a brand for which they are used, but can be part of an artist's visual identity. Brands can identify with the values of such an artist and ›borrow‹ their visual language for a project. The chapter also shows how the potential of emojis can be used for free projects by using the application and technology of digital stickers.

The chapter does not deal with how a visual identity is created through a visual language or how a visual language is structured in detail. Rather, the focus is on how emojis function as part of a visual identity or a visual language.

Fig. 699 **elements of a visual language**

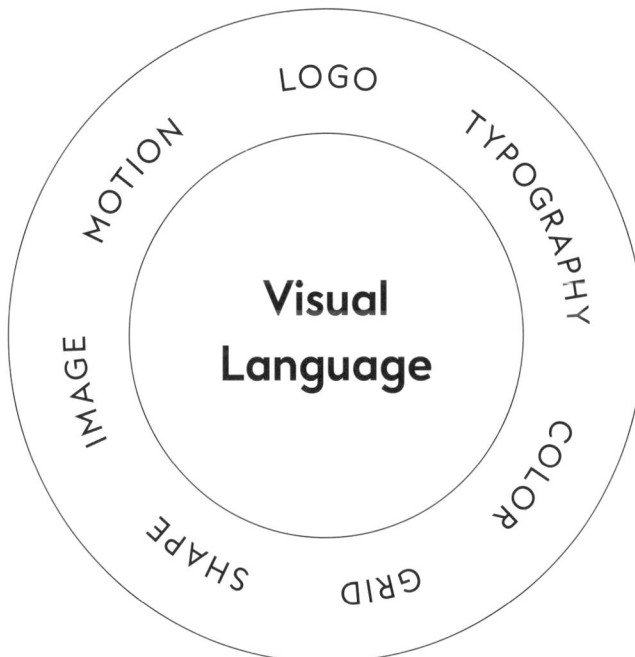

The graphic shows which elements can be used to create a visual language. The designer has the task of combining the visual elements into a coherent, functional and well thought-out over-all construct that visualizes and supports the identity of a company, organization, institu-tion, product, campaign, event or person. The graphic (Fig. 699) is formally inspired by the graphic about corporate identity by Lorenz (2021: 12). In terms of content, it is based on the explanations by Helmann 2017: 29–36) with the addition of animations, which have become an increasingly important component of visu-al identities in recent years. Animations and images not only refer to motifs, but also to the application of a certain style. The term ›image‹ is a broad category into which illustrations or pictorial signs can also be classified.

Emojis as an Integral Part of a Brand

Visual language forms the foundation of a visual identity and has a major influence on the perception of a brand. This subchapter is dedicated to the question of how the rise and spread of emojis can be used for brand design. With the spread of emojis, many projects have emerged that use emojis as an integral part of a brand. They are thus part of their identity and act as an element of the visual language. In the following, projects are presented that use the potential of emojis in different ways as part of brand communication and thus use emojis as part of the visual identity.

Projects featured in this subchapter:

Waze
Pentagram New York

Visible
Pentagram New York

Tutti Frutti
Schultzschultz

Angelina Schmücker
707Krea

Channel 4
Pentagram London

Emojis have become an important means of communication in social interaction. Emojis can be used individually and thus contribute to a personal writing style or generate new meanings through their use (cf. Enzmann 2023a: 171). According to the autonomy thesis, the choice of emojis used can influence communication and generate meaningful content (see pages 115–117).

The rise and spread of pictorial signs also offers potential for the design of brand identities. One of the most important foundations for the success of a brand identity is its recognition value through the visual language and the emotional connection that the customer establishes with a brand. The term brand identity is used below for the visual identity of a brand. It is therefore used specifically for brands, while the term visual identity can also be used for a person such as an artist.

The first project presented, ›Waze‹, shows how emojis can become an integral part of a brand by using their branded emojis for communication within the app. The use of mascot-like characters creates a connection to the rise of kawaii aesthetic (see pages 65–95).

The next two projects – Visible and Tutti Frutti – take up the aesthetics of pre-emojis and use them creatively for the word mark of the respective brand. By taking up the formal characteristics of text-based emojis, Visible creates a visual reference to emoji communication. Tutti Frutti uses individual letters – similar to the characters in the fairy tale Scheuche (see page 27) – to create a brand.

In the fourth example, emojis are used as a visual element of a subbrand to create an emotional connection with the consumer. By anthropomorphizing fruits, they form an imaginary counterpart (see also page 72 f.).

The last project – the 4mojis – shows how emojis can be used as an integral part of a brand font and thus form part of the brand's visual language.

The aim of the subchapter is to show ways in which emojis can be used in different ways in the implementation of design tasks and thus become an integral part of a brand. The projects shown are just a few examples of applications; the potential of emojis as integral part of a brand is far from complete. The projects serve as inspiration and are intended to inspire how the potential of emojis can be used.

Brand Identity System Waze

PENTAGRAM
Design studio

»The brand identity system unifies the look of the Waze brand while supporting its joyful sense of individual expression.«

(Pentagram 2024a)

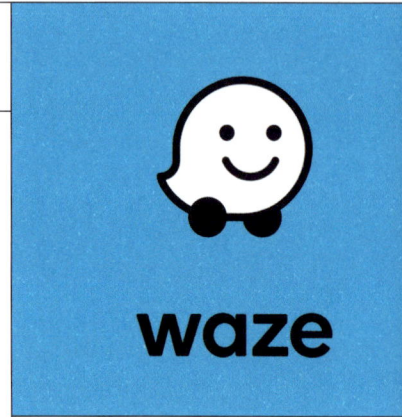

Fig. 700 **Waze brand** (Pentagram 2024a)

Pentagram is known for its innovative graphic design. Unsurprisingly, they recognized the potential of emojis and used them in several projects in different ways. One of these is the visual brand identity they created for Waze.

Office
New York

Partner
Natasha Jen

Waze's Creative Director
Jake Shaw

Project team
Yotam Hadar
Ran Zheng
Javier Arizu
Taylor Holland
John Sampson
Diego Prestes

Pentagram refreshed the brand identity for the navigation app Waze. They developed a sophisticated system for the brand with various revisions of the visual elements. The form of the logo (Fig. 700) takes on the shape of the speech bubble to visualize the app's focus on communication. The sans-serif font ›Boing‹ with its rounded corners reinforces the friendly look. In addition to revamping the logo, they introduced a series of new characters that allow users to communicate their mood and share their driving experiences (see 181 ff.).

The app combines a classic navigation app with social networking features, allowing users to update travel information in real-time. The aim is to use the connection to solve traffic problems in a way that is fun and functional. For this reason, Pentagram developed a colorful and inviting visual identity that reinforces a sense of individual expression.
To achieve this, the designers used a series of visual aids, all based on the same square grid (see Fig. 701, Fig. 706 and Fig. 707). The shapes based on this grid, which are used as a visual element of the brand in various applications, are inspired by the structure of the city grid (Fig. 705). These shapes form a flexible system that can be rearranged depending on the application.
The visual identity is characterized by its modular and flexible basis, which is built on a geometric grid.

»The system introduces a visual language called ›Block by Block‹, inspired by the modular design of the city grid.«

(Pentagram 2024a)

The basis is a square pattern in which the individual modules are connected to create a city-like structure (Fig. 704). The resulting shapes, which can range from simple to very hectic structures, are combined with vibrant colors (Fig. 705). These forms are used in various communication media, including the website, advertising materials, and moving formats such as animations.

Fig. 701 **the grid** (Pentagram 2024b)

Fig. 702 **excerpt from the style guide illustrating the application of the grid** (ibid.)

Fig. 703 **various sizes of grid units** (ibid.)

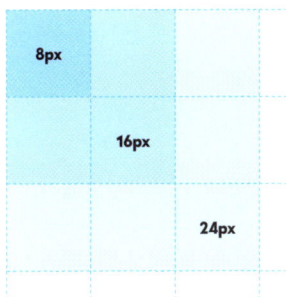

8px

16px

24px

Fig. 704 **excerpt from the style guide featuring a flexible basis** (ibid.)

Fig. 705 **the structure of the city grid with the transformation of shapes from Waze's visual language** (ibid.)

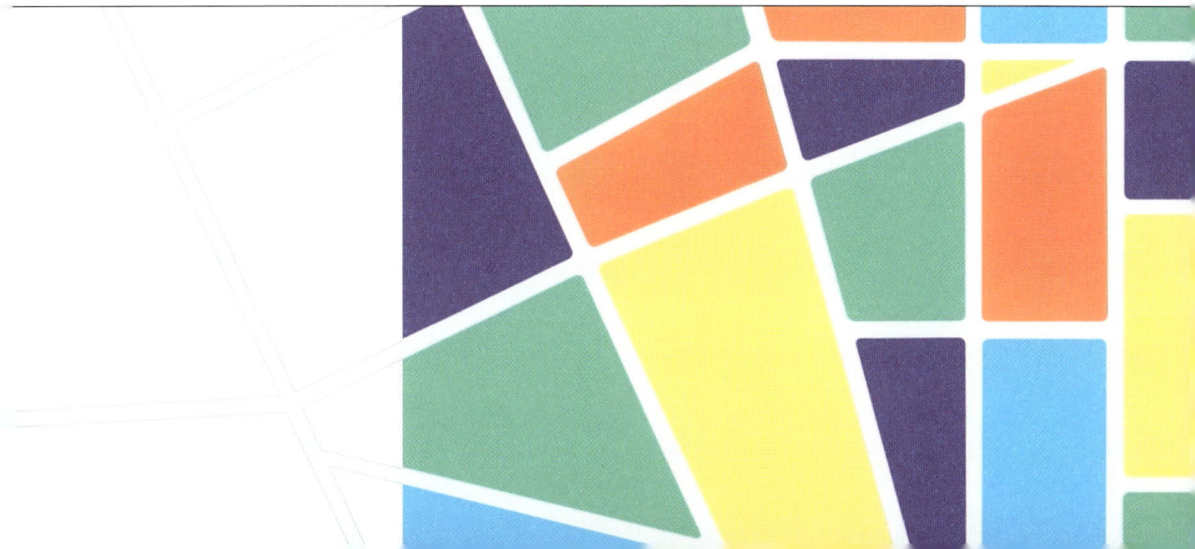

Fig. 706 **logo construction** (Pentagram 2024a)

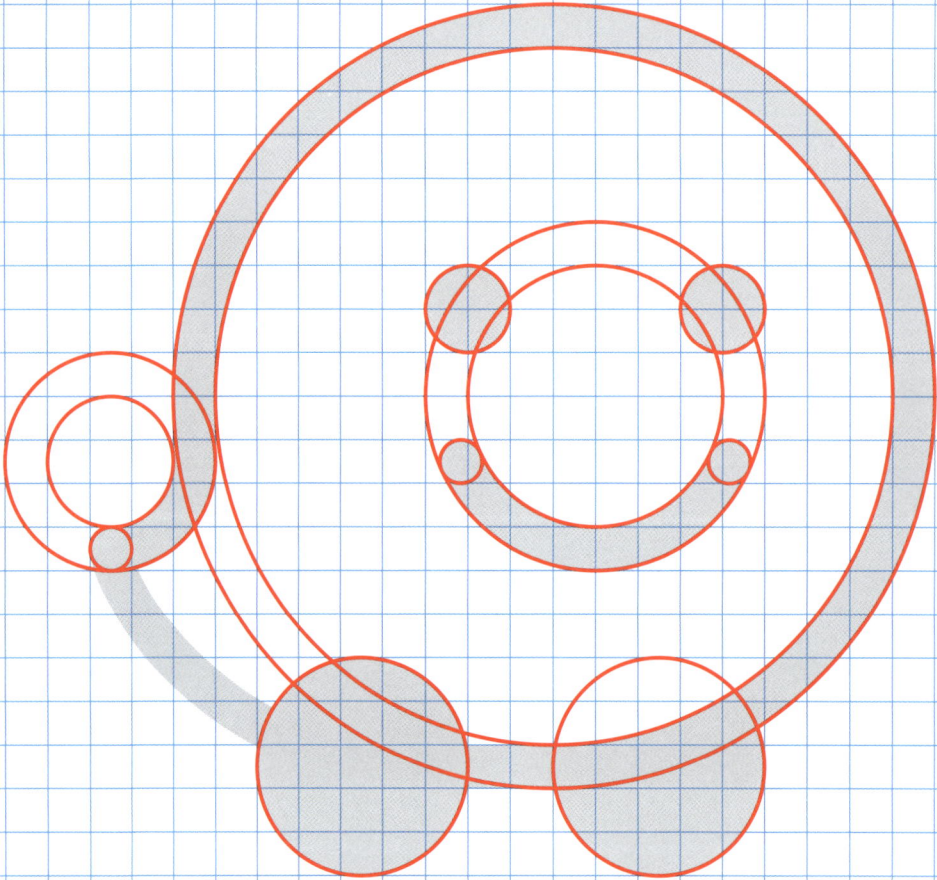

They also act as containers for the placement of photos. The colored shapes are used in combination with Waze's various mascot-like characters. The set of different characters serves to convey the emotional experience of driving (Fig. 708– Fig. 736). Derived from the logo, these signs depict the character in various emotional states. They are designed in a reduced, linear, geometric style with bold color. These humorous depictions reflect the variety of emotions a driver can experience while on the road. Moreover, these signs not only contribute to Waze's visual identity but also serve important communicative functions within the app.

In many characters, a clear reference to emojis and kawaii culture is recognizable. For example, characteristic facial expressions of emojis have been adopted, and typical features such as the rounded arch for the eyes are reminiscent of the

Fig. 707 **construction of Fig. 726** (according to Pentagram 2024a)

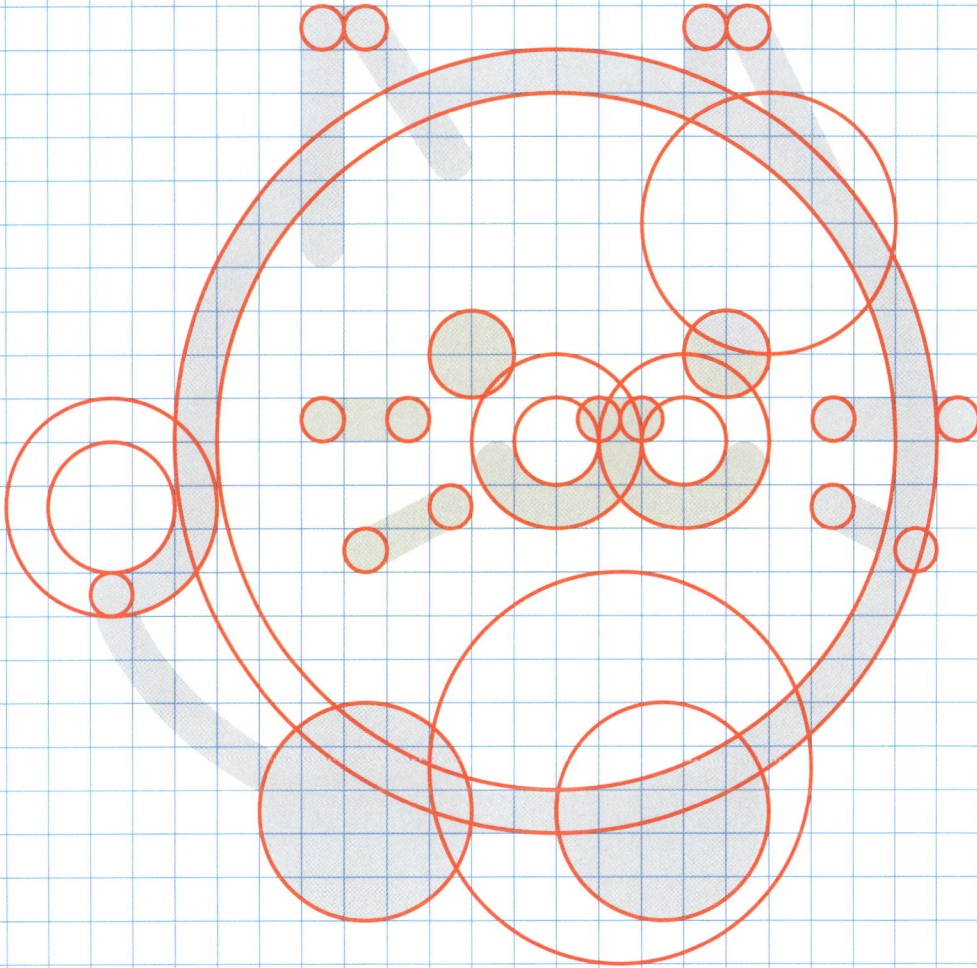

horizontal text-based emoji ^_^ (see page 44). How is the semiotic potential used? The illustrative elements are related to human behavior. However, the signs are not necessarily icons. For example, the American football helmet (Fig. 722), which stands for combative behavior, is not just an image of an American football helmet but is primarily associated with the act of football and linked to behavior in road traffic. It is not possible to derive the meaning of the sign from the image of the helmet alone; you have to know the sport associated with it to guess the meaning. The sign thus iconically depicts an American football helmet on the road but symbolically – through learned knowledge – refers to the sport of football and the ›combative‹ characteristic associated with it. In this way, the signs use the semiotic potential of emojis in different ways.

Fig. 708

Fig. 709

Fig. 710

Fig. 711

Fig. 712

Fig. 713

Fig. 714

Fig. 715

Fig. 716

Fig. 717

Fig. 718

Fig. 719

Fig. 720

Fig. 721

Fig. 722

Fig. 723

Fig. 724

Fig. 725

Fig. 726

For the creation of the numerous emojis used in Waze, research was conducted with 13,000 drivers to determine which emotions were essential in describing the daily commute (cf. Pentagram 2024b). These moods were designed in collaboration with FIG agency (cf. ibid.).

Fig. 727

Fig. 728

Fig. 729

Fig. 730

Fig. 731

Fig. 732

Fig. 733

Fig. 734

Fig. 735

Fig. 736

Fig. 737	Fig. 738	Fig. 739	Fig. 740	Fig. 741	Fig. 742

Fig. 743	Fig. 744	Fig. 745	Fig. 746	Fig. 747	Fig. 748

Fig. 749 **the navigation system in use** (Pentagram 2024a)

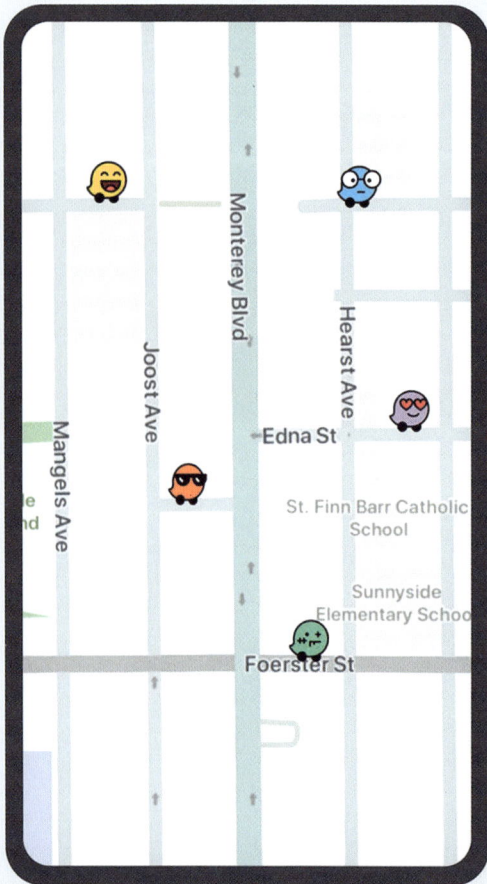

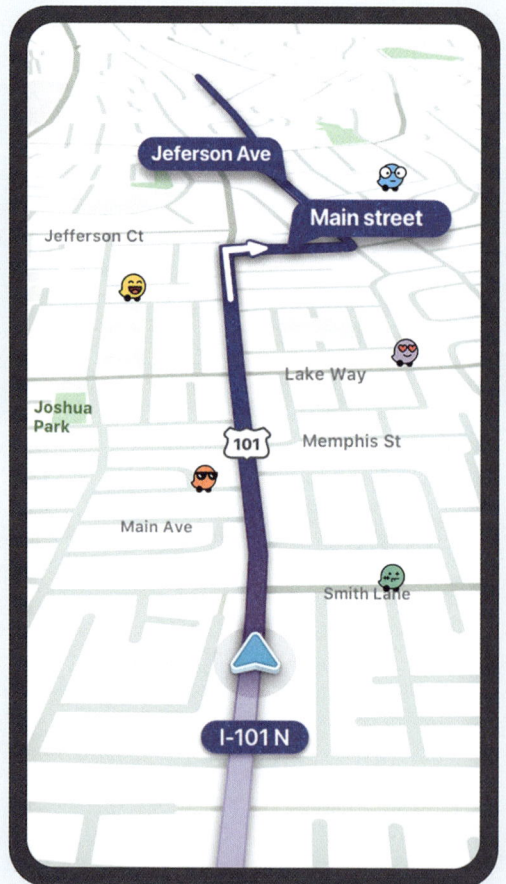

Fig. 750 **various illustrations for the app** (Pentagram 2024a)

Fig. 737 **police**
Fig. 738 **traffic**
Fig. 739 **roadside help**
Fig. 740 **hazard**
Fig. 741 **closure**
Fig. 742 **road construction**
Fig. 743 **gas prices**
Fig. 744 **map chat**
Fig. 745 **crash**
Fig. 746 **map issue**
Fig. 747 **camera**
Fig. 748 **place**
(Pentagram 2024a)

Fig. 751 **interface design of the report creation** (Pentagram 2024a)

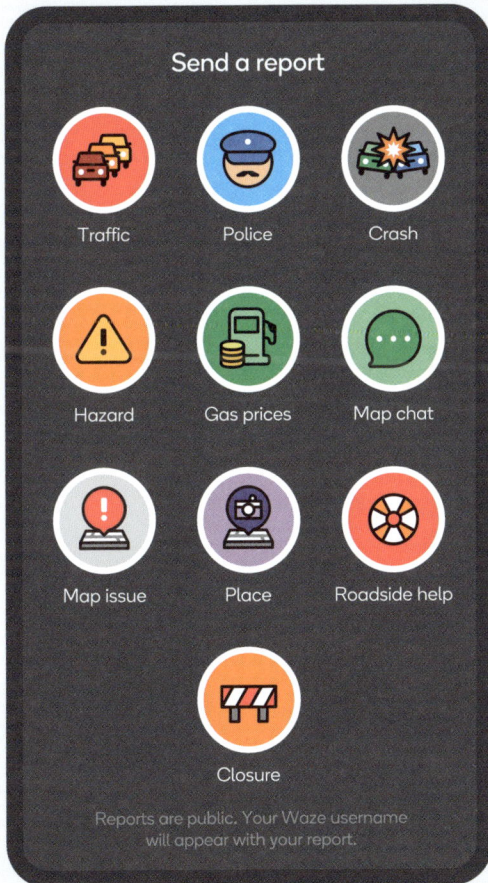

The visual language developed by Pentagram for Waze runs through the entire project. All visual elements are based on the grid, as well as the development of a series of icons (Fig. 737–Fig. 748). The colors and linear style are retained, but the illustrations are more oriented towards pictograms and contain typical traffic sign shapes, such as the triangle for hazard (Fig. 740) or the location sign (Fig. 748) to add a photo of a location for other users. The project contains numerous illustrations and icons (e.g., Fig. 750), which are based on the same principle and are partly animated.

The project demonstrates how a new development like the rise of emojis can be combined with fundamental design principles. Pentagram New York created a unique visual language for Waze, characterized by its linear style and bold colors. The use of different characters added an interpersonal layer, allowing users to interact and get real-time information about traffic. In addition, the characters provide entertainment and encourage active participation.

Waze is not the only project from Pentagram that utilizes the potential of emojis.[23] Another one, for example, takes up the formal language of text-based emojis and uses them to design a logo for a mobile phone provider. The project is presented and explained in detail on the following two pages.

23   There are other projects in their portfolio that use emojis in visual communication, such as Fisher-Price or Earthmojis, see also page 194.

Brand Identity Visible

vsble

Fig. 752 **Visible brand** (Pentagram 2024c)

»*The twin dots create a generative space where different icons can live – the face can smile, frown, laugh, wink and grin.*«

(Pentagram 2024c)

Office
New York

Partner
Natasha Jen

Project team
Joseph Han
Georgina McDonald

Visible is a wireless provider that offers its entire service in an app. Pentagram created a brand identity for Visible that is inspired by text-based chats, see also page 64. In doing so, they are addressing the fact that current text-based communication is characterized by the use of emojis.

»*We live in a smartphone-mediated world where texting is a prime means of communication, and through the use of emoticons and emojis, alphabets and pictures are increasingly one and the same.*«

(Pentagram, 2024d)

The fusion of letters and images is demonstrated with the font ›Sans Futura Heavy‹. By removing the stems of the letters ›i‹, space is created for an anthropomorphic element that speaks immediately to the viewer. The remaining i-dots function as a generative space that allows different facial expressions to be interpreted and created (cf. Pentagram 2024d). By combining letters and picture signs, they deliberately play with the iconic categorization threshold, see also page 110.

While the word Visible is below the iconic categorization threshold, the recognition of a face is above the categorization threshold.

Semiotically, the construct is also interesting, as the individual elements make use of different types of signs. By removing the letter elements, the word Visible is still legible, and the two i-dots as eyes create a kind of imaginary counterpart and communicate directly with the viewer – which in turn creates sympathy and a unique selling point. If a face is recognized in the logo, we are dealing with an iconic sign relation. If the face is in turn associated with an emotion, we speak of an indexical relationship. The recognition of the lettering, on the other hand, is based on a learned and symbolic language. This means that the sign relation is symbolic.

The creators from Pentagram intentionally play with the different sign relations by showing the logo or part of it animated. Short animations reflect the logo idea and show various emotions that can be created through the combination of font fragments (see Fig. 753, Fig. 755).

Fig. 753 **different facial expressions** (Pentagram 2024c)

Fig. 754 **combination of graphic language with photography** (Pentagram 2024c)

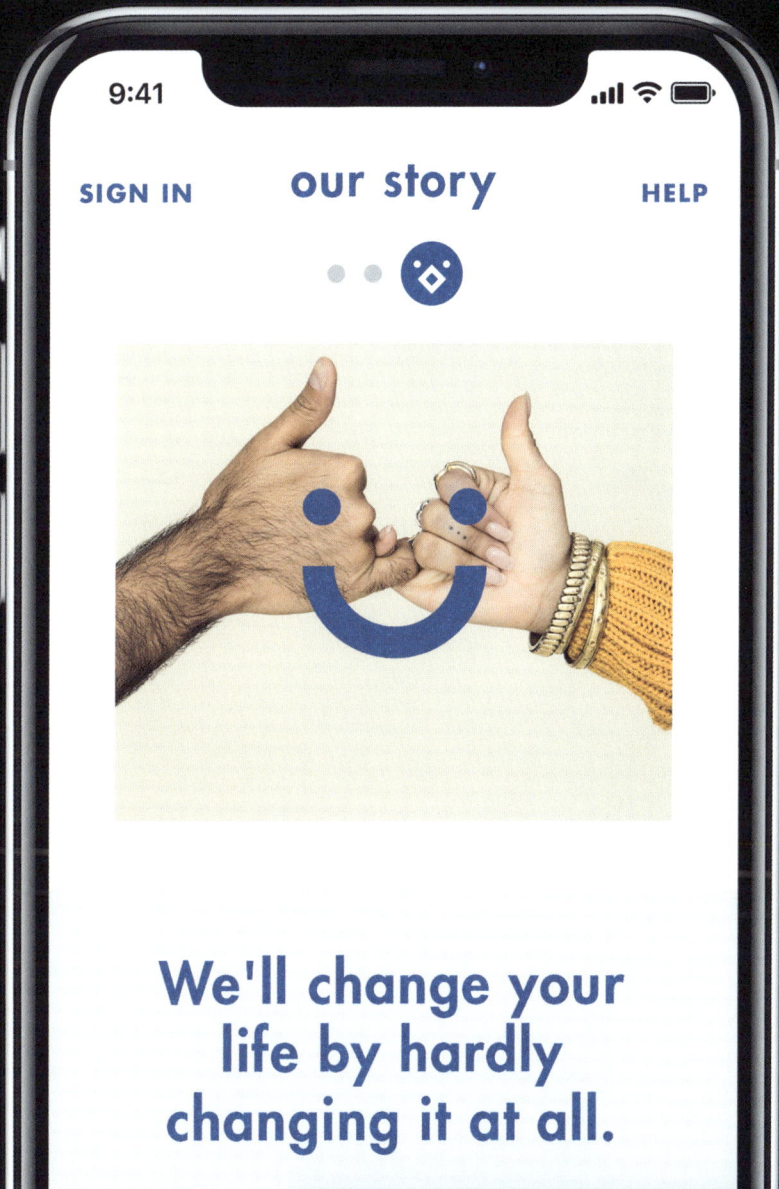

Fig. 755 **frames of the logo animation** (Pentagram 2024c)

Fig. 756

Brand Identity Tutti Frutti

SCHULTZSCHULTZ
Design studio

»The typographic constellation reflects the playful naming by creating a picture-like pattern through its arrangement.

Studio Schultzschultz is characterized by an experimental and innovative approach to typography based on a profound knowledge of type design. For the pizzeria ›Tutti Frutti‹, they created a logo that forms a pizza from elements of the name. The typographic approach is reminiscent of the typesetters' earlier creations (see pages 24–27).

Client
Tutti Frutti

Design
Schultzschultz

Year
2016

Marc Schütz and Ole Schulte founded Studio Schultzschultz in Frankfurt am Main in 2007. They are known for their abstract and often pattern-like use of typography, which is frequently based on technologically innovative methods and tools.

Schütz, a passionate typographer with a distinct sense for details and complex type design, created the Tutti Frutti logo (Fig. 756).

As with text-based emojis, the arbitrary letters are put together to form an image – the pizza – through their constellation. In addition to the text-based emojis, the typographical approach is also reminiscent of the anthropomorphized letters in the fairy tale ›die Scheuche‹ (see page 27). While in the fairy tale the individual letters became figures, in the Tutti Frutti logo the rounded and stencil-like letters are arranged in a circle similar to a pizza topping and thus form a pattern-like structure in which the word ›Tutti Frutti‹ can be read. The interruption of the line at the top left serves as a kind of reading orientation aid, as it makes it

easier for the viewer to recognize the beginning of the word, as Schütz discovered during the design process.

The letters themselves are considered symbolic, as they have to be learned in order to be understood. Through their arrangement, however, they are iconically recognized as pizza and thus liberated from their symbolic meaning. As the individual letters are not chosen randomly but represent the name of the pizzeria, the letters have a double function: on the one hand, they represent the restaurant's signature product and, on the other, they function as a word mark.

The project is a great example of how typographic constellations can be used to benefit from the advantages of pictorial representations. According to Frutiger, despite the internalization of language, we find it easier to look at a picture than to understand a spoken or written message (cf. Frutiger 2004: 224).

Fig. 757 **pizza by Tutti Frutti on the pizza plate by Schultzschultz**

Subbrand Angelina Schmücker

707KREA
Design office

»Kawaii embodies joy and the happiness we experience in everyday life — just like a good glass of wine. «

Fig. 758 **brand of Angelina Schmücker**

707Krea from Frankfurt designed the brand identity for Angelina Schmücker and its subbrand ›Urban‹ with customized emojis for the wine.

Client
Angelina Schmücker

Design
707Krea

Fig. 759 **derivation of the brand idea**

Schmücker + Angelina =

Terroir + Craft + Enjoyment =

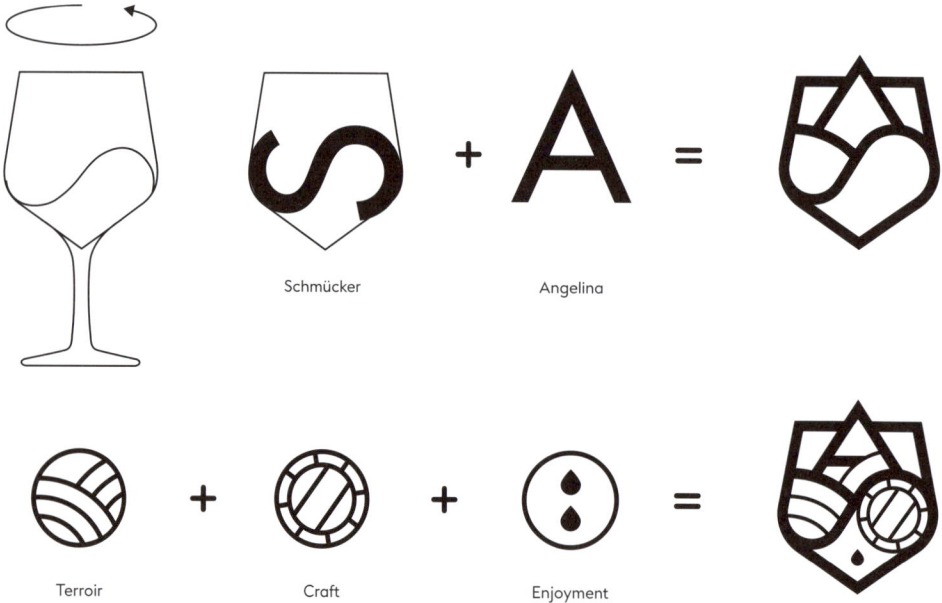

Fig. 760 **primary color**   50%   25%

Fig. 761 **baseline** (photo by Claudio Briguglio)

This project aims to demonstrate how emojis can be integrated as part of a subbrand. The Urban subbrand was created for the winemaker Angelina Schmücker, who aimed to target a younger audience with a new line of wines. The subbrand is intended to stand out from the standard visual language of Schmücker's brand identity, but remain recognizable as part of it. To provide better insight into the brand identity, Schmücker's visual language is presented before the subbrand.

The wine industry is characterized by a long tradition. Angelina Schmücker is a young winemaker with a lot of passion and energy. It is important to her to keep traditions, but still establish her own signature. 707Krea created a visual identity that embodies tradition and modernity. The tradition of winemaking is presented in the form of a coat of arms (Fig. 758). The shape is derived from the wine glass and the initials of the winemaker (see Fig. 759). The winemaker's work above and below ground is visualized by the elements terroir, the wine barrel, which stands for the work in the wine cellar and the two drops that stand for enjoyment. The linear and geometric visual language, paired with the strong color turquoise, embodies the modernity of the winemaker. There is a reduced and a more detailed version of the brand. The reduced logo is used for reasons of space or for certain wine lines.

The design for the subbrand ›Urban‹ was created with the aim of creating a wine line that is fun and appeals to a younger audience. The development of a new visual language should consciously stand out from the brand design, but be easy to integrate. 707Krea developed its own visual language for this, which is based on the existing brand design but has clear unique selling points. The geometric basis and the linear style were adopted and combined with playful elements, like a free-drawn lettering and emojis that stand for the joy, sociality and spontaneity of wine drinking.
The free-drawn Urban lettering is based on circles and has a consistent thickness (Fig. 762). To create sympathy, the circle was chosen as the basic element for the construction of the letters.

The flexibility of the young generation is visualized by a flowing design approach and gives the font a modern touch. In addition, the shape is reminiscent of liquid and the dancing play of the letters stands for the joy of drinking wine. The rounded and fluid character of the lettering supports the message of the subbrand. Pastel colors (Fig. 765) were chosen that harmonize well with the primary color (Fig. 760) of the brand. To visualize the taste of the wine, two fruits were assigned to each wine (Fig. 766-Fig. 771).

One of these was anthropomorphized in the kawaii aesthetic to communicate cheerfulness, friendliness and joy.

All elements of the subbrand are based on the same circle sizes (see page 192 f.), whereby the geometric and linear style of the corporate design is continued in the subbrand.

The fruit emoji are not only used in print, but also as animated stickers in social networks to strengthen the identity of the subbrand.

Fig. 762 **construction of the lettering urban with circles**

Fig. 763 **construction of the flavour strawberry with six basic circles**

Fig. 764 **structure of the characters in the style of Risograph aesthetics**

Fig. 765 **secondary colors**

FLAVOUR EMOJIS ROSÉ		FLAVOUR EMOJIS SAUVIGNON BLANC		FLAVOUR EMOJIS PINOT GRIS	
Fig. 766 **strawberry**	Fig. 767 **blueberry**	Fig. 768 **gooseberry**	Fig. 769 **pear**	Fig. 770 **apple**	Fig. 771 **apricot**
Fig. 772 **Rosé**		Fig. 773 **Sauvignon Blanc**		Fig. 774 **Pinot Gris**	

Fig. 775 **apple with six basic circles**

Fig. 776 **pear with six basic circles**

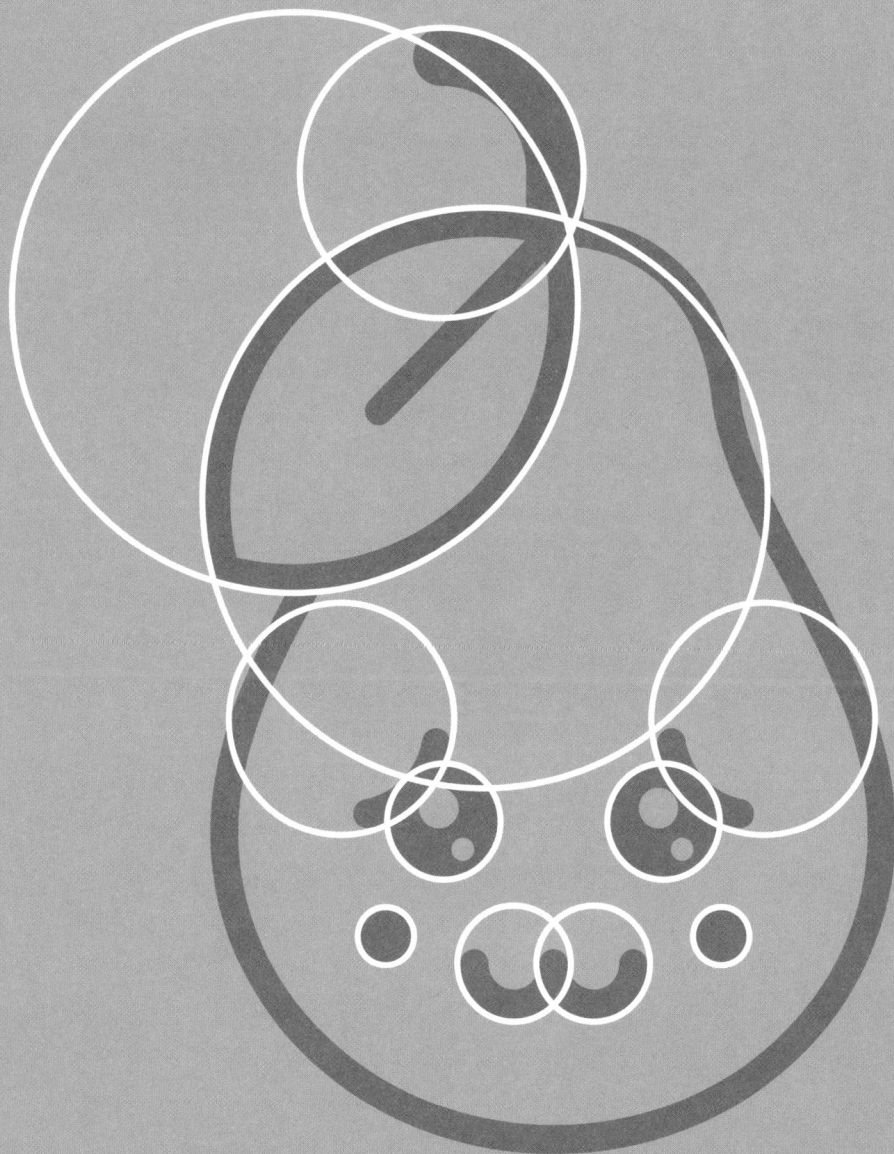

Brand Identity Channel 4

PENTAGRAM
Design studio

»Designed with practicality at its forefront, consistent typography and layout principles are coupled with playful moments that reveal Channel 4's mischievousness, such as the 4mojis integrated with the brand typefaces.«

(Pentagram 2024e)

Fig. 777   **Channel 4 logo** (Pentagram 2024e)

The creative minds at Pentagram London created a master brand for the British broadcaster ›Channel 4‹ that unites all channel brands, content and streaming services under one roof. They designed a stringently thought-out system that impresses with the integration of numerous details, such as the 4mojis. Movement, interaction and composition principles form the basis of the visual language.

Client
Channel 4

Pentagram Office
London

Partners
Luke Powell
Jody Hudson-Powell
Naresh Ramchandani

Collaborators
NaN
Found Studio
Stink Studio
Factory Studios and
Siren
Mat Heinl

Project team
Nav Bhatia
Jack Llewellyn
Ashley Johnson
Luis Gutiérrez
Alice Sherwin
Hazal Ozkaya
Isla Wickham
Kate Heller
Robyn Siân Cusworth
Zoë Gibson Quirk

Fig. 778   **the identity is built around three-dimensional cube spaces** (Pentagram 2024e)

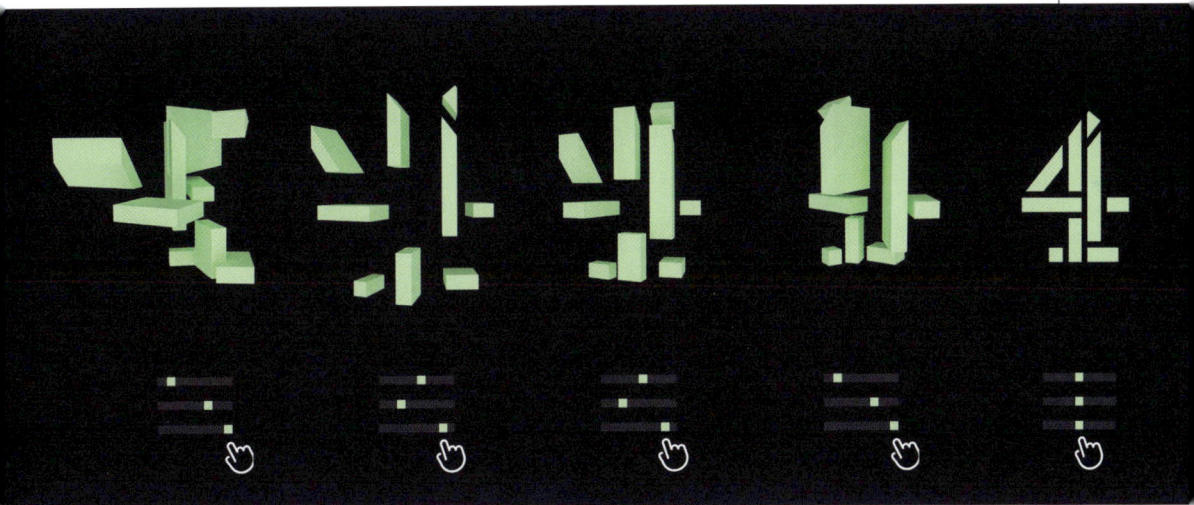

Fig. 779　**4 logo parametric motion behavior** (Pentagram 2024e)

Fig. 780　**the colorful worlds form the heart of the masterbrand** (ibid.)

Fig. 781 **pen branding** (Pentagram 2024e)

Fig. 782 **bucket hatbranding** (ibid.)

The brand identity centers on the 4 logo (Fig. 777). The logo is used both statically and in animated form (Fig. 779). The movements of the logo are based on a variable parametric system that can react to the different moods and functions of Channel 4 (cf. Pentagram 2024e). ›4 is a traveler‹ serves as a brand narrative as Channel 4 guides its viewers through different cube-based worlds, like a traveler guiding us through a universe of content. The colorful worlds form the heart of the masterbrand (Fig. 780). The theme of travel is also emphasized visually with camera movements that characterize the brand. The camera moves through the different cubes using core movement principles (Fig. 778), bringing the viewer into the universe of content, guided by the 4 logo.

While the colors green and black are mainly used to signify the core brand (Fig. 781, Fig. 782), the individual worlds are very colorful, like the channel's programming. The immersive color gradients and the shrill spectrum of the brand colors bring the universe to life. In this way, they reflect Channel 4's diverse content. The brand typeface includes standard, condensed and extended styles, each in eight different weights. The typeface was enriched with a set of pictorial signs – the ›4mojis‹ (see pages 198–199). The motifs of the pictorial signs allow use in both functional applications and expressive marketing contexts.

The 4mojis design language aligns with the typographic features of the brand fonts so that they work well in combination with the typography.

Fig. 783 **keynote template for the brand** (ibid.)

Current: Slide 1 of 54   Speaker notes

According to Pentagram, they point to the mischievousness of Channel 4 and offer a playful approach to the brand (ibid.).

Pentagram provides several examples of emoji usage in the application (see Fig. 783). Below, we discuss one example using the descriptive framework and Peirce's semiotics to establish a theoretical connection (see page 11 and pages 102–107).

In the example, sparkles are placed after ›Speaking now‹ This could suggest Emily Todd's speech has been anticipated. The emojis, depicting three stars, can represent the idea of stars or celebrities speaking. That sparkles can stand for celebrities is based on a convention and can be described as symbolic. If we were to interpret the stars as an image of celestial bodies, they would be iconic. However, they also function as an index when indicating enthusiasm for an upcoming event or conveying a positive sentiment. According to the descriptive framework, the emojis serve the function 📍 when indicating the audience anticipation for Emily Todd's speech or ⊗ when signifying an exciting programme underway.

With the design of the brand, Pentagram has created a bold and minimalist graphic language, peppered with playfulness through the 4mojis and color gradients. Pentagram has developed a system of behavioral principles that connects the brand's identity across all platforms (cf. Pentagram 2024e).

Fig. 784

Fig. 785

Fig. 792

Fig. 786

Fig. 787

Fig. 788

Fig. 789

Fig. 790

Fig. 791

Fig. 793

Fig. 794

Fig. 795

Fig. 796

Fig. 797

Fig. 798

Fig. 799

Fig. 800

Fig. 801

Stream tonight
Coming soon ⊙⊙

Fig. 802

Fig. 803

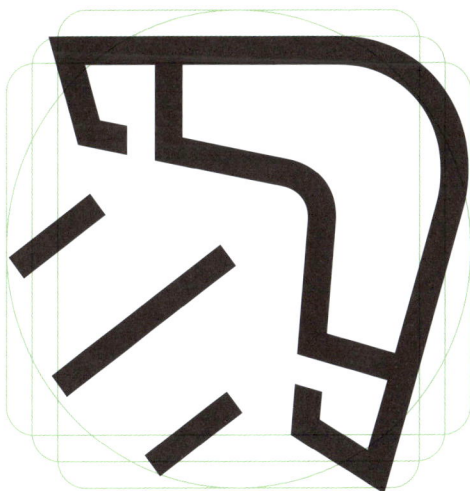

The 4mojis are used throughout brand applications, such as on screen presentation, web, social media, and classic print media in combination with the brand typefaces.

Most of the motifs are based on the emojis that are coded in Unicode. For example, ›sparkles‹ (Fig. 784), ›framed picture‹ (Fig. 786), ›performing arts‹ (Fig. 787), ›index finger pointing to the right‹ (Fig. 788), ›alien‹ (Fig. 790), ›rocket‹ (Fig. 791), ›smiling face with horns‹ (Fig. 792), ›video camera‹ (Fig. 795), ›index finger pointing downward‹ (Fig. 796), ›high voltage‹ (Fig. 797), ›house with garden‹ (Fig. 799), ›grinning face with big eyes‹ (Fig. 798), ›popcorn‹ (Fig. 800), ›eyes‹ (Fig. 802) and ›boomerang‹ (Fig. 803).

The character set also contains custom emoji motifs or modified emojis (see Fig. 785, Fig. 789, Fig. 794, Fig. 801).

Fig. 784–Fig. 791 **4mojis**
Fig. 792–Fig. 793 **4mojis in the grid**
Fig. 794–Fig. 801 **4mojis**
Fig. 802 **use of a 4moji for a program announcement**
Fig. 803 **4moji in the grid**

All 4mojis come from Pentagram and were designed as part of the brand identity design process for Channel 4.

(Emoji-)Stickers in Illustration and Art

With the emergence and constant change of new media, a visual identity must be able to react flexibly to different requirements. One way to reinforce and flexibly apply the presence of visual identities is to create sticker packs. Such stickers do not have to function directly as an integral part of a brand, but can take up selective elements of the visual language to refer to a visual identity. In the following, design projects are presented that illustrate the use of sticker packs to support and reinforce the visual identity with different approaches.

Projects featured in this subchapter:

YouTube Shorts
Mat Voyce

Locale Stickers
Mat Voyce

Arigato Nippon
Sarah Furrer

Summer Campaign for Kiehl's
Dan Woodger

As this book shows, emojis have formally developed in different directions in the process of their spread. Technical limitations have created further possibilities for how emojis can be used, as the Zouzoukwa project shows, for example. From a formal perspective, it is difficult to distinguish when a sign should be classified as an emoji and when as an illustration. However, based on the technical use of the signs, a distinction can be seen between (emoji-)stickers and illustrations. By using pictorial signs in a digital context to fulfil the same or similar functions as emojis, the signs can be seen as part of emojization. Although the signs are not created like conventional emojis from a design perspective, the technical possibilities of the development are used to utilize them.

The first project shows how digital stickers can be part of an overall brand language for an event to reinforce its visibility on different platforms while still keeping the designer's signature – in this case mainly through the animation style – recognizable. Such an approach offers a flexible application of stickers that are not directly part of the brand, as in the projects from the previous chapter, but which pick up on significant features of the brand, such as the logo, typography or colors, and communicate the visual language of the brand. The second project is by the same designer as the first, but

expresses its own visual language even more clearly by using fewer visual elements of the brand.

The third project demonstrates how stickers can utilize an additional level of communication for the project that has been established through the spread of digital stickers. With this project, the artist shows how a visual language in the form of digital stickers can be used to express visual language of the book and the visual identity of the artist.

The fourth project shows how digital stickers are used in the context of a collaboration, a brand and an artist, where the stickers represent the philosophy and background of the brand through the choice of motifs, but the visual language is clearly associated with the visual identity of the artist.

The application of the stickers extends across various digital platforms, including websites, social media and animations. The versatile integration makes it possible to present visual identities in a dynamic way, with the individual stickers picking up on parts of the visual identity and interacting with them on different channels. Stickers allow images or videos to be enriched with a visual language and to be assigned more directly to an identity.

Due to their mostly animated form, they create constantly moving visual elements that transcend the static boundaries of traditional corporate designs and can become part of a flexible system.

Sticker Pack YouTube Shorts Drive Thru

MAT VOYCE
Type Designer & Animator

»It's got to the point where I feel strange about sharing illustration and typography that doesn't move or animate. I now design something with motion in mind, even if it's supposed to be static!«

(Voyce in: May 2020)

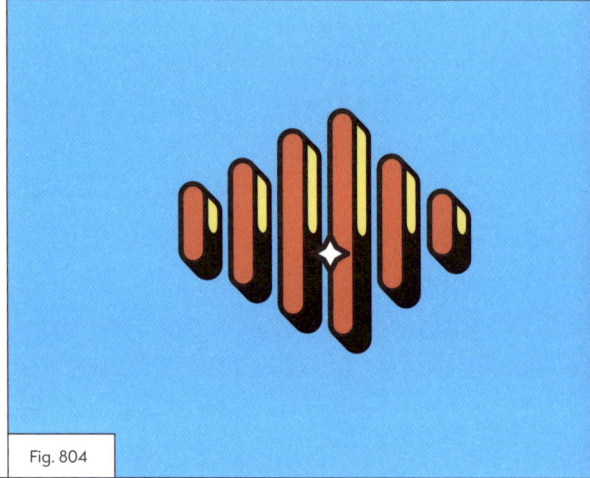

Fig. 804

As part of the ›YouTube Shorts Drive Tru‹ at the video convention ›VidCon‹, various stickers were created that pick up on and visualize the brand and the event concept. The stickers were proposed by Voyce for the event and take up different brand characteristics of YouTube and its presence at the video convention.

Client
YouTube

Event
YouTube Shorts Drive Thru
(for VidCon 2022)

Year
2022

Design & Motion
Mat Voyce
Saint Urbain

Mat Voyce is definitely a specialist in the creation of sticker packs with his unique animation style, see also pages 154–155. His stickers are mostly short, concise loops that are realized in the form of GIFs. His animation style is characterized by the use of different layers that move with a time delay. This gives his animations their dynamic and unmistakable style. The minimalist movements are skillfully created and are complemented by visual elements such as stars (e.g. Fig. 804), which are based on visual forms of representation from comics, see page 109.

He develops a wide variety of sticker packs for clients, which reflect their visual identity in different ways.[24] Despite constantly changing visual elements and different color palettes, the presence of Voyce's unmistakable style runs through the diversity of his colorful creations. His sticker creations are mostly used in social media, on websites, in advertising or in videos.

In 2022, he created a sticker pack for the ›YouTube Shorts Drive Thru‹, their activation at VidCon that year. According to Voyce, these stickers are proposed to be part of an overall brand language that falls under a 90s theme, sticker-bombing various set elements and aligning with the graphics, typography, and imagery that were key to that era. The stickers use various elements of the brand, such as

24   See for example his sticker pack for Lacoste (Voyce 2024c) or his fictional stickers for Nike, Netflix and Star Wars (Voyce 2024d).

the logo (Fig. 810), the event visual (see Fig. 805, Fig. 806 or Fig. 814) or the brand colors red and black. Although he adapts his style to the respective brand, his own visual language is present. This can be seen not only in the animation language, but also, for example, in the use of his linear and geometric illustration style. He uses cartoon-like illustrations, such as the white glove (Fig. 809), which is reminiscent of Mickey Mouse. To create, in addition to the logo and the colors, another level of connection to the YouTube brand, the stickers also incorporate visual elements of the film, such as a film reel (Fig. 813), the pictorial sign for a soundtrack (Fig. 804) or for a clapperboard (Fig. 808). In order to provide a kind of cinema experience, he also incorporates elements associated with the cinema, such as an admission ticket (Fig. 809) or typical cinema snacks (Fig. 805 or Fig. 811). The stickers reflect the brand on different levels. On the one hand, by picking up on the visual brand-relevant characteristics, such as the colors or the logo, and on the other hand, by responding to motifs that are linked to the brand, such as elements that are linked to the topic of film.

The project is a good example of how digital stickers can be used to reflect a visual language in order to make the visual identity visible on different channels and respond flexibly to different uses.

Fig. 804–Fig. 814 Stickers from Voyce proposed as part of ›YouTube Shorts Drive Thru‹ and their activity at VidCon 2022.

Fig. 805

Fig. 806

Fig. 807

Fig. 808

Fig. 809

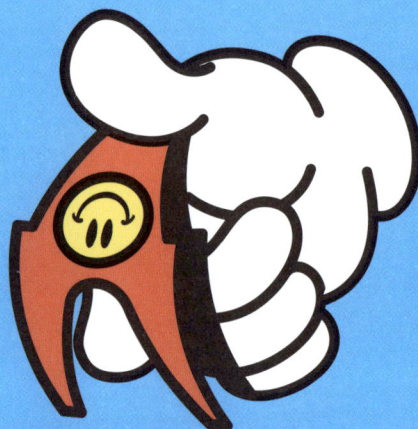

Fig. 810

Fig. 811

Fig. 812

Fig. 813

Fig. 814

GIPHY Locale Stickers

Voyce designed locale stickers for ›GIPHY‹, which are made available by the platform as animated GIF files on social media.

Client
Giphy

Year
2020

Design & Motion
Mat Voyce

The 15 location stickers designed by Voyce are based on cities and countries from around the world. Various pictorial signs are combined with the name of the respective city or country to form a sticker. The pictorial signs represent local features or landmarks. From the CN Tower in Toronto (Fig. 825) to the noodles of Bangkok (Fig. 820) and the crown of England (Fig. 835), the signs cover a wide variety of areas. Most of the pictorial signs can be considered iconically. For example, Fig. 824 shows the image of a snowflake. The pictorial sign can be interpreted as an sign for snow and is therefore iconically.

In contrast, however, a snowflake can also be indexical for cold, in that the snow is interpreted as a sign for cold. There is a causal connection between snowflakes and cold.

The Japanese flag on the local sticker of Tokyo (Fig. 822) is also initially an image of the flag. However, the flag is symbolic of the country and must be learned in order to be understood.

Depending on how a sign is interpreted in relation to the country or the respective culture, the semioticity changes, see also pages 102–107.

PICTORIAL SIGNS FOR CDMX (Voyce 2024e)

Fig. 815

Fig. 816

Fig. 817

PICTORIAL SIGNS FOR BANGKOK (ibid.)

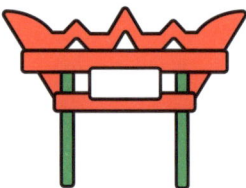

Fig. 818

Fig. 819

Fig. 820

Fig. 821 **local sticker for India** (ibid.)

Fig. 822 **local sticker for Tokyo** (ibid.)

PICTORIAL SIGNS FOR CANADA (ibid.)

Fig. 823

Fig. 824

Fig. 825

PICTORIAL SIGNS FOR NORWAY (ibid.)

Fig. 826	Fig. 827	Fig. 828

PICTORIAL SIGNS FOR AUSTRALIA (ibid.)

Fig. 829	Fig. 830	Fig. 831
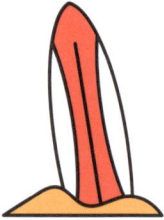		

Fig. 832 **local sticker for Hong Kong** (ibid.)

PICTORIAL SIGNS FOR LONDON (ibid.)

Fig. 833

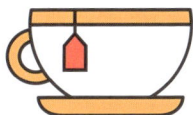

Fig. 834

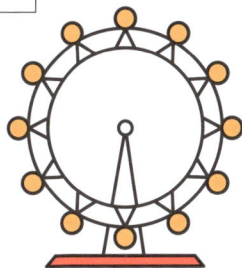

Fig. 835

Fig. 836 **local sticker for Dubai** (ibid.)

PICTORIAL SIGNS FOR SWEDEN (ibid.)

Fig. 837

Fig. 838

Fig. 839

Arigato Nippon

SARAH FURRER
Illustrator & Mural Artist

»Some Japanese see culture as a process from gradual disappearance of traditional, natural darkness to modern illumination. This is in Arigato Nippon expressed through the fusion of analog and digital media.«

Fig. 840 **Sarah Furrer**

Arigato Nippon is an illustrated book that offers an insight into Japanese culture. It contains a mix of analog and digitally animated stickers that not only reflect the visual language of the book, but also capture the unique visual identity of the creator.

Design & concept
SAFU Sarah Furrer

Text
Kevin Bloch
Yoko Inaba
Arisa Sigrist

Animation
Klub Galopp

Artist support
somewhere LAB

Print
Drucken3000

In her book, Furrer offers insights into her impressions and experiences during a trip to Japan. She illustrates traditional elements and visualizes them in her signature style. The illustrations and short texts contain lively narratives that capture the nuanced and often humorous experiences, making each illustration part of a larger story.

In addition to the artist's subjective experiences and lots of information about Japanese culture, the book also contains insights in the form of interviews with locals on relevant topics such as the importance of feminism in Japan.

Some of the illustrations were realized as analog and digital stickers. By animating a few of the illustrations, the author uses an additional layer of communication that has become established through the spread of digital stickers. The minimalist animations for the book were created as digital stickers and their appearance clearly illustrates the visual language of the book.

The book is consistently presented in the colors red and black and is complemented by graphic elements and the unique illustrations. Furrer creates her illustrations in an analog way before coloring them digitally.

To realize the book, Furrer resorted to the traditional Japanese stencil printing process of risography. The resulting typical aesthetic reflects the theme of the book, but also the artist's visual identity, which was influenced early on by manga and anime and is clearly recognizable in her style.

The project is a great example of how illustrations or visual elements from a project can be used to spread a visual language, for example on social media, and establish the artist's visual identity.

Fig. 841 **cat** (Furrer 2023: 81)

Fig. 842 **rest of japanese breakfast** (ibid.: 81)

Fig. 843 **Arigato Nippon** (ibid.: 86-87) photo by Laura Egger

Fig. 844 **illustration from Arigato Nippon** (Furrer 2023: 74)

Fig. 845 **maneki-neko with koinobori** (ibid.: 81)

Fig. 847 **uchiwa** (ibid.: 79)

Fig. 846 **kokeshi** (ibid.: 81)

Fig. 848 **inu-hariko** (ibid.)

Fig. 849 **dango** (ibid.: 29)

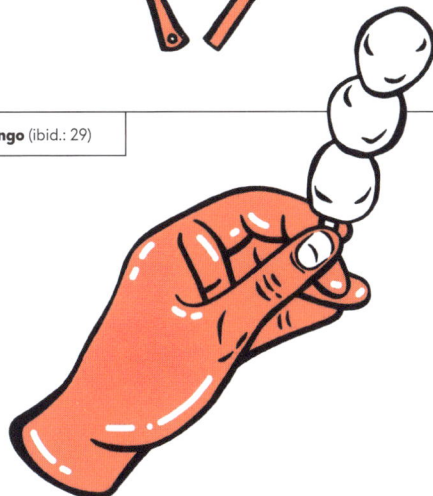

Fig. 850 **gyoza** (Furrer 2023: 14)

Fig. 851 **matcha set** (ibid.: 14)

Fig. 852 **anmitsu** (ibid.: 29)

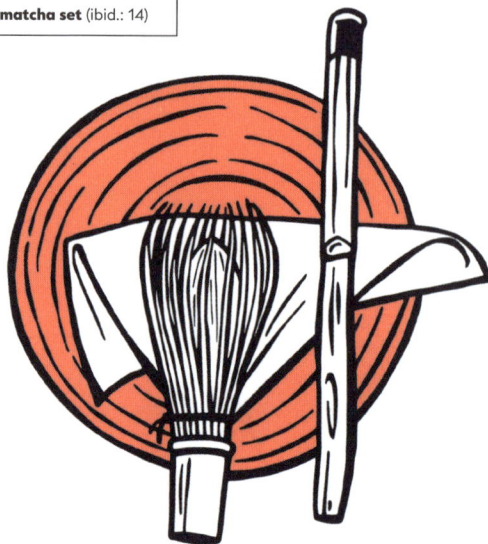

Fig. 853 **rice** (ibid.: 14)

Fig. 854 **nigiri sushi** (ibid.: 24–25)

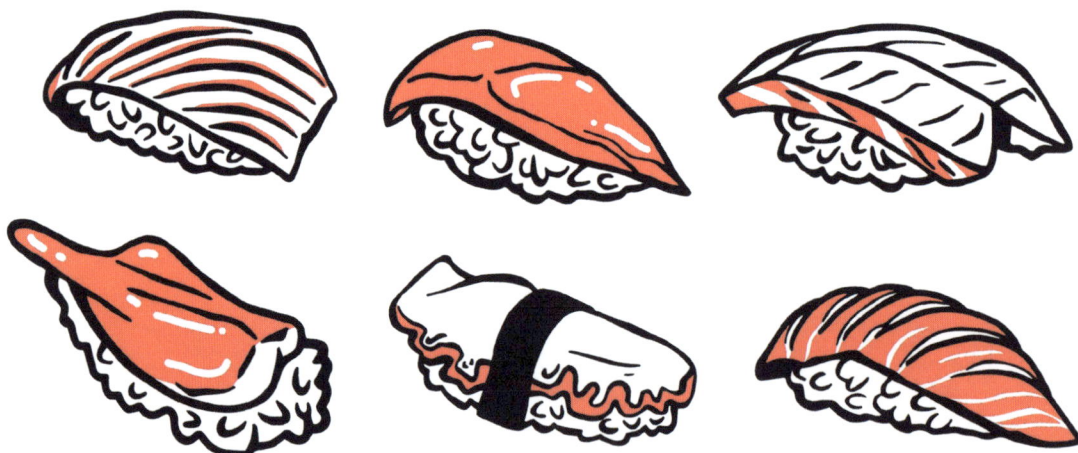

Fig. 855 **illustration from Arigato Nippon** (ibid.: 20)

Summary Campaign Kiehl's

DAN WOODGER
Illustrator & animaton director

»I create colourful, playful, character-based work designed to brighten your day and make you smile.«

(Woodger 2024b)

Fig. 856

Woodger created a series of illustrations for the summer campaign for Kiehl's. He realized some characters from his artworks as digital stickers. These have his distinctive signature, which shows his visual identity as an artist.

Client
Kiehl's

Year
2023

Illustration
Dan Woodger

Animation
Dan Woodger
Jordan Pledge
Ben Marsh

3D visualizations
Studio Yatta

The skin care brand Kiehl asked Woodger to design a summer campaign. The joyful campaign was launched for China's 6.18 Shopping Festival.

With the collaboration, Woodger lent his style to the skincare brand, using his colorful creations to convey the core philosophy of the campaign and the background of the brand.
His illustrations clearly reflect his style, although the artist's choice of motifs is based on both the history of the brand and the upcoming festival. As the products have a scientific background, many of the illustrations are based on this and visualize the work in the research laboratory. In addition to elements that reflect the shopping (Fig. 866, Fig. 867) and festival experience (Fig. 862, Fig. 863), there are numerous illustrations that depict the skincare process in a humorous way (Fig. 868). Woodger also designed limited edition products and the associated packaging design, such as gift boxes, make-up bags (Fig. 859) and shopping bags.

The illustrations were also realized as digital stickers and used for advertising. The result is a colorful, imaginative world that playfully focuses on the products.

Characteristic of Woodger's illustrations is the skillful fusion of geometric shapes with the liveliness of comic figures and the narrative flair of comics.

»Inspired by a childhood diet of 90's cartoons my work is an invitation to never grow up and to always find humour in the stupid world around us.«

(Woodger 2024b)

The illustrations act as Woodger's authentic visual language and humorously reflect the spirit of the cheerful campaign.
The choice of motifs created a connection to the brand, while Woodger's distinctive style remains recognizable as his visual language and represents his visual identity as an artist.

Fig. 857

Fig. 858

Fig. 859 **packaging design for Kiehl's**

Fig. 860

Fig. 861

Fig. 862

Fig. 864

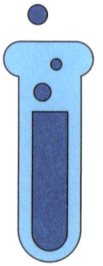

Fig. 865

Fig. 863

The illustrations are based on basic geometric shapes such as circles and rectangles, which are combined with dynamic cartoon elements. One example of this is the illustration Fig. 868, whose head is based on the basic shape of the circle. The dramatic, steadfast pose, accompanied by oversized feet and hands, emphasizes the central message of careful skin care.

The faces of the figures are highly stylized and depicted from a clear perspective, allowing the viewer a high degree of identification (see pages 110–117). In terms of the iconic categorization threshold, the illustrations are classified at roughly above the level of graphic emojis, see page 110. In addition, Woodger uses the anthropomorphiza-tion of objects (Fig. 862, Fig. 870) to create a kind of imaginary counterpart and thus arouse sympathy (see page 114). In combination with the bold and saturated colors, Woodger creates a lively and energetic atmosphere with a good mood.

The project demonstrates how the artist's unique visual language is kept and communicated and perceived as a colloboration even though the collaboration with the Kiehl's brand. In addition, the project illustrates how the potential of digital stickers can be used to create a certain mood and thus support a brand philosophy. The versatile use on different media also enables a flexible approach to visual communication.

Fig. 866

Fig. 867

Fig. 868

Fig. 869

Fig. 870

Fig. 871

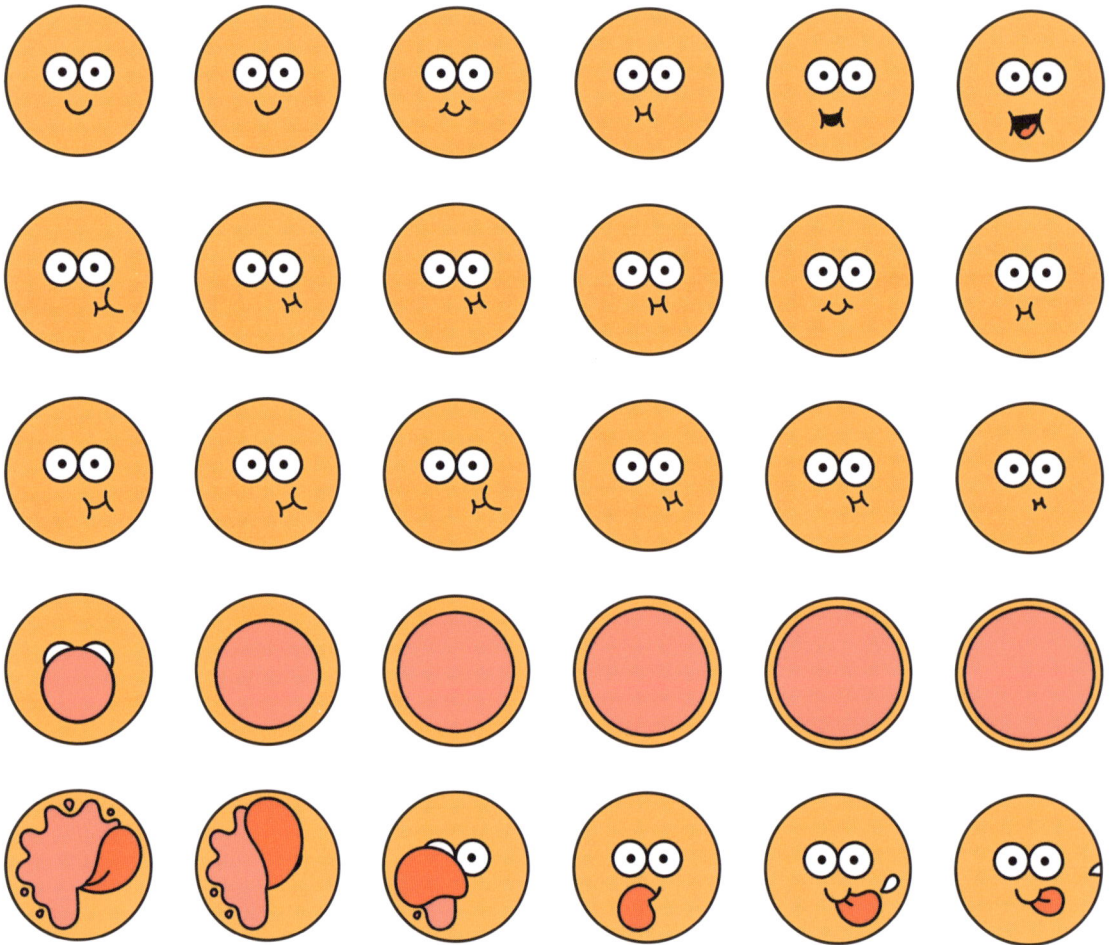

Fig. 872 **frames from the Woodger logo animation** (Woodger 2024b)

The projects presented in this sub-chapter show how digital stickers can be used in design projects to pick up and convey a visual language.

In the case of Voyce, the reference to the YouTube brand is established through the integration of the logo, the use of the brand colors and the integration of brand-relevant motifs. The linear and geometric representation gives some stickers a certain neutrality (e.g., Fig. 812, Fig. 813), but this is broken up by the animation style, which creates a link to the visual language of the artist Voyce. His unique animation style with geometric and mostly linear shapes has become an integral part of his visual language. His typical animation style is also recognizable in the Giphy stickers, but the stickers depict fewer brand-relevant attributes. Rather, it is the overall appearance that is reminiscent of the brand: linear style and bright colors.

In Furrer's project, the reference to the book is created through the colors red and black, while the visual language is picked up through the illustration style. Her signature illustration style has become an integral part of her visual language. By using motifs from the book as digital stickers, she creates a visual reference to her product.

Woodger takes typical motifs from the Kiehl's

brand, such as the brand's scientific background or numerous motifs from the cosmetics sector, and implements them in his own style. Woodger does not adapt his illustration style to the style of the brand, but borrows the values of his visual language from the Kiehl's campaign, so to speak. The brand chose Woodger's visual language for its campaign because it can identify with it.

The projects presented in this sub-chapter demonstrate how digital stickers can be used in various design contexts. There are no limits to the formal design of the stickers. They can range from geometrically reduced representations, as in the sticker

pack for YouTube, to very detailed illustrations, as in Arigato Nippon. Furrer's illustrations cross the iconic categorization threshold further than those of Woodger or Voyce.

The stickers presented are characterized by their moving form. The type of movement can itself become part of the visual language (see Fig. 699), as is the case with Voyce, for example.

These projects demonstrate how digital stickers not only serve as decorative elements, but also provide a way to convey the visual language or message of a brand or product.

Conclusion

Emojization shows that the potential of emojis in visual communication is used in different ways. The design of the signs and in particular the degree of abstraction are used for different purposes and have an influence on the perception and interpretation of the signs. In the course of emojization, it can be seen that form is increasingly becoming content.

What is the essence of this book?

What can we learn from emojis?

The historical reconstruction shows that the desire for means to compensate for the lack of paralinguistic and non-verbal means of expression in writing did not only arise with the rise of CMC. Since the spread and standardization of writing, the desire for corresponding signs has been constant. Authors attributed disadvantages to writing as a medium of communication long before the emergence of CMC. It is not the function of writing as a tool for storing information that is criticized. What is criticized is the lack of paralinguistic and non-verbal means of expression.

However, it was the emergence of digital communication systems and, above all, the use of text-based emojis that began the process of emojization. Starting with the facial expression rotated by 90 degrees, which was primarily intended to avoid misunderstandings, see page 43, an enormous variety of pictorial signs developed – both qualitatively and quantitatively. Cultural backgrounds, such as the emergence of kawaii culture, had a significant influence on the form and use of the signs.

From a historical perspective, emojis have evolved from the medium of writing to the medium of images. The more pictorial the signs became, the more the form gave rise to different discourses. Emojis have not only become an important means of expression for the individual, but also reflect social, economic or political conditions and trends (cf. Freedman 2020: 53). With the emergence and spread of emojis, discourses on the diversity of pictorial signs are increasingly coming to the foreground. The desire for diversity in terms of content and form can be seen in numerous projects by designers. On the one hand, projects have emerged that deal with the diversity of the content of the emoji sign set, such as Zouzoukwa or variable emojis. On the other hand, there are projects that deal with formal diversity, such as OpenMoji or GT Maru. In addition, some projects combine both tendencies, such as Diglû or the ›1000 Emojis Project‹. In the creation and dissemination of emojis through various design projects, two main tendencies can be distinguished, which are based on the current state of technology: On the one hand, emojis are designed as glyphs and thus an integral part of a font with a tendency towards reduced design means. In formal terms, they tend to be based more on pictograms or icons. On the other hand, they are used as stickers, which are primarily designed in more detail and are more reminiscent of illustrations. The latter are usually also animated, which offers further creative possibilities.

The creative potential of emojis also contributes to the design of visual identities. By using emojis as an integral part of a brand, they can function as part of its visual language. Projects that have emerged in recent years show how emojis are used in different ways in the creation of visual identities. For example, they act as part of a corporate font, as with Channel 4, or take on important communicative functions within an application, as with Waze. The emojis individually designed for the brand take on different functions. In most cases, they are designed to make communication friendlier and more individual and thus strengthen the consumer's identification with the brand.

Another part illustrates how the emergence and spread of emojis can be used in illustration or artwork projects. Digital stickers can take up the visual language of an artist and be used in different contexts. It will be shown how they can be used in free projects to draw attention to a product, as with Arigato Nippon. Or how digital stickers can be used in cooperation with a brand without being an integral part of it, for example by picking up on the content or formal characteristics of the brand, as with the sticker pack for YouTube Shorts Drive Thru or the stickers for Kiehl's.

It can be determined that the formal properties of emojis can have an influence on the perception, effect and meaning of the characters. The formal properties of an emoji can therefore influence the intensity of a sign, for example. Such a process is dynamic, individual and depends on cultural, social and situational factors. The formal aspects of emojis bring with them communicative attributes that can be traced back to their pictorial constitution. Formal aesthetic attributes from cartoon and kawaii aesthetics were identified. On the basis of McCloud's cartoon concept, it could be established that emojis experience a dissolution of individuality through abstraction and thus achieve a formally conditioned universality.

The use of emojis makes it clear that it is possible to express yourself very precisely with emojis, but also to remain very vague. Emojis offer an extended repertoire of expression that exceeds that of standard language. These possibilities are due to the pictorial constitution of emojis and can have an impact on the interpretation of the signs. Semiotic analyses of the sign process show that emojis take on far more than iconic functions in the sense of images or metaphors. Depending on how they use the sign, the sender is able to use an emoji iconically, indexically or symbolically. The semioticity of emojis depends heavily on how they are used.

The consideration of semiotic and formal-aesthetic concepts explains the influence of form on the effect and thus the content of the signs.

Using McCloud's cartoon concept, it was possible to determine that emojis experience a dissolution of individuality through abstraction and thus achieve a formally conditioned universality. Emojis that require a high level of identification by being used like a kind of mask to project an emotional or mood state are made up of reduced geometric shapes and depicted with a clear perspective. Others, which require less or no identification by the user, are designed in much greater detail. According to McCloud, they allow the user to immerse themselves in a world full of sensual stimuli. Emojis therefore utilize the potential of abstraction and realistic representation in different ways.

It can be stated that emojis generate a kind of immediate comprehensibility due to the cognitive types included in the medium by associating the medium with an object on an iconic level. In contrast to standard language, emojis are therefore able to communicate an entire sentence, create a positive mood or a virtual counterpart with just one sign. Due to this polyfunctionality, an emoji can be preferred over written characters. The polyfunctionality of the characters is favored by the pictorial substance of the emojis, which enables a kind of coexistence; the basic constitution of iconic types requires coexistence, which in turn can have an impact on the perception of the entire communication. Coexistence brings with it its own aesthetic, which in the case of emojis extends to all areas of life.

Viewing the signs from a formal perspective shows, that the aesthetics of emojis are designed to create an innocent and positive mood. Depictions such as the frontal view and the right degree of crossing the iconic threshold offer users optimal identification with the visual counterpart. The further an emoji crosses the iconic categorization threshold, the more autonomous and coexistent it becomes and the more the form can become the content.

References and Image Credits

Abdullah, Rayan/Hübner, Roger (2006):
›Pictograms, Icons, and Signs. A Guide to Informations Graphics‹, Thames & Hudson, London

Abel, Jonathan E. (2020):
›Not Everyone's: Or, the Question of Emoji as ›Universal‹ Expression‹. In: Giannoulis, Elena/ Wilde, Lukas R.A. (Eds.) (2020), pp. 25–43

Alt, Matthew (2016):
›The Secret Lives of Emoji. How Emoticons Conquered the World‹ Kindle Edition

&Walsh (2020): [online]
www.andwalsh.com/work/all/designer-emoji [July 8, 2024]

Apple (2024): [online]
www.apple.com/de/
a) apple-events
b) newsroom/2024/06/introducing-apple-intelligence-for-iphone-ipad-and-mac [July 8, 2024]

Arens, Roman (2002):
›i-mode persönlich‹, Books on Demand GmbH, Norderstedt

Arntz, Gerd (2007): [online]
www.gerdarntz.org [July 8, 2024]

Bazin, Hervé (1966):
›Plumons l'oiseau‹, Grasset, Paris

Beißwenger, Michael/Pappert, Steffen (2023):
›Language Decline due to Emojis? How Graphicons Contribute to Digital Communication Culture: A Pragma-Linguistic Approach‹. In: IMAGE, the interdisciplinary journal of image sciences 38, 2023/2, pp. 158–177, Herbert von Halem Verlag

Beißwenger, Michael/Pappert, Steffen (2020):
›Small Talk mit Bildzeichen. Der Beitrag von Emojis zur digitalen Alltagskommunikation‹ In: Zeitschrift für Literaturwissenschaft und Linguistik 50, Springer, pp. 8–114

Beißwenger, Michael/Pappert, Steffen (2019):
›Handeln mit Emojis. Grundriss einer Linguistik kleiner Bildzeichen in der WhatsApp-Kommunikation‹, Universitätsverlag Rhein-Ruhr, Duisburg

Benenson, Fred (2010):
›Emoji Dick or 🐋‹, Edited and compiled by Fred Beneson

Bergerhausen, Johannes/Helmig, Ilka (2020):
›Picto-, Ideo-, Bildzeichen, Begriffszeichen wörtlich, übertragen‹. Publication on the occasion of the exhibition ›Piktogramme, Lebenszeichen, Emojis: Die Gesellschaft der Zeichen‹, Leopold-Hoesch Museum Düren, Museum für Neue Kunst Freiburg

Bergerhausen, Johannes (2019):
›Mit Bildern schreiben. Keilschrift, Piktogramm, Emoji‹. At: ›Emojisierung – wie das digitale Schreiben unsere Kommunikation verändert.‹ Interdisciplinary symposium on June 7, 2019 at the saasfee*pavillon in Frankfurt am Main

Bergerhausen, Johannes (2014):
›Digitale Keilschrift‹, Verlag Hermann Schmidt, Mainz

Bergerhausen, Johannes/Poarangan, Siri (2011):
›decodeunicode – Die Schriftzeichen der Welt‹, Verlag Hermann Schmidt, Mainz

Blagdon, Jeff (2013):
›How emoji conquered the world‹, [online] www.theverge.com/2013/3/4/3966140/how-emoji-conquered-the-world [July 17, 2024]

Blanke, Börries (2003):
›Vom Bild zum Sinn: das ikonische Zeichen zwischen Semiotik und analytischer Philosophie‹, 1st ed., Deutscher Universitätsverlag Wiesbaden

Brown, Ryan Lenora (2019):
›Drawing West Africa, one emoji at a time‹ [online] www.csmonitor.com/World/Africa/ 2019/1210/Drawing-West-Africa-one-emoji-at-a-time [April 29, 2024]

Burge, Jeremy (2019):
›Correcting the Record on the First Emoji Set‹ [online] www.blog.emojipedia.org/correcting-the-record-on-the-first-emoji-set [March 2, 2021]

Burghagen, Otto (1898):
›Auszug aus der Schreibmaschinen-Zeitung. Monatsschrift für das gesamte Schreibmaschinenwesen‹, Volume 1, No. 3, September 15, 1898, Hamburg

Cartwright, James (2014):
›Dan Woodger works slavishly to create 1000 brilliant emoji in over 1000 hours!‹ [online] www.itsnicethat.com/articles/dan-woodger-bts [July 8, 2024]

Danesi, Marcel (2017):
›The Semiotics of Emoji. The Rise of Visual Language in the Age of the Internet‹, Bloomsbury Academic, London

Dear, Brian (2017):
›The Friendly Orange Glow. The Untold Story of the Rise of Cyberculture‹, Vintage Books, A Division of Penguin Random House LLC, New York Trade

Dear, Brian (2010):
[online] www.platohistory.org [July 8, 2024]

Dear, Brian (2002):
[online] www.platopeople.com/emoticons.html [June 24, 2024]

De Brahm, Alcanter (1899):
›L'ostensoir des ironies‹ Essai de metacritique. Bibliotheque d'art de la critique, Paris. In: Open Library, Internet Archive [online] www.openlibrary.org/books/OL25615210M/L%27ostensoir_des_ironies [June 24, 2024]

Eco, Umberto (1977):
›Zeichen, Einführung in einen Begriff und seine Geschichte‹, Suhrkamp, Frankfurt am Main

Eichinger, Ludwig M./Kallmeyer, Werner (Eds.) (2005):
›Standardvariation. Wie viel Variation verträgt die deutsche Sprache?‹ Jahrbuch des Instituts für Deutsche Sprache 2004, De Gruyter, Berlin

Emojipedia: [online]
www.emojipedia.org/
a) softbank/1997
b) face-with-tears-of-joy#designs
c) grimacing-face
d) person-with-foldedhands
e) diamond-with-a-dot
f) pouring-liquid
g) hamsa
h) apple
i) samsung
j) facebook
k) de/animoji [June 8, 2024]

Encalado, Jean-Claude (2005):
›Le point d'ironie d'Alcanter de Brahm‹. In: La Cause freudienne, Les nouvelles utopies de la famille 2005/2 (N° 60), pp. 217–218, Éditions L'École de la Cause freudienne

Englmann, Felicia (2015):
›Bedeutende Briefe: Die aussergewöhnlichsten deutschen Schriftstücke‹, mvg Verlag, Munich

Enzmann, Deborah (2023a):
›Emojisierung: Eine historische und semiotische Studie zu Emojis‹, niggli Verlag, Salenstein

Enzmann, Deborah (2023b):
›Analyzing Emojis Semiotically: Towards a Multi-Dimensional, Theoretical Model Inspired by Charles S. Peirce‹. In: IMAGE, the interdisciplinary journal of image sciences 38, 2023/2, pp. 178–195, Herbert von Halem Verlag

Erunyan (2024):
Interview by Hiromi Shirai & Deborah Enzmann, February 9, 2024, cf. Harajuku, Shibuya, Tokyo

Fahlman, Scott E. (2021):
›The Birth, Spread, and Evolution of the Smiley Emoticon‹ [online] www.cs.cmu.edu/~sef/Smiley2021.pdf [April 9, 2024]

Fahlman, Scott E. (2002):
›Original Bboard Thread in which :-) was proposed‹, [online] http://www.cs.cmu.edu/~sef/Orig-Smiley.htm [May 3, 2021]

Feigl, Walter/Windholz, Sascha (Eds.) (2011):
›Wissenschaftstheorie, Sprachkritik und Wittgenstein. In memoriam Elisabeth und Werner Leinfellner‹, Verlag De Gruyter

Flusser, Vilém (2002):
›Die Schrift. Hat Schreiben Zukunft?‹, 5th ed., European Photography

France Soir (1972):
Paris-Presse, Saturday January 1, 1972 edition

Freedman, Alisa (2020):
›Cultural Literacy in the Empire of Emoji Signs‹. In: Giannoulis, Elena/Wilde, Lukas R.A. (Eds.) (2020), pp. 44–66

Friedrich, Thomas/Schweppenhäuser, Gerhard (2010): ›Bildsemiotik: Grundlagen und exemplarische Analysen visueller Kommunikation‹, Birkhäuser Verlag AG, Basel

Frutiger, Adrian (2004):
›Der Mensch und seine Zeichen‹, 9th edition, Marix Verlag, Wiesbaden

Frutiger, Adrian (1989):
›Signs and Symbols. Their Design and Meaning‹, Nostrand, New York

Frutiger, Adrian (1980):
›Type Sign Symbol‹, ABC Verlag, Zurich

Giannoulis, Elena/Wilde, Lukas R.A. (Eds.) (2020): ›Emoticons, Kaomoji and Emoji. The Transformation of Communication in the Digital Age‹, Routledge Research in Language and Communication, London

Giesecke, Michael (1991):
›Der Buchdruck in der frühen Neuzeit. Eine historische Fallstudie über die Durchsetzung neuer Informations- und Kommunikationstechnologien‹, Suhrkamp, Frankfurt am Main

Gruppo Due:
[online] www.gruppo-due.com [May 3, 2021]

GT Maru (2024):
[online] www.gt-maru.com [April 16, 2024]

Hadley, Paul (1948):
›Keyboard Art‹. In: Popular Mechanics Magazine, Oktober 1948

Hammond, Kenneth J./Richey, Jeffrey L. (2014): ›The Sage Returns: Confucian Revival in Contemporary China‹, SUNY Press

Hartmann, Frank/Bauer Erwin K. (2006):
›Bildersprache. Otto Neurath Visualisierungen‹, 2nd ed., Facultas Verlags- und Buchhandels AG, Wien

Hawgood, Alex (2019):
›A Student Who Make African Emojis‹. In: New York Times [online] www.nytimes.com/by/alex-hawgood [April 29, 2024]

Helmann (2017):
›Rhetoric of Logos: A Primer for Visual Language‹, Niggli, imprint of bnb media gmbh, Zurich

Herrmann, Ralf (2013):
[online] www.typografie.info/3/artikel.htm/wissen/interrobang [May 3, 2021]

HfG Gmünd (2018):
›Openmoji – Emojis von Designern für alle‹ [online] www.hfg-gmuend.de/aktuelles/openmoji-emojis-von-designern-für-alle [April 4, 2024]

Houston, Keith (2013):
›Shad Characters; Ampersands, Interrobangs and Other Typographical Curiosities‹, Penguin Group, London

ifak:
›Partizipa City – ein Planspiel zu antimuslimischem Rassismus‹ [online] www.ifak-goettingen.de/projekte/partizipa-city [April 4, 2024]

Janßen, Barbara (1995):
›Medienkritik bei Platon und Medienkritik heute‹, Editorial Board LINSE, University of Duisburg-Essen, Faculty of Humanities, German Studies/Linguistics

j-fashion:
[online] www.j-fashion.fandom.com/wiki/Jirai_Kei [April 9, 2024]

Kakao Friends: [online]
https://kakaofriends-business.com/
a) kakaoFriends
b) kakaoFriends/choonsik
c) niniz [July 8, 2024]

Kanto Bus:
[online] www.kanto-bus.co.jp/kannyan/profile.html [May 21, .2024]

Katsuno, Hirofumi/Yano, Christine R. (2002): ›Face to Face: On-Line Subjectivity in Contemporary Japan‹. Asian Studies Review 26 (2): 205-233

Kavanagh, Barry (2020):
›A Cultural Exploration of the Use of Kaomoji, Emoji, an Kigo in Japanese log-Post Narratives‹. In: Giannoulis, Elena/Wilde, Lukas R.A. (Eds.) (2020), pp. 148–167

Kilchör, Fabienne (2020):
›Archäologie visualisieren. Entwicklung einer standardisierten Zeichenschrift zur Analyse und Vermittlung archäologischer Funde und Befunde‹. In: Winfried Orthmann, Jan-Waalke Meyer, und Mirko Novák (Eds.): Schriften zur vorderasiatischen Archäologie, Volume 15, Harrassowitz Verlag, Wiesbaden

Kinsella, Sharon (1995):
›Cuties in Japan‹. In: Skov, Lise/Moeran, Brian (eds.): Women, Media and Consumption in Japan. Curzon Press, London, pp. 220–254

Kreisblatt (1893):
›Kreisblatt für den Kreis Malmedy‹, Issue Saturday, September 2, 1893, No. 70, Volume 28, Doepgen Verlag, St. Bith (Eifel)

Kringiel, Danny (2011):
›Smiley-Erfinder: Millionen für ein Lächeln‹. In: Der Spiegel Geschichte [online] www.spiegel.de/einestages/smileyerfinder-millionen-fuer-ein-laecheln-a-947164.html [June 24, 2024]

Le Moign, Vincent (2022):
›Designing icon sets: A masterclass from Streamline‹ [online] www.bootcamp.uxdesign.cc/designing-icon-sets-a-masterclass-from-streamline-d331c4876de8 [May 15, 2024]

LINE: [online]
https://store.line.me/stickershop/product/
a) 1915067/en
b) 10306/en
c) 27059657/en
d) 27059657/en [July 2, 2024]

Lobo, Sascha (2017):
›Symbole des Fortschritts: Emojis, die beste Sprache der Welt ;-)‹ (27.12.2017). In: Spiegel [online] www.spiegel.de/netzwelt/web/emojis-warum-die-symbole-ein-gesellschaftlicher-fortschritt-sind-a-1185165.html [June 24, 2024]

Lorenz, Martin (2021):
›Flexible Visual Systems: The Design Manual for Contemporary Visual Identities‹, Slanted Publishers, Karlsruhe

Matsuda, Risa (2020):
›Construction of Iconicity in Scenes of Kaomoji‹. In: Giannoulis, Elena/Wilde, Lukas R.A. (Eds.) (2020), pp. 197–207

May, Tom (2020):
›14 graphic designers and illustrators explain why they moved into motion design‹ [online] www.creativeboom.com/inspiration/reasons-to-switch-to-motion-design [May 6, 2024]

McCloud, Scott (2006):
›Understanding comics: the invisible art‹, Lettering Bob Lappan, William Morrow, New York

McCloud, Scott (2001):
›Comics richtig lesen: Die unsichtbare Kunst‹, Carlsen Verlag, Hamburg

McVeigh, Brian J. (2000):
›Wearing Ideology: Stale, Schooling an Self-Presentation‹, Berg, Oxford

Merta, David (2017): [online]
www.archaiabrno.org/home_cs/?acc=zapisnicek&blog_id=785&blog_date=2017-03-01 [June 24, 2024]

Michel, Paul (Eds.) (2005):
›Unmitte(i)lbarkeit, Gestaltungen und Lesbarkeit von Emotionen, Schriften zur Symbolforschung‹, Volume 15, Pano Verlag, Zurich

Moeller, Hans-Georg/Wohlfart, Günter (Eds.) (2014): ›Laughter in Eastern and Western Philosophies: Proceedings of the Académie du Midi‹, Verlag Karl Alber, Freiburg/Munich

Müller, Marion G. (2003):
›Grundlagen der visuellen Kommunikation. Theorieansätze und Methoden‹, UVK Verlagsgesellschaft, Konstanz

Müller-Brockmann, Josef (1996):
›Grid systems in graphic design. A visual communication manual for graphic designers, typographers and three dimensional designers‹, 4th revised edition, Niggli Verlag, Sulgen/Zurich

Murphy, Zoe Loring (2021):
›Grilli Type's Latest Drop Is A Joyful New Typeface Stemming From Japanese & Latin Shapes‹, April 27, 2021 [online] www.type-01.com/grilli-types-latest-drop-is-a-joyful-new-typeface-stemming-from-japanese-latin-shapes [April 23, 2024]

Nagl, Ludwig (1992):
›Charles Sanders Peirce‹, Reihe Campus, Einführungen, Band 1053, Campus Verlag, Frankfurt am Main

Neurath, Otto (1980):
›International picture language, A facsimile reprint of the [1936] English edition‹, Department of Typography & Grapic Communication, University of Reading

Nielsen, Philipp/Weirich, Maxim (2021):
›Turn Over Signs: Die stetige Neuausrichtung der Bildzeichen‹. In: Düren Leopold-Hoesch-Museum (Eds.) (2021): ›Piktogramme, Lebenszeichen, Emojis: Die Gesellschaft der Zeichen‹, Ausst. Kat. Leopold-Hoesch-Museum, Düren, Museum für Neue Kunst, Städtische Museen, Freiburg, Verlag der Buchhandlung König

Nittono, Hiroshi (2016:
›The two-layer model of ›kawaii‹: A behavioural science frame work for understanding kawaii and cuteness‹, East Asian Journal of Popular Culture, Volume 2, Issue 1, Apr 2016, p. 79 - 95

Nöth, Winfried/Bishara, Nina/Neitzel, Britta (2008):
›Mediale Selbstreferenz: Grundlagen und Fallstudien zu Werbung, Computerspiel und den Comics‹, Herbert von Halem Verlag, Köln

Nöth, Winfried (2000):
›Handbuch der Semiotik‹, 2nd ed., J.B. Metzler Verlag, Stuttgart [u.a.]

Oberwinkler, Michaela (2020):
›Emoticons in Social Media: The Case of Japanese Facebook Users‹. In: Giannoulis, Elena/ Wilde, Lukas R.A. (Eds.) (2020), pp. 104–123

OpenMoji (2024):
[online] www.openmoji.org/
a) styleguide
b) library [May 13, 2024]

Osterwalder, Markus (2020):
›Olympic Games – the design: design history of the Olympic Games since Athens 1896‹, niggli Verlag, Salenstein

Otterstein, Ben (2018):
[online] www.maclife.de/ratgeber/ios-12-mehrere-memojis-erstellen-verwalten-100108475.html [July 5, 2024]

Oxford Languages (2024):
[online] https://languages.oup.com/word-of-the-year/2015/ [July 5, 2024]

Peirce, Charles S. (2000a):
›Semiotische Schriften, Band 1 (1865-1903)‹, Kloesel, Christian J.W.; Helmut Pape (Eds.), 1st ed., Suhrkamp, Frankfurt am Main

Peirce, Charles S. (2000b):
›Semiotische Schriften, Band 2 (1903-1906)‹, Kloesel, Christian J.W.; Helmut Pape (Eds.), 1st ed., Suhrkamp, Frankfurt am Main

Peirce, Charles S. (2000c):
›Semiotische Schriften, Band 3 (1906-1913)‹, Kloesel, Christian J.W.; Helmut Pape (Eds.), 1st ed., Suhrkamp, Frankfurt am Main

Peirce, Charles S. (1983):
›Phänomen und Logik der Zeichen‹, Pape, Helmut (Ed.), 1st ed., Suhrkamp, Frankfurt am Main

Packard, Stephan/Rauscher, Andreas/Sina, Véronique/Thon, Jan-Noël/Wilde, Lukas R. A./Wildfeuer, Janina (2019):
›Comicanalyse: eine Einführung‹, J.B. Metzler Verlag, Stuttgart [u.a.]

Parkes, Malcolm B. (1992):
›Pause and effect: an introduction to the history of punctuation in the West‹, Scolar Press, Aldershot, Hants

Pentagram (2024): [online]
www.pentagram.com/work/
a) waze
b) waze/story
c) visible
d) visible/story
e) channel-4
f) channel-4/story [April 9, 2024]

Pentagram (2023):
[online] www.pentagram.com/news/paula-scher-type-is-image-opens-at-die-neue-sammlung [June 6, 2024]

Petronzio, Matt (2012):
›A Brief History of Instant Messaging‹ [online] www.mashable.com/2012/10/25/instant-messaging-history/#rr5ESdTIZkqk [June 24, 2024]

Plamper, Jan (2012):
›Geschichte und Gefühl. Grundlagen der Emotionsgeschichte‹, Siedler Verlag, Munich

Puck Magazine (1881):
Number 2012, from March 30, 1881

Queneau, Raymond (1933):
›Le Chiendent‹, Gallimard, Paris

Ratcliffe, Rebecca (2019):
›New emoji set aims to shatter image of Africa as zone of famine and war‹ in: The Guardian (18.11.2019) [online] www.theguardian.com/global-development/2019/nov/18/new-emoji-set-aims-to-shatter-image-of-africa-as-zone-of-famine-and-war [June 24, 2024]

Runkehl, Jens/Schlobinski, Peter/Siever, Torsten (1998): ›Sprache und Kommunikation im Internet: Überblick und Analysen‹, Westdeutscher Verlag, Opladen

Sandner, Günther (2008):
›Demokratisierung durch Bildpädagogik, Otto Neurath und Isotype‹, SWS-Rundschau, 48.Jh., Heft 4/2008

Schlobinski, Peter/Watanabe, Manabu (2006):
›Mündlichkeit und Schriftlichkeit in der SMS-Kommunikation. Deutsch – Japanisch kontrastiv‹. In: Neuland, Eva (Ed.) ›Variation im heutigen Deutsch: Perspektiven für den Deutschunterricht‹ Frankfurt am Main, pp. 403–416

Schmidt, Wolfgang (1992):
›Worte und Bilder‹. Anke Jaaks [Eds.], Verlag Hermann Schmidt, Mainz

Schmitz, Ulrich (1995):
›Neue Medien und Gegenwartssprache. Lagebericht und Problemskizze‹. In: Osnabrücker Beiträge zur Sprachtheorie (OBST), Vol. 50 (1995), pp. 7–51

Scholz, Oliver R. (2009):
›Bild, Darstellung, Zeichen: Philosophische Theorien bildlicher Darstellung‹, 3rd ed., Klostermann, Frankfurt am Main

Schönrich, Gerhard (1999):
›Semiotik; Zur Einführung‹, 1st ed., Junius, Hamburg

Schwitters, Kurt/Steinitz, Käte/Doesburg, Theo van (1971):
›Die Scheuche‹ Märchen, Reprint 1971, Biermann + Boukes, Frankfurt am Main

Sevilla, Gadjo (2018):
[online] www.blog.bestbuy.ca/smartphones-accessories/create-use-ar-emojis-samsung-galaxy-s9-s9 [June 24, 2024]

Shirai, Hiromi (2024):
Interview by Deborah Enzmann, February 9, 2024, cf. Harajuku, Shibuya, Tokyo

Shirai, Hiromi (2019):
›Kawaii Kultur und deren Einfluss auf die Ka-waicons‹. At: ›Emojisierung – wie das digitale Schreiben unsere Kommunikation verändert.‹ Interdisciplinary symposium on June 7, 2019 at the saasfee*pavillon in Frankfurt am Main.

Shirai, Hiromi (2009):
›Eine kontrastive Untersuchung zur deutschen und japanischen Chat-Kommunikation‹, Lang, Frankfurt am Main

Shirai, Hiromi (2005):
›Kawaiiheit überall in der Welt? Zur Ausbreitung und zum semantischen Spektrum von kawaii‹. In: KG Germanistik. Annual Report of the German Department of the University of Kwansei-gakuin, Nishinomiya (Japan), pp. 53–68

Shorley, Christopher (1985):
›Queneau's Fiction: An Introductory Study‹, Cambridge University Press

Siever, Christina Margrit (2020):
›'Iconographetic Communication' in Digital Media. Emoji in WhatsApp, Twitter, Instagram, Facebook – From a Linguistic Perspective‹. In: Giannoulis, Elena/Wilde, Lukas R.A. (Eds.) (2020), pp. 127–147

Siever, Christina Margrit (2016):
›Von Bildzeichen und Zeichenschrift‹, VSAO Journal ASMAC, Nr. 5, Oktober 2016

Smileysnetwork [online]
www.smileysnetwork.com/en/kaoani-smileys.php [July 2, 2024]

Šmíd, Milan (2018):
[online] www.twitter.com/mfkşmid/status/1019553135088594944 [June 24, 2024]

Stefanowitsch, Anatol (2017): ›Es knirscht im Zeichensatz‹. In: Frankfurter Allgemeine [online] www.faz.net/aktuell/feuilleton/debatten/debatten-um-emojis-es-knirscht-im-zeichen-satz-14930000.html [June 24, 2024]

Suzuki, Kōji (2007):
›The History of Japanese Emoticon‹, Meikai Japanese Language Journal 12, pp. 91–96

Todd, Sarah (2017): ›Tokyo's adorable police mascot Pipo-kun is basically cuteness, weaponized‹ [online] www.qz.com/1164167/tokyos-adorable-police-mascot-pipo-kun-is-basically-cuteness-weaponized [May 21, 2024]

Trautsch, Christian und Wu, Yixin (2012):
›Die Als-ob-Struktur von Emotikons im WWW und in anderen Medien‹. In: IMAGE, Issue 16, Special Issue on Semiotics, 7/2012, pp. 47–60

Ulrich, Wolfgang (2006):
›Bilder auf der Weltreise. Eine Globalisierungs-kritik‹, Wagenbach, Berlin

Voyce, Mat (2024):
[online] www.matvoyce.tv/
a) personal
b) youtube-vidcon-22
c) lacoste
d) what-if-i-worked-for
e) giphy [May 6, 2024]

Walther, Elisabeth (1974):
›Allgemeine Zeichenlehre, Einführung in die Grundlagen der Semiotik‹, Deutsche Verlags-Anstalt, Stuttgart

Waze (2024):
Navigation und Verkehr, Version 4.101.2 (iOS) [Mobile app] www.waze.com [April 9, 2024]

Weirich, Maxim (2021):
›Piktogramme, Lebenszeichen, Emojis: Die Ge-sellschaft der Zeichen.‹ Lecture evening for the exhibition on January 22, 2021

Wiethölter, Waltraud (2008):
›Ikono-Graphie‹. In: Bohnenkamp, Anne/Wiet-hölter, Waltraud (2008): ›Der Brief – Ereignis & Objekt‹, pp. 117–190, Stroemfeld, Frankfurt am Main

Wikimedia Commons (2019):
[online] https://commons.wikimedia.org/wiki/File:Cute_Japanese_handwriting.png [June 24, 2024]

Wilde, Lukas R. A. (2020):
›The Elephant in the Room of Emoji Research: Or, Pictoriality, to what Extent?‹. In: Giannou-lis, Elena/Wilde, Lukas R.A. (Eds.) (2020), pp. 171–196

Wilde, Lukas R. A. (2019):
›Bildlichkeit von Emojis: Cartoonisierung und Manga-Symboliken‹. At: ›Emojisierung – wie das digitale Schreiben unsere Kommunika-tion verändert.‹ Interdisciplinary symposium on June 7, 2019 at the saasfee*pavillon in Frank-furt am Main

Wilde, Lukas R. A. (2018):
›Im Reich der Figuren. Meta-narrative Kommu-nikationsfiguren und die ›Mangaisierung‹ des japanischen Alltags‹, Herbert von Halem Ver-lag, Köln

Wilkins, John (1668):
›An Essay Towards a Real Character, and a Phi-losophical Language‹ [online] www.archive.org/details/AnEssayTowardsARealCharacterAndA-PhilosophicalLanguage [January 14, 2021]

Witte, Hannah (2021):
›Typohacks: Handbuch für gendersensible Sprache und Typografie‹, Verlag form, Frankfurt am Main

Wittgenstein, Ludwig (1968):
›Vorlesungen und Gespräche über Ästhetik, Psychologie und Religion‹, Barrett, Cyril (Eds.); Bubser, Eberhard (trans.), Vandenhoeck & Rup-recht, Göttingen

Woodger, Dan (2024):
[online] www.danwoodger.com/work/
a) line-emoji
b) app-store [April 30, 2024]

Woolley, David R. (1994):
[online] www.just.thinkofit.com/talkomatic [May 3, 2021]

Yuki et al. (2007):
›Are the windows to the soul the same in the East and West? Cultural differences in using the eyes and mouth as cues to recognize emotions in Japan and the United States‹, Journal of Ex-perimental Social Psychology 43(2), pp. 303–311

YouTube (2020):
[online]www.youtube.com/watch?v=Q4m6bQ-95KNk [June 14, 2024]

36 Days of Type (2023):
[online] www.36daysoftype.com [May 12, 2024]

Behind the book

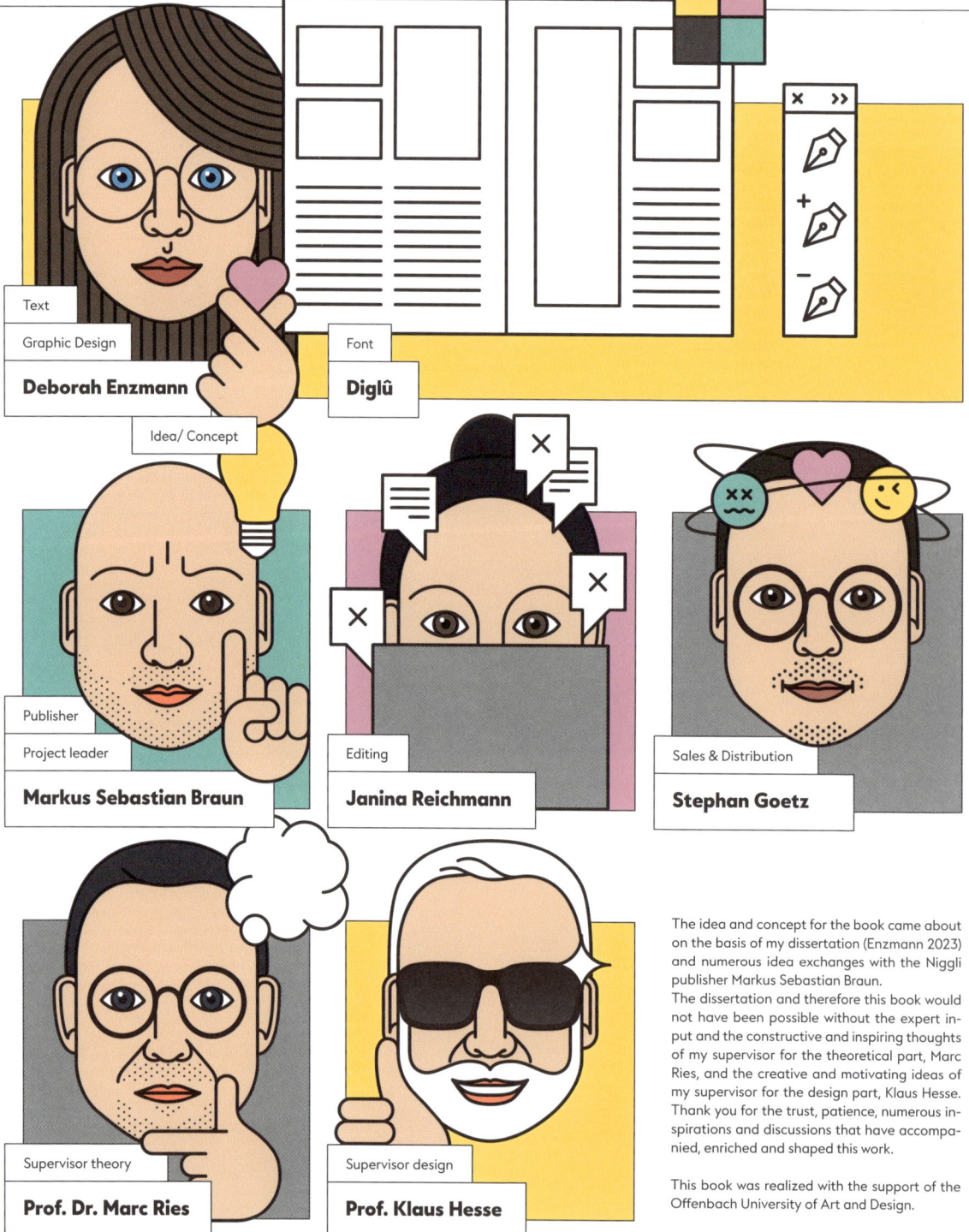

Text

Graphic Design

Deborah Enzmann

Font

Diglû

Idea/ Concept

Publisher

Project leader

Markus Sebastian Braun

Editing

Janina Reichmann

Sales & Distribution

Stephan Goetz

Supervisor theory

Prof. Dr. Marc Ries

Supervisor design

Prof. Klaus Hesse

The idea and concept for the book came about on the basis of my dissertation (Enzmann 2023) and numerous idea exchanges with the Niggli publisher Markus Sebastian Braun.
The dissertation and therefore this book would not have been possible without the expert input and the constructive and inspiring thoughts of my supervisor for the theoretical part, Marc Ries, and the creative and motivating ideas of my supervisor for the design part, Klaus Hesse. Thank you for the trust, patience, numerous inspirations and discussions that have accompanied, enriched and shaped this work.

This book was realized with the support of the Offenbach University of Art and Design.

My special thanks go to

King of solutions

Musti & Juna Enzmann

Chef of all cute illustrations

The true reason this book exists

Franziska & Jörg Enzmann

Tokyo travel buddy

Sarah Furrer

Networker

Remo Weiss

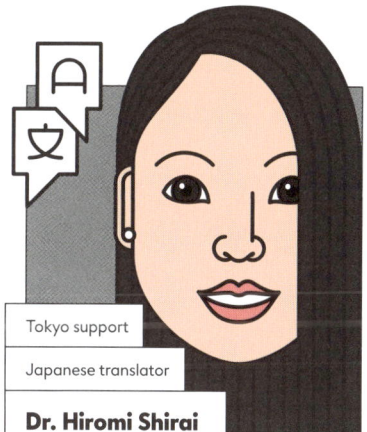

Tokyo support

Japanese translator

Dr. Hiromi Shirai

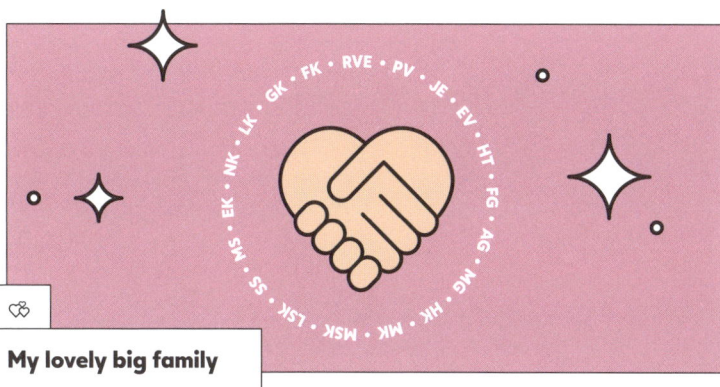

SMS · EK · NK · LK · GK · FK · RVE · PV · JE · EV · HT · FG · AG · NG · HK · MK · MSW · LSK · SS

My lovely big family

I thank my lovely big family, who support and motivate me in all situations and are always there for me, even in difficult times. I am very happy to have you in my life.

A special thanks to my parents who laid the foundation for this book by always believing in me, giving me the freedom and instilling the values that allowed me to follow this path.

An equally big thank you goes to my husband, who believes in me unwaveringly and supports me with his overwhelming commitment to have my back as often as possible.

Thank you all for your understanding and your love – without you, this work would not have been possible.

The Deutsche Nationalbibliothek lists this publication in the Deutsche Nationalbibliografie;
detailed bibliographic data are available on the
Internet at http://dnb.dnb.de

ISBN 978-3-7212-1037-8
© 2025 Niggli,
imprint of Braun Publishing AG, Salenstein

n'li

www.niggli.ch

1st edition 2025

Editing: Janina Reichmann
Graphic Concept, Layout: Deborah Enzmann

AI-based tools were used to translate and enhance the wording of the text. No information
relevant to the content of the book was generated by AI. All information comes from the
sources cited in the book or from the author.